Inferno

Inferno

Dante Alighieri

Translated by J.G. Nichols

ET REMOTISSIMA PROPE

Hesperus Poetry

Hesperus Poetry
Published by Hesperus Press Limited
4 Rickett Street, London SW6 1RU
www.hesperuspress.com

This translation first published by Hesperus Press Limited, 2005
Foreword © Ian Thomson, 2005
Introduction © M.R. McLaughlin, 2005
Introductory summaries, notes, afterword and English language translation
© J.G. Nichols, 2005

Every effort has been made to contact the copyright holder/s of 'Illustration of Dante's Inferno', and the Publisher invites such persons to be in touch with them directly.

Designed and typeset by Fraser Muggeridge
Printed in Jordan by Jordan National Press

ISBN: 1-84391-111-6

CONTENTS

FOREWORD

The boil and hiss of Dante's *Inferno* is hard for us to imagine today. As a singer of other-wordly horror, Dante has no equal. Yet, in spite of our distance from medieval theology, the poet's 700-year-old journey through hell remains one of the essential books of mankind. At least fifty English versions of the *Inferno* – the first part of Dante's *Divine Comedy* – appeared in the twentieth century alone. One inferno is enough, you might think. But now we have another – a striking version – by the poet and Italian translator J.G. Nichols.

If Dante's genius has often been obscured in the English-speaking world, part of the blame must lie with the Victorians. Clergymen, civil servants and other worthies translated the poet's crystalline cantos into pious fustian, full of cod moral sobriety. The original was nothing like this. Recast as Victorian hymnology, Dante's *Inferno* became the most solemn of poems. Even Longfellow's 1865 translation, much admired, is like drinking flat champagne with its timid expurgations and literalisms. There was a message for contemporary society in the *Inferno* which Christians such as John Ruskin saw it as their duty to convey. What happens to adulterers? Look no further than Canto V, where Paolo and Francesca are twisting without hope in a black whirlpool.

Dante Alighieri began the *Inferno* in about 1307, five years after he was exiled from Florence for corruption and embezzlement. The charges against him were false, but he never set foot in his native city again. Instead he worked with gleeful concentration on his private vision of hell. Much of the *Inferno* is 'awful' in that archaic sense of the word (still valid in Italian) of inspiring 'awe'. The 1935 Hollywood melodrama *Dante's Inferno* contains a ten-minute reconstruction of Dante's underworld, modelled on Gustave Doré's God-fearing illustrations. The damned are wedged 'arsy-versy' against each other in a stinking hell-pit, 'watering their bottoms with their tears', as Samuel Beckett put it. Spencer Tracey starred in the film; there is nothing like it in cinema history. In Britain perhaps only Peter Greenaway has interpreted the *Inferno* so adventurously. Computerised leopards slouch across the screen in his *TV Dante* as John Gielgud darkly intones: 'Abandon all hope, ye who enter.'

As every Italian schoolchild knows, the *Inferno* opens on Good Friday in a supernatural forest at nightfall. Dante, a figure in his own work, has lost his way in middle age and is alone and frightened in the woods. The Latin poet Virgil, sent by the mysterious Beatrice, is about to show him Hell. Little is known of Beatrice ('Bice') Portinari, who died in Florence in 1290; in the poem she is an allegory of divine grace, and first appears before the speechless Dante with improbably lustrous eyes ('brighter than the stars'). The love of Dante's life, Beatrice was worshipped by the Pre-Raphaelites as a dewy-eyed damsel, tender as a marshmallow. Rossetti's *Beata Beatrix*, now in Tate Britain, illustrates the lachrymose Victorian ideal.

Yet, awkwardly for the Victorians, parts of the *Inferno* are decidedly ribald. How translators must have agonised over Canto XXI, where Muckrake (Dante's 'Malacoda', literally 'Evil Tail') makes a 'bugle' of his arse by breaking wind musically. The Reverend Henry Boyd comically rendered the devil's farts in his 1802 version as 'loud Aeolian fifes', after the Greek god of wind. Dante's burlesque was much more vulgar; when William Burroughs' *Naked Lunch* was prosecuted for obscenity in Boston in 1965, the *Inferno* was cited in the novel's defence.

In order to reach a wider audience, Dante chose to write the *Inferno* in vernacular Italian instead of Latin (his overthrow of Latin preceded Geoffrey Chaucer's by eighty years). Inevitably Dante became a national institution in Italy. As a teenager in Turin during the 1930s, Primo Levi took part in 'Dante Tournaments' where boys showed off their knowledge of the *Inferno*; one contestant recited a canto and his opponent scored a point if he knew its continuation. Later, in *If This is a Man*, Levi relates how he tried to remember lines from the *Inferno* at Auschwitz. Dante had reached out to a condemned man many times before Levi. In 1882, while on a lecture tour of America, Oscar Wilde was impressed to find a copy of the *Inferno* in a Nebraska death-row cell. ('Oh dear, who would have thought of finding Dante here?') Many years later, the disgraced politician Jeffrey Archer chose to subtitle his prison diary 'Hell', to be followed by the equally presumptuous (if blatantly Dantesque) titles 'Purgatory' and 'Paradise'.

Interestingly, *The Divine Comedy* has often been put to political use. In the mid-60s the Italian poet and film director Pier Paolo Pasolini rewrote Dante's austere trilogy to form a critique of Italy's consumer society. Published in the year of his murder – 1975 – *The Divine Mimesis* bristles with Pasolini's abhorrence of American-style materialism and political opportunism. Like Dante before him, Pasolini fulminated against politicians, grafters and humbugs who had ruined Italy (so he believed). For others, T.S. Eliot among them, the *Inferno* was the highest expression of Christian civilisation. Dante's brimstone poem encouraged Eliot in his conviction that modern man is spiritually shipwrecked. 'I had not thought death had undone so many', we read of those lifeless rush-hour commuters in *The Wasteland* (words that Eliot cribbed directly from Canto III of the *Inferno*).

I first read Dante as a twenty-year-old in Rome, where I was then living. A beautiful second-hand edition of *The Divine Comedy*, fortified with Doré's copperplate etchings, had caught my eye. If any work has a claim to the universal, I thought, this must be it: all life is written in its burning pages. (The book was the size of a large encyclopaedia.) Though the medieval belief in infernal retribution has lost its power to terrify, we still respond to the *Inferno*. Samuel Beckett kept a copy of the poem by his bedside as he lay dying in a Paris hospice. Another tenacious *dantista*, the Russian poet Osip Mandelstam, never left his Moscow flat without a paperback *Inferno*. Dante's epic of sin and salvation endures powerfully.

– Ian Thomson, 2005

INTRODUCTION

The number of translations into English of Dante's *Divine Comedy* far outstrips that of any other Italian literary work, and the number of English translations of Dante's *Inferno* is considerably higher than those of the *Comedy* as a whole. Yet Dante's popularity in Anglo-American culture is a relatively recent phenomenon, starting only around 1800. As late as the last quarter of the eighteenth century Dante's poem was considered a 'whimsical poem', and as for an English version of it, in 1782 an influential critic was still capable of stating that 'the extreme inequality of this Poet would render such a work a very laborious undertaking, and it appears very doubtful that such a version would interest our country'.[1] Yet in that same year the first translation of Dante's *Inferno* (by Charles Rogers) appeared in English; within twenty years of that statement the first complete translation of the whole poem appeared (by Henry Boyd in 1802); and by 1814 the most influential English version of the work, H.F. Cary's *The Vision*, was published, the version that made Dante's work known to the chief Romantic poets: Byron, Coleridge, Keats and Shelley. By 1900 no fewer than fifteen translations of the *Comedy* had been published in Britain and four in North America.

What caused this sudden rise in Dante's fortunes? It is clear from the bald statistics above that the Romantic turn at the end of the eighteenth century swept away the neoclassical distaste for Dante's 'whimsical' poem and its gothic horrors. But there were other reasons for the poet's extraordinary hold on the British imagination. In the 1840s Carlyle's championing of Dante as an 'artist-hero' at the beginning of the decade and then the emergence of the Pre-Raphaelite movement in the late 1840s helped to secure Dante's iconic position in Victorian culture, thanks particularly to the paintings (and translations) of Dante Gabriel Rossetti. Exactly halfway through the nineteenth century, the high priest of Pre-Raphaelitism, John Ruskin, could champion Dante in *The Stones of Venice* (1851–3) as 'the central man of all the world, as representing in perfect balance the imaginative, moral and intellectual faculties, all at their highest'.[2] Ruskin was also in close

1. William Hayley, *Essay on Epic Poetry* (1782), cited in Beatrice Corrigan (ed.), *Italian Poets and English Critics, 1755–1859. A Collection of Critical Essays* (Chicago-London: University of Chicago Press, 1969), p. 9, n. 11.
2. *Comments of John Ruskin* on the Divina Commedia, ed. George P. Huntington, introduction by Charles Eliot Norton (Boston-New York: Houghton Mifflin, 1903), 3.

contact with Charles Eliot Norton when the latter translated the *Vita nova* in 1859, and since T.S. Eliot was taught by Norton, then it is clear that this Ruskin-Norton-Eliot line was the path that led to the high road of the twentieth-century cult of Dante in English, from Eliot and Pound at the beginning of the century to Seamus Heaney at the end of it. While we take this for granted now, it is interesting to note that Dante's fortune in English could have been that of his great rival in the next generation, Petrarch (1304–74): that other poetic masterwork of the Italian middle ages, Petrarch's *Canzoniere*, had just two complete translations in the nineteenth century, which were not much read, and had to wait until 1976 for the first complete version to achieve considerable circulation.

Instead translations of the *Comedy*, particularly of the *Inferno*, have continued to flourish in these two centuries. But writers in English do not just turn to Dante to read him in translation; their own creative works are often inspired by him, from Tennyson's *Ulysses*, a recasting of Dante's (as well as Homer's) Ulysses (Canto XXVI), and T.S. Eliot's reworking of the Brunetto Latini episode (Canto XV) in 'Little Gidding' (No. 4 of *Four Quartets*) to Heaney's refashioning of *Purgatorio* in *Station Island* (1984). The opening of the twenty-first century has seen no let-up in translations of the whole poem and of the *Inferno*, and so it is into this two-century-old tradition of Dante worship that J.G. Nichols' new translation of the *Inferno* fits.

It is extremely difficult to read any classic work afresh, in a defamiliarised way, but perhaps that is one of the advantages of a new translation: that it gives a fresh voice to a familiar text, like the restoration of the colours in an old master painting. It is important for the English reader trying to achieve that sense of freshness to remember that Dante's *Comedy* emerges from the mists of the middle ages almost without precedent. Before this epic undertaking, all that the newly formed Italian vernacular had produced were short poetic forms like sonnets or *canzoni*, whose content was either love poetry (by authors such as Cavalcanti and Dante himself), religious poetry, or a kind of streetwise verse known as 'comic-realistic' poetry, in which poets would exchange insulting sonnets with each other. It could be argued that Dante's *Comedy*, and in particular the *Inferno*, with its realistic portrayal of landscape and character, has no single precedent in Italian literature but draws on all three of these poetic traditions, the erotic, the religious and the comic. But we must always remember the sheer poetic originality and daring of Dante's undertaking, to write a poem of epic dimensions, in the Italian vernacular and not in Latin, based on a vision of the Christian afterlife. There was nothing predictable about that; and perhaps it is to compensate for this audacious gesture that he gives such an important role to the major representative of the classical tradition, Virgil. The classical poet appears both as a character and as a major source for the *Inferno*, in which Dante's portrayal of the underworld owes so much to Virgil's depiction of it in *Aeneid* VI.

Whether the reader of this translation is reading Dante for the first time, or simply trying to read him as if it were the first time, I would suggest four points to bear in mind. Firstly, although this is a religious poem which begins with the poet-protagonist in the dark wood of sin, and ends with the divine vision of God at the end of *Paradiso*, yet it is also a very earthly poem, with strongly voiced criticism of the Papacy (see in particular the chain of corrupt Popes in Canto XIX), a wonderfully crude comic scene with devils and pitchforks (Cantos XXI–XXII), and considerable moral complexity in its major figures. The poet does not simply adopt a sequence of encountering sinners of increasing moral turpitude as he descends into the pit of hell; instead the first major sinner he meets, Francesca da Rimini (Canto V), is one of the most 'sympathetic' characters in the poem – so full of sympathy is the pilgrim to her plight that he faints, as if suggesting that he too was someone who knew only too well the dangers of lust and literature. Similarly, in one of the lower regions of Hell, Ulysses (Canto XXVI) also earns part of our approval as he attempts to explore the known universe, while in the bottommost zone of *Inferno*, amongst those who were treacherous to their country, we meet the last major sinner of the poem, Ugolino della Gherardesca, the counterpart to Francesca at the beginning, and like her speech, so Ugolino's words have a power to conjure up extraordinary sympathy in the reader for this traitor betrayed by his enemy. We are far here from the black-and-white morality of the *Chanson de Roland*, which at one point simply states that Christians are right and pagans are wrong.

A second key feature of the poem is that, like many medieval works, this is a vision poem with an allegorical dimension. This is particularly clear in the opening canto, but this rather heavy allegorical machinery of dark wood, Virgil as reason, the beasts as different kinds of sin, soon gives way to the first adumbrations of psychological realism in Western literature: apart from the morally complex characters mentioned above, look at the portrayal of the politically obsessed Farinata (Canto X), who even ends up in a slanging match with Dante, or Pier delle Vigne's paranoid account of how he was jealously trapped by his enemies at court (Canto XIII), or the pathos of the portrayal of Dante's old teacher, Brunetto Latini, condemned to the punishment meted out to the sodomites (Canto XV).

The third element to strike the reader is Dante's knowledge of the ancient world. Yet although we may be impressed with his classical erudition, and there are many sophisticated intertextual allusions to classical texts (Canto III is the most heavily indebted to *Aeneid* VI), it is worth noting that he modifies this classical 'baggage' in two ways: he transforms Virgil's mythological monsters into medieval Christian demons (Minos, Phlegyas, Nessus), the best example of this being Virgil's surly boatman, Charon, who in Canto III turns into a snarling devil, like a demon from a medieval fresco of the Last Judgement. On the other hand, there is a very personal inflection to this classical lore: Dante the character enjoys an almost personal relationship with Virgil (throughout, this is very much a father-son relationship, and there is a particularly good example of the fluctuating emotions on the pupil's part in Canto III).

Lastly it is worth noting the medieval obsession with structure and number symbolism. In order to tie his huge poem together Dante constructs a tight overarching structure: the whole work is constructed around a system based on a mixture of 3 and 1, obviously echoing the Divine Trinity which contains three persons in the one Godhead. On a macroscopic level there is an introductory canto (Canto I) followed by 33 canti for each of the three canticas (*Inferno*, *Purgatorio* and *Paradiso*), thus totalling 100 canti for the whole poem. Each cantica ends on the symbolically uplifting word 'stelle' (stars). Dante thus invents not only the idea of a cantica and a canto but also his own rhyme scheme, each canto containing a certain number of tercets in 'terza rima' (i.e. a rhyme scheme of *aba, bcb, cdc,* etc.), followed by a final single line at the end: thus each canto is a microcosm of the 1 plus 3 structure of the whole *Comedy*.

One final point is how much the English reader is missing in reading a translation and not the original. In this edition there is the great advantage of having Dante's original text on the facing page for those who want to check translation against original: even T.S. Eliot learnt to read Italian this way. But one of the marvels of Dante's poetry is its concreteness and economy: there could be nothing more concrete or economical than that opening line of *Inferno*, 'Halfway along our journey to life's end'; and the final line of each canto is nearly always a striking example of poetic energy (the alliterative energy of the final line is well preserved here in Cantos III, V, and XXI). Similarly Dante's ability to conjure up a three-dimensional character and his or her tragic story in a short speech is unrivalled in Italian poetry and has been paralleled rightly with his contemporary Giotto's capacity to produce from an otherwise non-realistic context the first realistic narrative paintings in Western Europe. Dante himself was aware of how much is lost in translating poetry, but because the virtues of Dante's poetry are close to the best virtues of prose, there is certainly less lost in translating Dante than in translating his great successor Petrarch. This new translation by J.G. Nichols has preserved those crucial Dantesque virtues of concreteness, economy and energy.

– Martin McLaughlin, 2005

Inferno

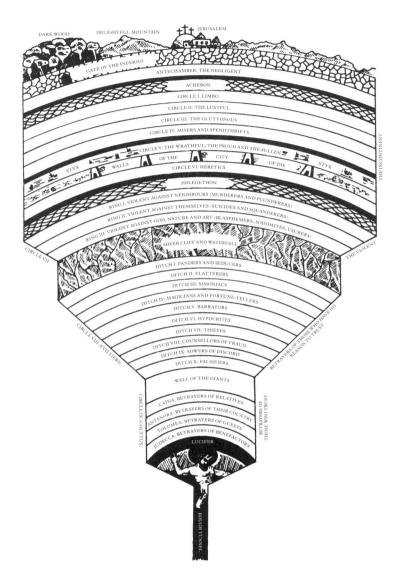

Illustration of Dante's Inferno

CANTO I

This canto, the prologue to Dante's journey through the Inferno, acts also as an introduction to *The Divine Comedy* as a whole.

At the age of thirty-five Dante realises he is lost in a dark, terrifying wood. He takes heart when he sees in front of him a hilltop shining in sunlight. But, as he starts to climb the hill, he is frightened by a leopard which obstructs him in a threatening manner, and then by an angry lion, and finally by a she-wolf – the most alarming animal of the three. So Dante is driven back into the darkness which – as we soon come to realise about everything in this poem – is both real and allegorical. (There are, throughout this poem, many kinds of allegory. For instance, the leopard, the lion, and the she-wolf – emblems rather than symbols, and therefore in need of interpretation – are of a different order from the dark wood, whose import is obvious.)

A human figure approaches, and Dante, uncertain whether it is a living being or a ghost, implores its help. The figure explains that he is the shade of Virgil. This is the poet whom Dante, as he is quick to declare, admires more than any other. Virgil encourages Dante, and explains that he must travel by a different road if he is to find a way out of his difficulties.

After making an obscure prophecy about the coming of a hound which will kill the she-wolf and also be the saviour of Italy, Virgil says that he will guide Dante through the realms of the Inferno, inhabited by the souls of the damned, who are beyond all hope; and also through Purgatory, where the souls of those now doing penance for their sins are residing, glad to suffer because they have the certain hope of going ultimately to Paradise. Virgil, because he was a pagan who lived and died before Christ and so could not believe in Him, cannot accompany Dante into Paradise. But he says there is another guide who will take Dante there.

Dante accepts Virgil's guidance, and they set off.

Nel mezzo del cammin di nostra vita   1
   mi ritrovai per una selva oscura,
   ché la diritta via era smarrita.
Ah, quanto a dir qual era è cosa dura
   esta selva selvaggia e aspra e forte
   che nel pensier rinova la paura!
Tant'è amara che poco è più morte;
   ma per trattar del ben ch'io vi trovai,
   dirò dell'altre cose ch'i' v'ho scorte.
Io non so ben ridir com'io v'entrai,   10
   tant'era pien di sonno a quel punto
   che la verace via abbandonai.
Ma poi ch'i' fui al piè d'un colle giunto,
   là dove terminava quella valle
   che m'avea di paura il cor compunto,
guardai in alto, e vidi le sue spalle
   vestite già de' raggi del pianeta
   che mena dritto altrui per ogni calle.
Allor fu la paura un poco queta
   che nel lago del cor[a] m'era durata   20
   la notte ch'i' passai con tanta pièta.
E come quei che con lena affannata
   uscito fuor del pelago alla riva
   si volge all'acqua perigliosa e guata,
così l'animo mio, ch'ancor fuggiva,
   si volse a retro a rimirar lo passo
   che non lasciò già mai persona viva.
Poi ch'èi posato un poco il corpo lasso,
   ripresi via per la piaggia diserta,
   sì che 'l piè fermo sempre era 'l più basso.   30
Ed ecco, quasi al cominciar dell'erta,
   una lonza leggiera e presta molto,
   che di pel macolato era coverta;
e non mi si partìa d'innanzi al volto,
   anzi impediva tanto il mio cammino
   ch'i' fui per ritornar più volte vòlto.[b]

---

a. A lyrical expression, lit. 'in the heart's lake', or (to quote Yeats) 'in the deep heart's core', the heart being the seat of the passions.

b. Lit. 'often turned to go back'; 'volte vòlto' exemplifies the figure of *traductio*, a play on words with similar sounds but different meanings.

Halfway along our journey to life's end   I
    I found myself astray in a dark wood,
    Since the right way was nowhere to be found.
How hard a thing it is to express the horror
    Of that wild wood, so difficult, so dense!
    Even to think of it renews my terror.
It is so bitter death is scarcely more.
    But to convey what goodness I discovered,
    I shall tell everything that I saw there.
How I got into it I cannot say: 10
    I'd fallen into such a heavy sleep
    The very instant that I went astray.
But when I came beneath a steep hillside –
    Which rose at the far end of that long valley
    That struck my stricken heart with so much dread –
I lifted up my eyes, and saw the height
    Covered already in that planet's rays[1]
    Which always guides all men and guides them right.
And then the fear I felt was somewhat less,
    Though it had filled my heart to overflowing   20
    The whole night I had spent in such distress.
And as somebody, trying to get his breath,
    Emerging from the sea, now safe on shore,
    Turns round to look at where he cheated death,
Just so inside my mind, which was still fleeing,
    I turned to look again upon that pass
    Which never left alive one human being.
When I'd rested my body for a time,
    I made my way across deserted foothills,
    Keeping my low foot always the more firm.[2]   30
And then, just where the hill began to rise,
    I saw a leopard, light upon its paws,
    Covered all over in a spotted hide![3]
It would not move, but stood in front of me,
    And so obstructed me upon my journey
    I kept on turning round to turn and flee.

1. According to the Ptolemaic system, accepted in Dante's time, the sun was one of several planets revolving round the earth. The dark wood and the comforting sunlight mark the beginning of that symbolism of light and darkness which runs through the whole *Comedy*.

2. He was climbing.

3. This leopard is an embodiment of the sin of lust, or sensuality in general, commonly associated with youth.

Temp'era dal principio del mattino,
    e 'l sol montava 'n su con quelle stelle
    ch'eran con lui quando l'amor divino
mosse di prima quelle cose belle;   40
    sì ch'a bene sperar m'era cagione
    di quella fera alla[c] gaetta pelle
l'ora del tempo e la dolce stagione;
    ma non sì che paura non mi desse
    la vista che m'apparve d'un leone.
Questi parea che contra me venisse
    con la test'alta e con rabbiosa fame,
    sì che parea che l'aere ne tremesse[d].
Ed una lupa, che di tutte brame
    sembiava carca nella sua magrezza,   50
    e molte genti fe' già viver grame;
questa mi porse tanto di gravezza
    con la paura ch'uscìa di sua vista,
    ch'io perdei la speranza dell'altezza.
E qual è quei che volentieri acquista,
    e giugne 'l tempo che perder lo face,
    che 'n tutt'i suoi pensier piange e s'attrista;
tal mi fece la bestia sanza pace,
    che, venendomi incontro, a poco a poco
    mi ripigneva là dove 'l sol tace.   60
Mentre ch'i' rovinava in basso loco,
    dinanzi alli occhi mi si fu offerto
    chi per lungo silenzio parea fioco[e].
Quando vidi costui nel gran diserto,
    'Miserere di me' gridai a lui,
    'qual che tu sii, od ombra od omo certo!'
Rispuosemi: 'Non omo, omo già fui,
    e li parenti miei furon lombardi,
    mantovani per patria ambedui.
Nacqui sub Julio, ancor che fosse tardi,   70
    e vissi a Roma sotto 'l buono Augusto
    nel tempo delli dei falsi e bugiardi.

c. 'dalla' in modern Italian.
d. Another reading is 'temesse' ('was afraid'); 'tremesse' is preferable: there are two further uses of the same expression (IV: 27 and 150); moreover there is here a clear reminiscence of a line by Dante's friend Guido Cavalcanti, 'che fa tremar di chiaritate l'âre' ('She makes the very air tremble with light').
e. 'Hoarse' and 'wan'. See l. 54 of the canzone 'Donna pietosa..' (from *Vita nova*): 'ed homo apparve scolorito e fioco' ('I saw a man appear, pale, hoarse, and wan'). The figure of Virgil appears 'hoarse' because the voice of reason (which Virgil represents) has long been silent to Dante. The figure also appears 'wan', or seen only dimly, through the dark atmosphere: the 'lungo silenzio' may be a metaphor, similar to that in l. 60 'dove 'l sol tace' ('where the sun is mute').

By then it was the first hour of the morning,
    With the sun rising in the constellation
    That came with him when stars we still see burning
Were set in motion by divine love first.[4]   40
    And so I had good cause to feel encouraged –
    About the lithe and gaily coloured beast –
By that glad time of day and time of year.
    But not so much encouraged that a lion
    Failed to inspire alarm as it drew near.
It seemed to me the beast was drawing near,
    With head held high, and so irate with hunger
    The air itself seemed shivering in fear.[5]
And then a she-wolf! Though she was so lean,
    She looked about to burst, being crammed with cravings, 50
    She who'd made many draw their breath in pain.[6]
The pain she caused me was so terrible,
    And such the terror coming from her sight,
    I lost all hope of climbing up the hill.
And like that miser, happy while he's gaining,
    Who when luck changes and he starts to lose,
    Gives himself up to misery and moaning –
That's how I was, faced by that restless brute,
    Which always coming nearer, step by step
    Drove me back down to where the sun is mute.[7]   60
Then suddenly, as I went slipping down,
    Someone appeared before my very eyes,
    Seemingly through long silence hoarse and wan.[8]
When I caught sight of him in that wide waste,
    'Take pity on me,' I shouted out to him,
    'Whatever you are, a real man or a ghost!'
He answered: 'Not a man, though I was once.
    Both of my parents came from Lombardy,
    And both of them were native Mantuans.
I came to birth *sub Julio*, rather late,[9]   70
    And lived in Rome under the good Augustus[10]
    When false, deceptive gods still held their state.

4. It was a common medieval belief that, when the world was created, the season was early spring, with the sun in the constellation of Aries.
5. The lion embodies the sins of wrath and pride, commonly associated with middle age.
6. The she-wolf embodies the sin of avarice, commonly associated with old age.
7. As an example of synaesthesia this may at first seem more striking than apt, but during the course of the *Comedy* light, or the lack of it, 'speaks' volumes.
8. This is the shade of someone who has been dead a long time.
9. When Julius Caesar was dominant in Rome, but too late to be acquainted with Caesar.
10. The Emperor Augustus.

Poeta fui, e cantai di quel giusto
    figliuol d'Anchise che venne di Troia
    poi che 'l superbo Ilión fu combusto.
Ma tu perché ritorni a tanta noia?
    perché non sali il dilettoso monte
    ch'è principio e cagion di tutta gioia?'
'Or se' tu quel Virgilio e quella fonte
    che spandi di parlar sì largo fiume?'   80
    rispuos'io lui con vergognosa fronte.
'O delli altri poeti onore e lume,
    vagliami 'l lungo studio e 'l grande amore
    che m'ha fatto cercar lo tuo volume.
Tu se' lo mio maestro e 'l mio autore:
    tu se' solo colui da cu' io tolsi
    lo bello stilo[f] che m'ha fatto onore.
Vedi la bestia per cu' io mi volsi:
    aiutami da lei, famoso saggio,
    ch'ella mi fa tremar le vene e i polsi.'   90
'A te convien tenere altro viaggio,'
    rispuose poi che lagrimar mi vide,
    'se vuo' campar d'esto loco selvaggio:
ché questa bestia, per la qual tu gride,
    non lascia altrui passar per la sua via,
    ma tanto lo 'mpedisce che l'uccide;
e ha natura sì malvagia e ria,
    che mai non empie la bramosa voglia,
    e dopo 'l pasto ha più fame che pria.
Molti son li animali a cui s'ammoglia,   100
    e più saranno ancora, infin che 'l veltro
    verrà, che la farà morir con doglia.
Questi non ciberà terra né peltro,
    ma sapienza, amore e virtute,
    e sua nazion sarà tra feltro e feltro[g].
Di quella umile Italia fia salute
    per cui morì la vergine Cammilla,
    Eurialo e Turno e Niso di ferute.

f. The high, or tragic, or sublime style, as distinguished from the middle style (chosen for general use in the *Comedy*) and the low style. The high style is used in Virgil's *Aeneid*, and for some moral and allegorical *canzoni* by Dante, written before 1300, which had earned him a reputation.
g. As so often with prophecies, the expression is deliberately enigmatic. It may refer to humble origins (felt being a cheap cloth), or to ecclesiastical origins (with reference to the Franciscan habit). It may also, if we use capitals, mean that this saviour originates from somewhere between Feltre and Montefeltro: there could be an allusion to Dante's patron Cangrande della Scala.

I was a poet, and I sang the good
    Son of Anchises who came out of Troy
    When Ilium was burnt down in all its pride.[11]
But you, why d'you go back to misery?
    Why don't you climb up the delightful mountain,
    The origin and cause of perfect joy?'
'Then are you Virgil, you, that spring, that stream
    Of eloquence, that ever-widening river?'   80
    I answered, red with reverence and shame.
'Oh every poet's glory and guiding light!
    May I be aided by the love and zeal
    That made me study your works by day and night.
You are my only master and my author,
    You only are the one from whom I took
    That style which has bestowed on me such honour.
You see the beast that made me turn in flight.
    Save me from her, O famous fount of wisdom!
    She makes the blood run from my veins in fright.'   90
'Now you must travel by a different road,'
    He answered when he saw that I was weeping,
    'If you wish to escape from this wild wood.
This beast, the reason that you cry out loud,
    Will not let people pass along this way,
    But hinders them, and even has their blood.
She is by nature such an evildoer
    Her avid appetite is never slaked,
    And after food she's hungrier than before.
And many are the beasts she's mating with,[12]   100
    And there'll be many more, until the hound[13]
    Arrives, to bring her to a painful death.
This hound will not be fed with land or pelf,
    But rather feed on wisdom, love, and valour.
    He will originate in folds of felt.[14]
He'll be the saviour of low-lying lands
    Of Italy for which Camilla died,
    Turnus, Nisus, Euryalus, of their wounds.[15]

11. This is Virgil, and the poem he refers to is his *Aeneid*, whose hero, Aeneas, a refugee from Troy (or Ilium), is the son of Anchises. The theme of the *Aeneid*, the events leading up to the foundation of Rome, was particularly dear to Catholic Europe because Rome eventually became the seat of the Papacy.
12. Many people will indulge in the sin of avarice.
13. Variously interpreted as a political or religious saviour (there are many candidates) or – most satisfactorily – as a prophecy left deliberately vague.
14. Again obscure, but as translated here it suggests a humble origin.
15. All characters in the *Aeneid*.

Questi la caccerà per ogni villa,
    fin che l'avrà rimessa nello 'nferno,   110
    là onde invidia prima dipartilla.
Ond'io per lo tuo me' penso e discerno
    che tu mi segui, e io sarò tua guida,
    e trarrotti di qui per luogo etterno,
ove udirai le disperate strida,
    vedrai li antichi spiriti dolenti,
    che la seconda morte ciascun grida[h];
e vederai color che son contenti
    nel fuoco, perché speran di venire,
    quando che sia, alle beate genti.   120
Alle qua' poi se tu vorrai salire,
    anima fia a ciò più di me degna:
    con lei ti lascerò nel mio partire;
ché quello imperador che là su regna,
    perch'io fu' ribellante alla sua legge,
    non vuol che 'n sua città per me si vegna.
In tutte parti impera e quivi regge –
    quivi è la sua città e l'alto seggio:
    oh felice colui cu' ivi elegge!'
E io a lui: 'Poeta, io ti richeggio   130
    per quello Dio che tu non conoscesti,
    acciò ch'io fugga questo male e peggio,
che tu mi meni là dove or dicesti,
    sì ch'io veggia la porta di san Pietro
    e color cui tu fai cotanto mesti.'
Allor si mosse, e io li tenni dietro.

---

h. 'The second death', possibly referring to a hope of annihilation, but more probably to the final
   sentence of damnation after the Last Judgement. Even if 'grida' means 'invokes', that fits the second
   interpretation, since the damned in a sense desire their damnation, see III: 125–6.

This hound will hunt that creature high and low
    Until he thrusts her back in the Inferno   110
    Whence envy freed her first and let her go.
I therefore think and judge it would be best
    For you to follow me. And I shall lead
    You to a region that will always last,
Where you will hear shrieks of despair and grief,
    And see the ancient spirits in their pain,
    As each of them begs for their second death.
And you'll see spirits happy in the fire,
    Because they live in hope that they will come,
    Sooner or later, where the blessèd are.   120
And if you wish to join that company,
    One worthier than I will take you up.[16]
    I'll leave you with her when I go away.
That emperor who has his kingdom there[17]
    Lets no one come through me into his city,
    Because I was a rebel to his law.[18]
He governs all creation, ruling where
    He has his capital and his high throne.
    Happy are those he chooses to have there!'
I answered: 'What I beg of you is this –   130
    By that God whom you never knew – so that
    I may escape this evil and much worse,
Take me to both those places as you said,
    To see the gate kept by St Peter,[19] and
    Those souls you say are desperately sad.'[20]
Then he set off. I followed on behind.

16. Beatrice, the woman loved by Dante in his youth and a lasting means of grace leading him to God. Dante's own account of his love, *Vita nova* (New Life), a work in prose with lyrics interspersed, is by far the best introduction to the *Comedy*.
17. God. In the Inferno God tends to be alluded to rather than named, while Christ is never named.
18. Virgil was a pagan.
19. Either the gate of Purgatory, guarded by an angel obedient to St Peter, or the gate of Paradise.
20. Those in the Inferno.

CANTO II

The sun is now setting. This is a time when most creatures settle down to rest. Dante, however, is preparing himself for the coming daylong journey and its hardships.

He invokes the Muses to help him give a true account of his journey. Then he tells Virgil how he doubts his own ability to complete the task, and expresses his perplexity as to why he has been chosen for such an unusual enterprise. He can understand why Aeneas was chosen, the man of destiny who was to found the race that founded Rome, the ruling city of a great empire, and the seat of the Holy See. But Dante cannot think that any such destiny is prepared for him. He can understand too why St Paul was taken temporarily into Heaven while still alive. But no one could believe that Dante is worthy of such a favour.

To these doubts Virgil replies by saying that Dante is simply afraid. To combat Dante's fear he will explain how he came to help him. Beatrice came to him in Limbo and asked for his help to save Dante from damnation. She promised in return to praise Virgil frequently in the presence of God. In answer to Virgil's question, Beatrice explains how she was not afraid to venture down from Heaven: the souls in bliss are not tormented by earthly things. Beatrice describes how Mary, the Mother of Christ, had asked Saint Lucy to help Dante, and Saint Lucy then asked her.

With three such ladies caring for him (an outstanding example of the communion of the saints, in contrast to the lack of a sense of community we find in the Inferno) Dante must have nothing to fear.

Duly encouraged, Dante sets off with Virgil.

Lo giorno se n'andava, e l'aere bruno   1
   toglieva li animai che sono in terra
   dalle fatiche loro – e io sol uno
m'apparecchiava a sostener la guerra
   sì del cammino e sì della pietate,
   che ritrarrà la mente che non erra.
O muse, o alto ingegno, or m'aiutate –
   o mente che scrivesti ciò ch'io vidi,
   qui si parrà la tua nobilitate.
Io cominciai: 'Poeta che mi guidi,   10
   guarda la mia virtù s'ell'è possente,
   prima ch'all'alto passo tu mi fidi.
Tu dici che di Silvio il parente,
   corruttibile ancora, ad immortale
   secolo andò, e fu sensibilmente.
Però, se l'avversario d'ogni male
   cortese i fu, pensando l'alto effetto
   ch'uscir dovea di lui, e 'l chi e 'l quale,
non pare indegno ad omo d'intelletto,
   ch'e' fu dell'alma Roma e di suo impero   20
   nell'empireo ciel per padre eletto:
la quale e 'l quale, a voler dir lo vero,
   fu stabilita per lo loco santo
   u' siede il successor del maggior Piero.
Per questa andata onde li dai tu vanto,
   intese cose che furon cagione
   di sua vittoria e del papale ammanto.
Andovvi poi lo Vas d'elezione,
   per recarne conforto a quella fede
   ch'è principio alla via di salvazione.   30
Ma io perché venirvi? o chi 'l concede?
   Io non Enea, io non Paulo sono:
   me degno a ciò né io né altri crede.
Per che, se del venire io m'abbandono,
   temo che la venuta non sia folle:
   se' savio – intendi me' ch'i' non ragiono.'

The light was failing, and the growing gloom   1
   Relieving every creature on the earth
   Of all its toil and trouble. I alone
Was getting ready to endure the stress
   Both of the road and the resultant anguish,
   Which never-erring memory will rehearse.
O Muses, O my genius, lend me aid!
   O memory, who wrote down what I saw,
   Here your capacity will be well tried!
I started: 'Poet, you who are my guide,   10
   Consider if I have the strength and skill,
   Before you set me on this rugged road.
The father of Silvius,[1] as you tell it, while
   He was corruptible, travelled beyond
   This world of ours, being still corporeal.
And, if the enemy of all that's bad
   Did favour him, because of who he was
   And what he was, and what at last he did,
That must, to men of sense, seem not unfair,
   Since he was chosen in the highest heaven   20
   As father of great Rome and Rome's Empire.
The City of Rome, to tell the truth of it,
   Was destined to become that sacred place
   Where his successor[2] sits in Peter's seat.
On this strange journey you ascribe to him,
   He heard of things that were to bring about
   His triumph and the papal power in Rome.
That is a road the Vessel of Election[3]
   Went upon also, strengthening the faith
   Which starts us on our journey to salvation.   30
But why should I go there? By whose decree?
   Aeneas[3] I am not, and not Paul either.
   That I am worthy no one would agree.
And so, if I agree to go that way,
   I am afraid of being overbold.
   You're wise. You understand more than I say.'

1. Aeneas, the hero of the *Aeneid*. In the sixth book of that poem Aeneas journeys through the underworld and is rewarded with a prophecy of the future glory of Rome.

2. Saint Peter's successor, the Pope.

3. Saint Paul, the 'chosen vessel' mentioned in Acts 9: 15. Paul himself describes how 'he was caught up into paradise' (2 Cor. 12: 2–4).

E qual è quei che disvuol ciò che volle
   e per novi pensier cangia proposta,
   sì che dal cominciar tutto si tolle,
tal mi fec'io in quella oscura costa,   40
   perché, pensando, consumai la 'mpresa
   che fu nel cominciar cotanto tosta.
'S'i' ho ben la parola tua intesa,'
   rispuose del magnanimo quell'ombra,
   'l'anima tua è da viltate offesa;
la qual molte fiate l'omo ingombra
   sì che d'onrata impresa lo rivolve,
   come falso veder bestia quand'ombra[a].
Da questa tema acciò che tu ti solve,
   dirotti perch'io venni e quel ch'io 'ntesi   50
   nel primo punto che di te mi dolve.
Io era tra color che son sospesi,
   e donna mi chiamò beata e bella,
   tal che di comandare io la richiesi.
Lucevan li occhi suoi più che la stella,
   e cominciommi a dir soave e piana,
   con angelica voce, in sua favella:
"O anima cortese mantovana,
   di cui la fama ancor nel mondo dura,
   e durerà quanto 'l mondo lontana,   60
l'amico mio, e non della ventura,
   nella diserta piaggia è impedito
   sì nel cammin, che volt'è per paura;
e temo che non sia già sì smarrito
   ch'io mi sia tardi al soccorso levata,
   per quel ch'i' ho di lui nel cielo udito.
Or movi, e con la tua parola ornata
   e con ciò ch'ha mestieri al suo campare
   l'aiuta, sì ch'i' ne sia consolata.
I' son Beatrice che ti faccio andare –   70
   vegno del loco ove tornar disio –
   amor mi mosse, che mi fa parlare.

---

a. 'ombra': here a verb ('darkness falls'), while in l. 44 it is a noun ('shade'): another instance of *traductio*, see notes to i: 36.

Just as one is who unmeans what he meant,
    Changing that mind of his on second thoughts,
    Wholly diverted from his first intent –
That's how I stood upon that gloomy slope: 40
    By thinking through it, I'd consumed the venture
    For which I was so eager starting up.
'If I have understood your words aright,'
    Answered the shade of that high-minded man,
    'Your cowardly soul has simply taken fright.
Fear often faces men with obstacles
    To make them turn from honourable endeavours,
    As beasts fear shadows when the daylight fails.
That you may lose this fear and so come through,
    I'll tell you why I came, and what I learnt   50
    At the first instant when I pitied you.
I was among those souls who are suspended.[4]
    A lady called to me, so bright and blest
    I asked her to make known what she commanded.
Her eyes were shining brighter than the stars.
    She spoke in her own tongue, in gentleness,
    And said in that angelic voice of hers:
"O Mantuan soul, the soul of courtesy,
    Whose glory is still current in the world,
    And shall endure till this world cease to be,   60
This friend of mine (though not a friend of fate)
    Is so encumbered on the lonely hillside
    He has been driven from his path in fright.
It could be that he has already strayed
    So far I'm here too late to give him succour,
    Judging by what in heaven I have heard.
Now go, and with your noted eloquence,
    And everything he needs for his escape,
    Come to his aid. I shall take comfort thence.
For I am Beatrice putting you to work.   70
    I come from where I'm anxious to return.
    Love urged me on to this – Love makes me speak.

4. In Limbo, described in IV. Limbo is the part of the Inferno reserved for those who had lived virtuously but were not baptised, and so are held in suspense between their desire for God and the impossibility of ever seeing Him.

Quando sarò dinanzi al Signor mio,
   di te mi loderò sovente a lui."
  Tacette allora, e poi comincia' io:
"O donna di virtù, sola per cui
   l'umana spezie eccede ogni contento
   di quel ciel c'ha minor li cerchi sui,
tanto m'aggrada il tuo comandamento
   che l'ubidir, se già fosse, m'è tardi: 80
   più non t'è uopo aprirmi il tuo talento.
Ma dimmi la cagion che non ti guardi
   dello scender qua giuso in questo centro
   dell'ampio loco ove tornar tu ardi."
"Da che tu vuo' saper cotanto a dentro,
   dirotti brievemente," mi rispose,
   "perch'io non temo di venir qua entro.
Temer si dee di sole quelle cose
   c'hanno potenza di fare altrui male –
   dell'altre no, ché non son paurose.   90
Io son fatta da Dio, sua mercé, tale
   che la vostra miseria non mi tange,
   né fiamma d'esto incendio non m'assale.
Donna è gentil nel ciel che si compiange
   di questo impedimento ov'io ti mando,
   sì che duro giudicio là su frange.
Questa chiese Lucia in suo dimando
   e disse: 'Or ha bisogno il tuo fedele
   di te, ed io a te lo raccomando.'
Lucia, nimica di ciascun crudele,   100
   si mosse, e venne al loco dov'i' era,
   che mi sedea con l'antica Rachele.
Disse: 'Beatrice, loda di Dio vera,
   ché non soccorri quei che t'amò tanto,
   ch'uscì per te della volgare schiera?
non odi tu la pièta del suo pianto?
   non vedi tu la morte che 'l combatte
   sulla fiumana onde 'l mar non ha vanto?'

When I'm once more in presence of my Lord,
    I'll sing your praises to him frequently."
    At that point she fell silent. Then I said:
"O lady full of virtue, and through whom
    The human race surpasses everything
    Beneath the narrow circle of the moon,[5]
I am so gratified by what you order,
    If I'd obeyed already I'd be tardy.   80
    There is no need to express your wishes further.
But tell me first the reason you don't spurn
    Descending to this centre from broad spaces[6]
    Where, as you say, you're anxious to return."
"Because you feel the urge to understand,
    I shall explain quite briefly," she replied,
    "Why I am not too frightened to descend.
We should be frightened of those things alone
    Which have the ability to do us evil.
    Things are not frightening if they do no harm.   90
I'm formed in such a fashion, by God's grace,
    That your unhappiness does not affect me.
    Nor do the fires that rage throughout this place.
A lady in heaven[7] has such great sympathy,
    Given the encumbrances through which I send you,
    That the stern judgement up above gives way.
She called on Lucy, and she said to her:
    'One who is faithful to you now has need
    Of you, and I commend him to your care.'
Saint Lucy[8], foe to all malignity,   100
    Rose at those words and, coming where I sat
    With venerable Rachel, said to me:
'Beatrice, veritable praise of God,
    Why do you not help him who loved you so
    That for your sake he stood out from the crowd?
Can you not hear his cries of misery?
    Can you not see him caught in a death-struggle
    Upon that flood as fearful as the sea?'

5. The moon was considered to be the planet nearest to the earth. All above its orbit was considered
   everlasting, and all below mortal.
6. 'This centre' is the earth, seen in the Ptolemaic system as the centre of the universe. The 'broad
   spaces' refers to the Empyrean, the highest heaven, the sphere furthest from the earth.
7. The Virgin Mary.
8. A saint to whom Dante was particularly devoted. Her name is derived from the Latin 'lux' meaning
   light.

Al mondo non fur mai persone ratte
    a far lor pro o a fuggir lor danno,   110
    com'io, dopo cotai parole fatte,
venni qua giù del mio beato scanno,
    fidandomi del tuo parlare onesto,
    ch'onora te e quei ch'udito l'hanno."
Poscia che m'ebbe ragionato questo,
    li occhi lucenti lacrimando volse,
    per che mi fece del venir più presto;
e venni a te così com'ella volse;
    d'innanzi a quella fiera ti levai
    che del bel monte il corto andar ti tolse.   120
Dunque che è? Perché, perché restai?
    Perché tanta viltà nel core allette?
    Perché ardire e franchezza non hai?
Poscia che tai tre donne benedette
    curan di te nella corte del cielo,
    e 'l mio parlar tanto ben ti promette?'
Quale i fioretti, dal notturno gelo
    chinati e chiusi, poi che 'l sol li 'mbianca
    si drizzan tutti aperti in loro stelo,
tal mi fec'io di mia virtute stanca,   130
    e tanto buono ardire al cor mi corse,
    ch'i' cominciai come persona franca:
'Oh pietosa colei che mi soccorse!
    e te cortese ch'ubidisti tosto
    alle vere parole che ti porse!
Tu m'hai con disiderio il cor disposto
    sì al venir con le parole tue,
    ch'i' son tornato nel primo proposto.
Or va', ch'un sol volere è d'ambedue:
    tu duca, tu segnore e tu maestro.'   140
    Così li dissi; e poi che mosso fue,
intrai per lo cammino alto e silvestro.

Nobody in the world was ever so quick
    To seek advantage and to run from loss   110
    As I, the instant I had heard her speak,
Was quick to leave my seat among the blest,
    Putting my faith in your fine honest speech,[9]
    Which honours you and those who read it best."
As soon as she had said these words to me,
    She turned her eyes, shining with tears, aside,
    Which made me the more eager to obey.
And so I came since she requested it,
    And saved you from that savage beast that barred
    The short way up the mountain of delight.   120
What is it then? Why do you hesitate?
    Why do you relish living like a coward?
    Why cannot you be bold and keen to start?
Are not three blessèd ladies, after all,
    Concerned and speaking up for you in heaven?
    And does not what I've said promise you well?'
As tiny blossoms, when the cold night air
    Has made them droop and close, lift up their heads
    And spread their petals once it's dawn once more,
So I did also, after being exhausted.   130
    And such great ardour streamed into my heart
    That like somebody freed from fear I started:
'Oh how compassionate to bring me aid!
    And you, how courteous you were! When she
    Spoke those true words, how swiftly you obeyed!
You have instilled such longing in my heart
    To come with you, because of all you say,
    That I have now gone back to my first thought.
Now go, for we are thoroughly at one.
    You are my leader, my master, and my lord.'   140
    Those were my words. And so, as he went on,
I started on that rugged, savage road.

9. Virgil's poetry, especially the *Aeneid*.

CANTO III

Dante sees the terrible words written over the gate of the Inferno, stressing divine justice and the everlasting nature of the punishment which it inflicts.

Dante is understandably perturbed, and Virgil has once again to remind him of the need for courage to face what lies ahead.

Inside the gate there is no light, no quiet, no rest. The damned are running continually, and to no purpose, after a banner whose significance is not specified. The souls here are of those who were neither for God nor against Him. Having shown neither the courage nor the energy to act decisively, they are now not good enough for heaven, and not evil enough for hell. So they exist in a sort of antechamber of the Inferno. As if to emphasise the contempt in which they should be held, not one of these souls is named.

Then Dante sees a crowd gathering on the bank of a river, the Acheron. A frightening, demonic boatman, Charon, comes towards them from the opposite bank to ferry them over. He curses them. He also tells Dante that, since he is still alive, he cannot go in this boat. Virgil silences Charon by mentioning the inescapable nature of the decision which has brought Dante there. He explains to Dante that normally only the damned can go that way.

As Charon's boat moves off, another crowd of damned souls is already gathering to be ferried across.

Suddenly, the earth quakes, there is thunder and lightning, and Dante falls down in a faint.

'Per me si va nella città dolente,   1
   per me si va nell'etterno dolore,
   per me si va tra la perduta gente.
Giustizia mosse il mio alto fattore:
   fecemi la divina potestate,
   la somma sapienza e 'l primo amore.
Dinanzi a me non fuor cose create
   se non etterne, e io etterno duro.
   Lasciate ogni speranza, voi ch'entrate.'
Queste parole di colore oscuro[a]   10
   vid'io scritte al sommo d'una porta –
   per ch'io: 'Maestro, il senso lor m'è duro[b].'
Ed elli a me, come persona accorta:
   'Qui si convien lasciare ogni sospetto –
   ogni viltà convien che qui sia morta.
Noi siam venuti al loco ov'io t'ho detto
   che tu vedrai le genti dolorose
   c'hanno perduto il ben dell'intelletto.'
E poi che la sua mano alla mia pose
   con lieto volto, ond'io mi confortai,   20
   mi mise dentro alle segrete cose.
Quivi sospiri, pianti e alti guai
   risonavan per l'aere sanza stelle,
   per ch'io al cominciar ne lagrimai.
Diverse lingue, orribili favelle,
   parole di dolore, accenti d'ira,
   voci alte e fioche, e suon di man con elle,
facevano un tumulto, il qual s'aggira
   sempre in quell'aura sanza tempo tinta,
   come la rena quando turbo spira.   30
E io, ch'avea d'orror la testa cinta,
   dissi: 'Maestro, che è quel ch'i' odo?
   E che gent'è che par nel duol sì vinta?'
Ed elli a me: 'Questo misero modo
   tengon l'anime triste di coloro
   che visser sanza infamia e sanza lodo.

a. 'Black' or 'darkly menacing'. See the following note.
b. The meaning of the words is 'duro' both in the sense of 'hard to understand' and 'hard to accept'.

'YOU GO THROUGH ME TO A CITY OF LAMENTATION.   1
    YOU GO THROUGH ME TO EVERLASTING PAIN.
    YOU GO THROUGH ME TO THE FORSAKEN NATION.
JUSTICE INSPIRED MY MAKER UP ABOVE.
    I WAS ESTABLISHED BY OMNIPOTENCE,
    THE HIGHEST WISDOM, AND THE PRIMAL LOVE.
NOTHING BEFORE ME WAS CREATED EVER
    BUT EVERLASTING THINGS.¹ AND I SHALL LAST.
    ABANDON HOPE ENTIRELY, YOU WHO ENTER.'
These were the very sentences I eyed,   10
    Set out in sombre black above a gate.
    Then I said: 'Master, this seems very hard.'
Then he to me, being quick to catch my mood:
    'Here all misgivings must be left behind,
    And all your cowardice be left for dead.
We come now to the region, as I said,
    Where you will see the people steeped in sorrow,
    Those who have lost all intellectual good.'²
And then, when he had looked at me and smiled
    And pressed my hand, from which I drew some comfort,   20
    He introduced me to the secret world.
From this point, sighs, laments, and piercing groans
    Were echoing throughout the starless air.
    Hearing them this first time, I wept at once.
Deformed and diverse tongues, terrible sounds,
    Words venting misery, outbursts of rage,
    Loud voices, soft ones, sounds of slapping hands
Combined into a turmoil always swirling
    Throughout that unrelieved black atmosphere,
    Like sand which rises at a whirlwind's whirling.   30
And I, my head surrounded by that horror,
    Said: 'Master, what's this noise that I can hear?
    Who are these people crushed by what they suffer?'
He said: 'This is the wretched way of these
    Sorry creatures: the lives they lived were such
    They earned no infamy, and earned no praise.

1. The angels were created first (creatures who, not being corporeal, are not subject to mortality), and the Inferno was created to receive those angels who rebelled against God.
2. Nothing but the truth, which is God, can satisfy the intellectual longings with which human beings are born.

Mischiate sono a quel cattivo coro
   delli angeli che non furon ribelli
   né fur fedeli a Dio, ma per sé foro.
Caccianli i ciel per non esser men belli,   40
   né lo profondo inferno li riceve,
   ch'alcuna gloria i rei avrebber d'elli.'
E io: 'Maestro, che è tanto greve
   a lor, che lamentar li fa sì forte?'
   Rispuose: 'Dicerolti molto breve.
Questi non hanno speranza di morte,
   e la lor cieca vita è tanto bassa,
   che 'nvidiosi son d'ogni altra sorte.
Fama di loro il mondo esser non lassa –
   misericordia e giustizia li sdegna –   50
   non ragioniam di lor, ma guarda e passa.'
E io, che riguardai, vidi un'insegna
   che girando correva tanto ratta
   che d'ogni posa mi parea indegna;
e dietro le venìa sì lunga tratta
   di gente ch'io non averei creduto
   che morte tanta n'avesse disfatta.
Poscia ch'io v'ebbi alcun riconosciuto,
   vidi e conobbi l'ombra di colui
   che fece per viltà il gran rifiuto.   60
Incontanente intesi e certo fui
   che questa era la setta de' cattivi,
   a Dio spiacenti ed a' nemici sui.
Questi sciaurati, che mai non fur vivi,
   erano ignudi e stimolati molto
   da mosconi e da vespe ch'eran ivi.
Elle rigavan lor di sangue il volto,
   che, mischiato di lagrime, ai lor piedi
   da fastidiosi vermi era ricolto.
E poi ch'a riguardare oltre mi diedi,   70
   vidi genti alla riva d'un gran fiume;
   per ch'io dissi: 'Maestro, or mi concedi

Now they are mingled with that wicked sort
    Of angels who were neither with the rebels,
    Nor true to God, but simply stood apart.
The heavens, lest their beauty should be flawed,   40
    Reject them, whom deep hell cannot receive
    Lest it should gain some glory on that head.'
I asked: 'What is it hitting them so hard
    That they must answer with such loud laments?'
    And he replied: 'I'll tell you in a word.
These people have no hope of dying ever,
    And their blind life is so contemptible
    That they would barter it for any other.
The world accords them not the least renown.
    Pity and justice scorn them equally.   50
    Enough of this – you've seen them, now pass on.'
I saw some kind of banner that was wheeled
    Around, and racing round at such a rate
    It seemed there was no breathing-time allowed.
And after it there ran so long a line
    Of people that I never would have thought
    That death had gathered such a number in.
When I had recognised some of them there,
    I saw and recognised the shade of him
    Who made the great refusal, out of fear.[3]   60
Immediately I understood how those
    Were members of that dire denomination
    Displeasing both to God and to his foes.
All these wretches, who'd never really existed,
    Went naked and were fiercely goaded on
    By blowflies and by wasps that buzzed and twisted.
These insects went on stinging them and streaking
    Their faces with their blood which, mixed with tears,
    Flowed down to where obnoxious worms were licking.
And then I saw, some way beyond all these,   70
    A crowd upon the bank of a broad river.
    That made me beg of Virgil: 'Master, please

3. There has been much discussion as to who this is. To mention only the most prominent candidates, some say it is Pope Celestine V (c.1214–96) who resigned the Papacy only five months after his election. Others suggest Pontius Pilate, who washed his hands at the trial of Christ. The second seems more appropriate, since this is the only shade in this canto who receives an individual mention, and Pilate's role in the Passion was so important. However, the essential point is that Dante leaves this character unnamed (in a poem which includes so many names) to imply that, since he is one of those who lived so unworthily that they 'never really existed', he does not deserve to be named.

ch'i' sappia quali sono, e qual costume
   le fa di trapassar parer sì pronte,
   com'io discerno per lo fioco lume.'
Ed elli a me: 'Le cose ti fier conte
   quando noi fermerem li nostri passi
   sulla trista riviera d'Acheronte.'
Allor con li occhi vergognosi e bassi,
   temendo no[c] 'l mio dir li fosse grave,   80
   infino al fiume del parlar mi trassi.
Ed ecco verso noi venir per nave
   un vecchio, bianco per antico pelo,
   gridando: 'Guai a voi, anime prave!
Non isperate mai veder lo cielo:
   i' vegno per menarvi all'altra riva
   nelle tenebre etterne, in caldo e 'n gelo.
E tu che se' costì, anima viva,
   pàrtiti da cotesti che son morti.'
   Ma poi che vide ch'io non mi partiva,   90
disse: 'Per altra via, per altri porti
   verrai a piaggia, non qui, per passare:
   più lieve legno convien che ti porti.'
E 'l duca lui: 'Carón, non ti crucciare:
   vuolsi così colà dove si puote
   ciò che si vuole, e più non dimandare.'
Quinci fuor quete le lanose gote
   al nocchier della livida palude,
   che 'ntorno alli occhi avea di fiamme rote.
Ma quell'anime, ch'eran lasse e nude,   100
   cangiar colore e dibattieno i denti,
   ratto che 'nteser le parole crude:
bestemmiavano Dio e lor parenti,
   l'umana spezie e 'l luogo e 'l tempo e 'l seme
   di lor semenza e di lor nascimenti.
Poi si ritrasser tutte quante inseme,
   forte piangendo, alla riva malvagia
   ch'attende ciascun uom che Dio non teme.

c. A Latin construction. Modern Italian would be 'temendo che'.

Tell me. Who are they? And what can incite
    Them with such eagerness to cross the river,
    As far as I can see in this dim light?'
And he replied: 'All will be made quite plain
    When we suspend our journey for a while
    Upon the gloomy banks of Acheron[4].'
So then, with eyes cast down and full of shame,
    Afraid that I might irk him with my speech,   80
    I kept from talking till we reached the stream.
At that there came towards us in a boat
    An old old man, whose hair was white with age.[5]
    'Woe to you, wicked souls!' he shouted out.
'Do not expect to see the sky again!
    I'm here to take you to the further bank,
    To everlasting darkness, ice, and flame.
And you, you over there, you living soul!
    Keep well away from these. All these are dead.'
    But when he saw I made no move at all,   90
He said: 'By other ways, another port,
    You will arrive on shore, and not this way.
    You must be carried in a lighter boat[6].'
My guide said: 'Charon, do not fret and fuss.
    This is wished there where whatsoever is wished
    Is always done. There's nothing to discuss.'
The shaggy jowls went silent. Nothing more
    Came from the pilot of the muddy river
    Who had around his eyes such rings of fire.
But those souls – every troubled naked wretch –   100
    Changed colour and their teeth began to chatter
    Soon as they heard his rough and ready speech.
They cursed their God, their parents in one breath,
    All humankind, the time, the place, the seed
    Of their conception and their very birth.
And they huddled together in a crowd,
    Weeping loudly beside that wicked river
    Which waits for all who have no fear of God.

4. The classical river of the dead, which must be crossed to reach the underworld. Its name is
   derived from a Greek word meaning 'pain' or 'distress'.
5. The classical ferryman of the dead. His Greek name is derived from his bright, fierce eyes.
6. The boat which carries the souls of the saved to the island of Purgatory.

Carón dimonio, con occhi di bragia,
    loro accennando, tutti li raccoglie –   110
    batte col remo qualunque s'adagia.
Come d'autunno si levan le foglie
    l'una appresso dell'altra, fin che 'l ramo
    vede alla terra tutte le sue spoglie,
similmente il mal seme d'Adamo
    gittansi di quel lito ad una ad una,
    per cenni come augel per suo richiamo.
Così sen vanno su per l'onda bruna,
    e avanti che sien di là discese,
    anche di qua nuova schiera s'auna.   120
'Figliuol mio,' disse 'l maestro cortese,
    'quelli che muoion nell'ira di Dio
    tutti convengon qui d'ogni paese:
e pronti sono a trapassar lo rio,
    ché la divina giustizia li sprona,
    sì che la tema si volve in disio.
Quinci non passa mai anima bona;
    e però, se Carón di te si lagna,
    ben puoi sapere ormai che 'l suo dir sona.'
Finito questo, la buia campagna   130
    tremò sì forte che dello spavento
    la mente di sudore ancor mi bagna.
La terra lagrimosa diede vento,
    che balenò una luce vermiglia
    la qual mi vinse ciascun sentimento –
e caddi come l'uom che 'l sonno piglia.

The demon Charon, eyes like glowing embers,
    Beckons to them and gathers them together,   110
    And with his oar he beats whoever lingers.
As in the autumn, when the leaves descend
    One after the other, till the boughs are left
    With all that clothed them lying on the ground,
In the same fashion Adam's evil seed
    Flew down towards the river one by one,
    At Charon's nod, as birds do when they're lured.
They move away across the murky river,
    And well before they reach the other bank
    Another crowd on this side starts to gather.   120
'My son,' my courteous master then explained,
    'Those who have died still subject to God's anger
    All come together here from every land.
And they are keen to reach the other shore,
    Because celestial justice spurs them on
    Until their fear is turned into desire.[7]
No soul that has been good passes this way.
    So now, if Charon was annoyed with you,
    You know exactly what he meant to say.'
The instant this was said, the darkened land   130
    Shuddered, so violently that once again
    I'm bathed in sweat, calling it back to mind.
Out of the tearful, sodden earth a wind
    Burst with the sound of thunder, sending up
    Sudden vermilion flashes. I was stunned,
And sank like someone overcome by sleep.

7. It is as though the damned, in a very human way, wish to get the suspense over with, even though they are going to their punishment. There is also here a hint of something which becomes clearer and clearer in the course of the poem: divine justice consists in allowing people to have what they really want, and the damned have chosen damnation.

CANTO IV

Dante is aroused by a clap of thunder, to find himself on the other side of Acheron. He and Virgil are on the edge of the abyss which is the Inferno proper. Dante's fear is increased by the sight of Virgil's pallor. However, as Virgil explains, this pallor is not the result of fear, but of compassion for those who are suffering below. And so they enter Limbo, the first circle of the Inferno.

Here nothing can be distinguished at first but the sighs of the damned, who are not here because they have sinned, but because they were not baptised. Virgil himself is one of them. They sigh because of their spiritual grief: they endure no physical pain, but a strong and hopeless desire for God.

Dante asks if anyone was ever taken from this place to bliss, and finds that Virgil understands what is in his mind. Virgil describes the Harrowing of Hell – the rescue by Christ, after His resurrection, of Old Testament patriarchs, one matriarch, and others too many to mention. These people worshipped the true God, even though they were not baptised, and they were the first to go to heaven.

Dante and Virgil see ahead of them a hemisphere of light, in which Dante imagines there may be great spirits. Virgil confirms this, and says a special place is allotted to them. A lone voice cries out to announce Virgil's return. Then they are approached by the shades of Homer, Horace, Ovid, and Lucan, who welcome Dante because he too is a poet.

When they reach the light, they see it is a castle with seven high walls and a moat. Inside the castle are the shades of many celebrated people. These include, apart from the four classical poets, Trojan and Roman heroes, pagan intellectuals, and three Muslims.

Dante and Virgil leave the four famous poets and go down to the second circle of the Inferno, where there is no light at all.

Ruppemi l'alto sonno nella testa   1
    un greve truono, sì ch'io mi riscossi
    come persona ch'è per forza desta;
e l'occhio riposato intorno mossi,
    dritto levato, e fiso riguardai
    per conoscer lo loco dov'io fossi.
Vero è che 'n sulla proda mi trovai
    della valle d'abisso dolorosa
    che truono accoglie d'infiniti guai.
Oscura e profonda era, e nebulosa,   10
    tanto che, per ficcar lo viso a fondo,
    io non vi discernea alcuna cosa.
'Or discendiam qua giù nel cieco mondo[a],'
    cominciò il poeta tutto smorto:
    'io sarò primo, e tu sarai secondo.'
E io, che del color mi fui accorto,
    dissi: 'Come verrò, se tu paventi
    che suoli al mio dubbiare esser conforto?'
Ed elli a me: 'L'angoscia delle genti
    che son qua giù nel viso mi dipigne
    quella pietà che tu per tema senti.   20
Andiam, ché la via lunga ne sospigne.'
    Così si mise e così mi fe' intrare
    nel primo cerchio che l'abisso cigne.
Quivi, secondo che per ascoltare,
    non avea pianto mai che di sospiri,
    che l'aura etterna facevan tremare.
Ciò avvenìa di duol sanza martìri
    ch'avean le turbe, ch'eran molte e grandi,
    d'infanti e di femmine e di viri.   30
Lo buon maestro a me: 'Tu non dimandi
    che spiriti son questi che tu vedi?
    Or vo' che sappi, innanzi che più andi,
ch'ei non peccaro – e s'elli hanno mercedi,
    non basta, perché non ebber battesmo,
    ch'è parte della fede che tu credi.

a. Not only is this 'blind world' physically obscure, but those in it are morally blind. See also l. 151 of this canto and X: 58; XXVII: 25.

A sudden thunder broke the heavy sleep   1
    I'd fallen into, and I shook myself,
    As people do when roughly woken up.
From side to side I moved my rested eyes,
    Standing erect, and staring fixedly,
    In an attempt to find out where I was.
The truth is I was standing on the brow
    Over the valley and the sad abyss,
    Receptacle of never-ending woe.
It was so deep, profoundly dark, and full   10
    Of mist that, though I peered and peered again,
    I could not make out anything at all.
'Now down into a world where all is blind,'
    Said then the poet, who was deathly pale.
    'I shall go first, you follow on behind.'
And I, who'd seen the pallor in his face,
    Answered, 'How can I come, when you're afraid
    Who've always comforted my fearfulness?'
Then he to me, 'The thought of those down there
    In misery has painted on my face   20
    That agony which you mistake for fear.
We must go now. The long way urges us.'
    And so he entered, and he made me enter
    On the first circle that goes round the abyss.[1]
So far as I could tell by listening, here
    There was no lamentation but of sighs,
    That trembled through the everlasting air,
Arising from the grief, which is not pain,
    Of all the innumerable multitudes
    Of babies and of women and of men.   30
'You do not ask,' my gentle master said,
    'Who these spirits are that you are looking at?
    You ought to know, before you go ahead,
They did not sin. And if they have some worth,
    That's not enough, since they were not baptised:
    Baptism is essential in your faith.[2]

1. The Inferno is in the shape of a hollow inverted cone. See the illustration on p.3.
2. The Jews of the Old Testament – those who worshipped the true God and lived in hope of a Messiah – are exempted from this requirement. The exclusion of unbaptised virtuous pagans from heaven clearly troubled Dante.

E se furon dinanzi al cristianesmo,
    non adorar debitamente a Dio:
    e di questi cotai son io medesmo.
Per tai difetti, non per altro rio,   40
    semo perduti, e sol di tanto offesi,
    che sanza speme vivemo in disio.'
Gran duol mi prese al cor quando lo 'ntesi,
    però che gente di molto valore
    conobbi che 'n quel limbo eran sospesi.
'Dimmi, maestro mio, dimmi, segnore,'
    comincia' io per voler esser certo
    di quella fede che vince ogni errore:
'uscicci mai alcuno, o per suo merto
    o per altrui, che poi fosse beato?'   50
    E quei, che 'ntese il mio parlar coperto,
rispuose: 'Io era nuovo in questo stato,
    quando ci vidi venire un possente,
    con segno di vittoria coronato.
Trasseci l'ombra del primo parente,
    d'Abèl suo figlio e quella di Noè,
    di Moisè legista e obediente;
Abraàm patriarca e David re,
    Israèl con lo padre e co' suoi nati
    e con Rachele, per cui tanto fe' –   60
e altri molti, e feceli beati –
    e vo' che sappi che, dinanzi ad essi,
    spiriti umani non eran salvati.'
Non lasciavam l'andar perch'ei dicessi,
    ma passavam la selva tuttavia,
    la selva, dico, di spiriti spessi.
Non era lunga ancor la nostra via
    di qua dal sommo, quand'io vidi un foco
    ch'emisperio di tenebre vincìa.
Di lungi v'eravamo ancora un poco,   70
    ma non sì ch'io non discernessi in parte
    ch'orrevol gente possedea quel loco.

They lived too early to be Christian,
    And failed to worship God as people should.[3]
    Among such spirits I myself am one.[4]
It is for such defects, not sin, we're here   40
    Among the lost, and punished but in this:
    That without hope we languish in desire.'
My heart was sickened when I caught his sense,
    Because I recognised some men of worth
    Inhabiting that limbo in suspense.
'Tell me, my master and my lord, tell me,'
    I said, because I wanted to be sure,
    With faith that conquers all uncertainty:
'Has anyone ever, through the good he did,
    Or others' help, gone out from here to bliss?'   50
    And he, who knew what I had left unsaid,[5]
Answered: 'When I'd arrived but recently
    I saw the coming of a mighty lord[6],
    Bearing the evidence of victory.[7]
He took from here our primal father's shade,[8]
    The shade of Abel and the shade of Noah,
    And Moses, who made laws and who obeyed,
The patriarch Abraham, David the King,
    Israel with his father and his children,
    And Rachel, won with so much labouring,[9]   60
And many others, whom he took to bliss.
    And you must know, no human spirits ever
    Were taken up to glory before this.'
While he explained these things, we did not pause,
    But kept on making progress through the wood –
    I mean the wood of shades crowded like trees.
When we had still not travelled very far
    From the circle's highest point, I saw a blaze
    That overcame a gloomy hemisphere.
As yet we were some way away from it,   70
    But not so far that I could not perceive
    That there were honoured people in that light.

3. That is, as was done by the Jews of the Old Testament who were faithful to their covenant with God.
4. The inclusion in Limbo of even Virgil, who was for centuries revered by Christians as a poet and a sage, stresses the limitations of human reason without God's grace.
5. Several times subsequently Virgil shows that he can tell intuitively what Dante is thinking.
6. Christ after His resurrection.
7. Medieval representations of the resurrected Christ often show him with a halo which encircles a cross.
8. Adam.
9. Jacob, later called Israel, served Rachel's father for fourteen years to win her as his bride.

'O tu ch'onori scienzia ed arte, .
   questi chi son c'hanno cotanta orranza
   che dal modo delli altri li diparte?'
E quelli a me: 'L'onrata nominanza
   che di lor suona su nella tua vita
   grazia acquista in ciel che sì li avanza.'
Intanto voce fu per me udita:
   'Onorate l'altissimo poeta: 80
   l'ombra sua torna, ch'era dipartita.'
Poi che la voce fu restata e queta,
   vidi quattro grand'ombre a noi venire:
   sembianza avevan né trista né lieta.
Lo buon maestro cominciò a dire:
   'Mira colui con quella spada in mano,
   che vien dinanzi ai tre sì come sire.
Quelli è Omero poeta sovrano;
   l'altro è Orazio satiro che vène;
   Ovidio è il terzo, e l'ultimo Lucano.   90
Però che ciascun meco si convene
   nel nome che sonò la voce sola,
   fannomi onore, e di ciò fanno bene.'
Così vidi adunar la bella scola
   di quel signor dell'altissimo canto
   che sovra li altri com'aquila vola.
Da ch'ebber ragionato insieme alquanto,
   volsersi a me con salutevol cenno;
   e 'l mio maestro sorrise di tanto.
E più d'onore ancora assai mi fenno,   100
   ch'e' sì mi fecer della loro schiera,
   sì ch'io fui sesto tra cotanto senno.
Così andammo in fino alla lumera,
   parlando cose che 'l tacere è bello,
   sì com'era 'l parlar colà dov'era.
Venimmo al piè d'un nobile castello,
   sette volte cerchiato d'alte mura,
   difeso intorno d'un bel fiumicello.

'O you who honour both knowledge and art,
    Who are these men who are so highly honoured
    Above the others that they're set apart?'
And he to me: 'Their honourable name,
    Still echoing throughout the world above,
    Wins grace in heaven and thus advances them.'
He'd scarcely finished when I heard a voice:
    'Give honour to the celebrated poet!   80
    His shade returns which had abandoned us!'
Then, when the voice had stopped and all was still,
    I saw four lofty shades approaching us.
    And they seemed neither glad nor sorrowful.[10]
My kindly master, when he saw them, said:
    'Look well at him who has a sword in hand,[11]
    And comes before the other three as lord.
Homer, the sovereign poet, is the first,
    Satirical Horace is the next to come,
    Ovid is third, and Lucan is the last.[12]   90
Since they, as well as I do, have by right
    That name[13] the single person has pronounced,
    They do me honour, and in that do right.'
And as I watch, the glorious circle gathers
    Around that master of the highest style[14]
    Who like an eagle soars above all others.
When they had talked a little while together
    They turned to me and made a sign of welcome,
    At which my master smiled in simple pleasure.
An even higher honour came my way,   100
    For they invited me to join their circle:
    I was the sixth, with such great minds as they.[15]
So we continued till we reached the light,
    Speaking of things of which I must be silent,
    Just as to talk about them then was right.
We came at last to a noble castle's foot,
    Surrounded seven times by soaring walls,[16]
    Round which a little stream served as a moat.

---

10. Because they were not physically tormented, but not in bliss either. Also, one traditional notion of a sage was of someone not subject to emotion.

11. Indicating his authorship of the warlike epic, *The Iliad*.

12. Homer's work was known to Dante only by reputation, but the three Roman poets were among his favourite writers.

13. The name of poet.

14. The epic style.

15. Dante is welcomed by them as a fellow-poet.

16. Opinions vary, but probably best interpreted as referring to the seven liberal arts – grammar, rhetoric, logic, arithmetic, music, geography, and astronomy.

Questo passammo come terra dura –
    per sette porte intrai con questi savi: 110
    giugnemmo in prato di fresca verdura.
Genti v'eran con occhi tardi e gravi,
    di grande autorità ne' lor sembianti:
    parlavan rado, con voci soavi.
Traemmoci così dall'un de' canti
    in luogo aperto, luminoso e alto,
    sì che veder si potean tutti quanti.
Colà diritto, sopra 'l verde smalto,
    mi fur mostrati li spiriti magni,
    che del vedere in me stesso n'essalto.   120
I' vidi Elettra con molti compagni,
    tra' quai conobbi Ettòr ed Enea,
    Cesare armato con li occhi grifagni.
Vidi Cammilla e la Pantasilea;
    dall'altra parte vidi 'l re Latino,
    che con Lavina sua figlia sedea.
Vidi quel Bruto che cacciò Tarquino,
    Lucrezia, Julia, Marzia e Corniglia;
    e solo, in parte, vidi 'l Saladino.
Poi ch'innalzai un poco più le ciglia,   130
    vidi 'l maestro di color che sanno
    seder tra filosofica famiglia.
Tutti lo miran, tutti onor li fanno:
    quivi vid'io Socrate e Platone,
    che 'nnanzi alli altri più presso li stanno;
Democrito, che 'l mondo a caso pone,
    Diogenès, Anassagora e Tale,
    Empedoclès, Eraclito e Zenone;
e vidi il buon accoglitor del quale,
    Dioscoride dico; e vidi Orfeo,   140
    Tullio e Lino e Seneca morale;
Euclide geomètra e Tolomeo,

We went across this stream as on dry land –
    I went through seven gateways with these sages.   110
    We reached a meadow growing green, and found
People there whose eyes were grave and slow:
    They looked as though they had authority –
    They seldom spoke, and then gently and low.
We drew apart onto some rising ground,
    Into an open area full of light,
    From which we could see everyone around.
In front of me, on the enamelled green,
    All those great spirits were revealed to me:
    I still rejoice to think what I have seen.   120
I saw Electra there, with all her seed,
    Among whom there were Hector and Aeneas,
    And Caesar, all in armour and hawk-eyed.[17]
I saw Camilla and Penthesilea,
    And King Latinus on the other side,
    Sitting beside his child, Lavinia, there.[18]
I saw that Brutus who drove Tarquin out,
    Lucrece and Julia, Marcia and Cornelia.
    And I saw Saladin, alone, apart.[19]
I had to raise my eyes somewhat to see   130
    Where the great master of the men who know[20]
    Sat with his philosophic family.
They all look up to him, all do him honour:
    I saw both Socrates and Plato there,
    Standing closer to him than any other,
Democritus, who puts all down to chance,
    Diogenes, Empedocles, and Zeno,
    Heraclitus and Thales, Anaxagoras.[21]
I also saw the worthy herbalist
    Dioscorides; Linus, and Orpheus,   140
    Tully, and Seneca the moralist,[22]
Euclid the geometer, and Ptolemy,

17. In this tercet: mother of Troy's founder; defender of Troy; refugee from Troy who founded the Latin race; Julius Caesar.
18. In this tercet: queen killed by Aeneas; Amazon killed by Achilles; King of Latium before Aeneas; Aeneas' third wife.
19. In this tercet: Junius Brutus; four virtuous women of republican Rome; Sultan of Egypt who inflicted severe defeats on crusaders, yet had a high reputation in Europe.
20. Aristotle, Greek philosopher of the fourth century BC, a pupil of Plato who was himself a pupil of Socrates.
21. Greek philosophers of the pre-Christian era.
22. In this tercet: Greek physician of the first century AD; two mythical Greek poets; Cicero (Roman statesman and orator); Roman tragedian (died 65 AD).

Ipocràte, Avicenna e Galieno,
    Averoìs, che 'l gran comento feo.
Io non posso ritrar di tutti a pieno,
    però che sì mi caccia il lungo tema
    che molte volte al fatto il dir vien meno.
La sesta compagnia in due si scema:
    per altra via mi mena il savio duca,
    fuor della queta, nell'aura che trema;   150
e vegno in parte ove non è che luca.

Hippocrates, Galen, and Avicenna,
Averroës who wrote the Commentary.[23]
I cannot now give details of them all:
My long theme urges me, and very often
What's said falls short of what there is to tell.
The company of six now disassembles.
My leader takes me on a different trail,
Out of that calm, into the air that trembles.   150
I come to where there is no light at all.

23. In this tercet: Greek mathematician (*c.* 300 BC); Greek astronomer (second century AD); Greek physician (*c.* 400 BC); Greek physician (second century AD); Arab philosopher (died 1037); Arab from Spain whose Commentary was on Aristotle.

CANTO V

Dante has left Limbo behind: now all the shades he meets
have damned themselves by their own actions. This second
circle contains the lustful: worse sins are punished lower
down in the Inferno. King Minos of Crete is here as judge,
and he consigns the damned to an appropriate circle of the
Inferno, winding his tail around himself a certain number of
times to indicate how many circles down the sinner must go.
Like Charon, he tries to warn Dante off, but is rebuked with
the same words which Virgil used to Charon.

This circle resounds with cries of lamentation, mixed with
the bellowing of opposing winds on which the spirits are
carried higgledy-piggledy, as once they allowed themselves to
be swept along by their passions.

Virgil names some of these spirits, all of them more or less
legendary people, for whom the reader may well feel sym-
pathy, so striking are their stories. But then Dante speaks to
two people who had certainly existed and died during his
lifetime – Paolo Malatesta and Francesca da Rimini. It is
clear why these two spirits are associated with the others: the
immediate cause of their sin was their reading of a romantic
episode of the Arthurian legends. Their fate is pitiful, and it
disturbs Dante so much (he has, after all, himself been much
concerned with literary depictions of love) that he faints.

This, justly one of the most famous episodes in the
Comedy, has itself become part of the literature of romantic
love. But a merely romantic interpretation of it would be
inadequate. Francesca is damned out of her own mouth. All
the souls have to reveal their unvarnished sins to Minos;
but when she is speaking to Dante Francesca tries subtly to
exculpate herself, revealing the very irresponsibility which led
to the damnable sinful act. We find ourselves sympathising
with Francesca, not because the judgement on her is too
hard, but because we have similar defects ourselves. The
seriousness of the sin, with its dreadful consequence of three
damnations, is neither glossed over by Dante nor blurred in a
legendary mist.

Così discesi del cerchio primaio   1
    giù nel secondo, che men luogo cinghia
    e tanto più dolor, che punge a guaio.
Stavvi Minòs orribilmente, e ringhia:
    essamina le colpe nell'entrata;
    giudica e manda secondo ch'avvinghia.
Dico che quando l'anima mal nata
    li vien dinanzi, tutta si confessa;
    e quel conoscitor delle peccata[a]
vede qual luogo d'inferno è da essa: 10
    cignesi con la coda tante volte
    quantunque gradi vuol che giù sia messa.
Sempre dinanzi a lui ne stanno molte:
    vanno a vicenda ciascuna al giudizio;
    dicono e odono, e poi son giù volte.
'O tu che vieni al doloroso ospizio,'
    disse Minòs a me quando mi vide,
    lasciando l'atto di cotanto offizio,
'guarda com'entri e di cui tu ti fide:
    non t'inganni l'ampiezza dell'entrare!'   20
    E 'l duca mio a lui: 'Perché pur gride?
Non impedir lo suo fatale andare:
    vuolsi così colà dove si puote
    ciò che si vuole, e più non dimandare.'
Ora incomincian le dolenti note
    a farmisi sentire – or son venuto
    là dove molto pianto mi percuote.
Io venni in luogo d'ogni luce muto,
    che mugghia come fa mar per tempesta
    se da contrari venti è combattuto.   30
La bufera infernal, che mai non resta,
    mena li spirti con la sua rapina:
    voltando e percotendo li molesta.
Quando giungon davanti alla ruina,
    quivi le strida, il compianto, il lamento –
    bestemmian quivi la virtù divina.

---

a. The word 'conoscitor' suggests a judge, in the legal sense. 'Peccata' is an example of a Latin-style neuter plural.

And so from the first circle I descended   1
    Into the second, which contains less space[1]
    And much more woe, whence shouts of pain ascended.
Minos[2] is there, most horribly, and grinding
    His teeth. He judges guilt as people enter,
    And places them according to his winding.
I mean that when the spirit born for ill
    Comes in his sight, it makes a full confession;
    And then that expert on all sin can tell
What depth of Hell is most appropriate,   10
    Winding his long tail round himself to number
    How many circles down it must be put.
Always there are large crowds. Each one in turn
    Must stand in front of him to hear his judgement.
    They speak, they hear, they're straight away sent down.
'O you, arriving where the wretched dwell,'
    Cried Minos when he saw me there, neglecting
    To carry out his task as usual,[3]
'Watch how you enter and in whom you trust!
    The entrance is so wide it may deceive you!'   20
    My leader answered him: 'Why this outburst?
Do not obstruct his fated journey thus.
    This is wished there where whatsoever is wished
    Is always done. There's nothing to discuss.'[4]
And now there is the sound of voices, loud
    With lamentation, and I have arrived
    Where outcries strike my ears from every side.
I have come somewhere where all light is mute,
    Where there is bellowing like a storm at sea,
    With wild opposing winds fighting it out.   30
This hellish storm, that does not slacken ever,
    Whirls all the spirits irresistibly
    Along with it, and beats and bowls them over.
And when they come where rocks have fallen down,[5]
    Why then what outcries, wailings, and laments!
    And how they curse the power that is divine.

1. All the circles become smaller as Dante descends further into the Inferno. See IV: 24 and note.
2. Mythical King of Crete, generally regarded as a just ruler who became judge of the dead in Hades.
3. His allocation of the damned to their appropriate circle.
4. See III: 95–6.
5. The result (as we are told in XII) of the earthquake which occurred at the time of the Crucifixion.

Intesi ch'a così fatto tormento
    enno[b] dannati i peccator carnali,
    che la ragion sommettono al talento.
E come li stornei ne portan l'ali   40
    nel freddo tempo a schiera larga e piena,
    così quel fiato li spiriti mali
di qua, di là, di giù, di su li mena;
    nulla speranza li conforta mai,
    non che di posa, ma di minor pena.
E come i gru van cantando lor lai,
    faccendo in aere di sé lunga riga,
    così vidi venir, traendo guai,
ombre portate dalla detta briga:
    per ch'i' dissi: 'Maestro, chi son quelle   50
    genti che l'aura nera sì gastiga?'
'La prima di color di cui novelle
    tu vuo' saper,' mi disse quelli allotta,
    'fu imperadrice di molte favelle.
A vizio di lussuria fu sì rotta,
    che libito fe' licito in sua legge
    per tòrre il biasmo in che era condotta.
Ell'è Semiramìs, di cui si legge
    che succedette a Nino e fu sua sposa:
    tenne la terra che 'l Soldan corregge.   60
L'altra è colei che s'ancise amorosa,
    e ruppe fede al cener di Sicheo;
    poi è Cleopatràs lussuriosa.
Elena vedi, per cui tanto reo
    tempo si volse, e vedi il grande Achille,
    che con amore al fine combattèo.
Vedi Parìs, Tristano,' e più di mille
    ombre mostrommi e nominommi a dito
    ch'amor di nostra vita dipartille.
Poscia ch'io ebbi il mio dottore udito   70
    nomar le donne antiche e' cavalieri,
    pietà mi giunse, e fui quasi smarrito.

---

b. A form of 'sono' still found in some Tuscan dialects.

I understood how all such torments are
    Destined for those whose sins are of the flesh,
    Those who subject their reason to desire.
And like a flock of starlings on the wing   40
    In the cold season, crowded all together,
    So the bad spirits in that blustering
Are carried here and there and up and down:
    They are not comforted by thoughts of rest,
    Or even diminution of their pain.
And like a flock of loud lamenting cranes
    Making themselves a long line in the air,
    I saw shades coming, and emitting groans,
Borne on the onrush of that windy war.
    So that I questioned: 'Master, who are these,   50
    Punished so hard in this black atmosphere?'
My master answered me: 'The first of those
    Of whom you wish to be informed was empress
    Of many lands and many languages.
She was so vicious, unrestrained, and lewd
    That she made licence licit in her laws
    To take away the blame she had incurred.[6]
She was Semiramis – we read of her
    That she was Ninus' wife and his successor.
    She ruled the land now in the Sultan's power.[7]   60
That other killed herself in love's despair,
    Breaking her faith with the ashes of Sychaeus.[8]
    Then Cleopatra[9] is the next one there.
See Helen[10], for whose sake the times were cursed
    With crime and woe, and see the great Achilles:
    He too was overcome by love at last.[11]
See Paris[12], and see Tristan[13].' And he showed
    A thousand shades and more to me, and named them,
    Of those whom love and lust had left for dead.
When I had heard my teacher to the end,   70
    Naming the ancient ladies and the knights,
    Such horror seized me that I almost swooned.

---

6. By her incest with her son.

7. Egypt.

8. In the *Aeneid*, Dido Queen of Carthage had vowed to remain faithful to the memory of her dead
    husband. She violated this oath by her love for Aeneas, and killed herself when Aeneas forsook her.

9. Queen of Egypt, lover of Julius Caesar and later Marc Antony, who killed herself to avoid falling
    into the hands of Octavius after the Battle of Actium.

10. Whose face, in Marlowe's words, 'launched a thousand ships' to avenge her abduction by Paris of Troy.

11. Because of his love for Polyxena, daughter of Priam King of Troy, he let himself be ambushed and killed.

12. See note 10 above.

13. The adulterous lover of Isolde, who was killed by her husband.

I' cominciai: 'Poeta, volentieri
    parlerei a quei due che 'nsieme vanno,
    e paion sì al vento esser leggieri.'
Ed elli a me: 'Vedrai quando saranno
    più presso a noi – e tu allor li priega
    per quello amor che i mena, ed ei verranno.'
Sì tosto come il vento a noi li piega,
    mossi la voce: 'O anime affannate,   80
    venite a noi parlar, s'altri nol niega!'
Quali colombe, dal disio chiamate,
    con l'ali alzate e ferme al dolce nido
    vegnon per l'aere dal voler portate,
cotali uscir della schiera ov'è Dido,
    a noi venendo per l'aere maligno,
    sì forte fu l'affettuoso grido.
'O animal grazioso e benigno
    che visitando vai per l'aere perso
    noi che tignemmo il mondo di sanguigno,   90
se fosse amico il re dell'universo,
    noi pregheremmo lui della tua pace,
    poi c'hai pietà del nostro mal perverso.
Di quel che udire e che parlar vi piace,
    noi udiremo e parleremo a voi,
    mentre che 'l vento, come fa, si tace.
Siede la terra dove nata fui
    sulla marina dove 'l Po discende
    per aver pace co' seguaci sui.
Amor, ch'al cor gentil ratto s'apprende,   100
    prese costui della bella persona
    che mi fu tolta – e 'l modo ancor m'offende.
Amor, ch'a nullo amato amar perdona,
    mi prese del costui piacer[c] sì forte
    che, come vedi, ancor non m'abbandona.
Amor condusse noi ad una morte:
    Caina attende chi a vita ci spense.'
    Queste parole da lor ci fur porte.

---

c. Both 'beauty' and 'pleasure', i.e. Paolo's beauty and the pleasure he gives to her and she to him.

I started: 'Poet, I would be inclined
    To talk with those two who go yoked together
    And seem to be so light upon the wind.'
Then he to me: 'You try it when those two
    Have come much nearer. Beg them by that love
    Which drives them on, and they will turn to you.'
Once they were blown towards us by the wind,
    I spoke: 'O terribly tormented souls,   80
    Come here and speak to us, if that's not banned!'
And just as doves, attracted by desire
    Into their nest, their wings outspread and still,
    Glide with a clear intention through the air,
So these two left the throng where Dido was,
    And came to us through that foul atmosphere,
    Such was the power of my affectionate cries.
'O living being, so gracious and so good
    That you come visiting, through pitch-black air,
    Us who once stained this world of ours with blood,   90
Oh, if the Lord of all were but our friend,
    We would appeal to him to give you peace,
    Since you show sympathy with our sad end.
And anything you wish to talk about,
    Whatever it is, we'll talk of it with you,
    In these few moments while the storm is mute.
I must explain my native city lies
    Upon that seacoast where the Po descends
    To the calm sea with all its tributaries.[14]
Love, kindling quickly in the noble heart,   100
    Seized him: he was enamoured of this body
    Killed in a way from which I suffer yet.[15]
Love, who insists all loved ones must requite
    Their lovers, seized me so with love's enjoyment
    That, as you see, love does not leave me yet.
Love chose a single death for both of us.
    Caïna[16] waits for him who took our lives.'
    Such were the words of hers which came across.

14. The speaker is Francesca da Rimini. She was married to Gianciotto Malatesta, but fell in love with
    his brother Paolo. Her husband came upon the guilty pair and killed them.
15. Not only was her death violent, but it allowed her no time to repent.
16. A zone of the lowest circle of the Inferno, reserved for those who betray their relatives (XXXII).
    It is named after Cain who murdered his brother Abel (Genesis 4: 8).

Quand'io intesi quell'anime offense,
  china' il viso, e tanto il tenni basso   110
  fin che 'l poeta mi disse: 'Che pense?'
Quando rispuosi, cominciai: 'Oh lasso,
  quanti dolci pensier, quanto disio
  menò costoro al doloroso passo!'
Poi mi rivolsi a loro e parla' io,
  e cominciai: 'Francesca, i tuoi martìri
  a lacrimar mi fanno tristo e pio.
Ma dimmi: al tempo de' dolci sospiri,
  a che e come concedette Amore
  che conosceste i dubbiosi disiri?'   120
E quella a me: 'Nessun maggior dolore
  che ricordarsi del tempo felice
  nella miseria – e ciò sa 'l tuo dottore.
Ma s'a conoscer la prima radice
  del nostro amor tu hai cotanto affetto,
  dirò come colui che piange e dice.
Noi leggiavamo un giorno per diletto
  di Lancialotto come amor lo strinse:
  soli eravamo e sanza alcun sospetto.
Per più fiate li occhi ci sospinse   130
  quella lettura, e scolorocci il viso –
  ma solo un punto fu quel che ci vinse.
Quando leggemmo il disiato riso
  esser baciato da cotanto amante,
  questi, che mai da me non fia diviso,
la bocca mi baciò tutto tremante.
  Galeotto[d] fu il libro e chi lo scrisse:
  quel giorno più non vi leggemmo avante.'
Mentre che l'uno spirto questo disse,
  l'altro piangea, sì che di pietade   140
  io venni men così com'io morisse –
e caddi come corpo morto cade.

---

d. The seneschal who, in the book which Paolo and Francesca are reading, encouraged Lancelot and
  Guinivere to reveal their love for each other, as the book does with Paolo and Francesca.

I, when I'd heard these stricken souls, inclined
   My head, and for a long time held it down.   110
   At length the poet asked: 'What's in your mind?'
Then I replied to him and said: 'Alas!
   How many pleasant thoughts, and how much ardour
   Have brought this wretched pair to such a pass!'
And then once more I turned to them to speak,
   And said: 'Francesca, seeing how you suffer
   Makes me weep tears of sympathy and grief.
But tell me: in the time of gentle sighs,
   By what and in what way did Love permit you
   To recognise your dubious desires?'   120
She said: 'There is no greater wretchedness
   Than calling back to mind a happy time
   In misery – and your teacher[17] knows this.
But, if you want to understand the root –
   Cause of our love – it seems you really want to –
   I'll tell you, though I weep describing it.
We were reading one day for delectation
   Of Lancelot and how love held him close.[18]
   We were alone and quite without suspicion.
At several points that reading drew our eyes   130
   Together, drained the colour from our cheeks.
   But one point only took us by surprise.
When we read how the smile of the belovèd
   Was kissed by such a celebrated lover,[19]
   This one[20], from whom I never will be severed,
Kissed me upon the mouth, trembling all over.
   That book's a pander, and the man who wrote it:
   And on that day we read in it no further.'
While the one spirit said all this to me,
   The other wept, and my disquietude   140
   Brought on a fainting fit. I seemed to die,
And fell down as a body does when dead.

17. Virgil.
18. The adulterous love of Lancelot for Guinevere, the wife of his lord King Arthur.
19. Guinevere was kissed by Lancelot.
20. Paolo.

CANTO VI

Dante is now in the third circle of the Inferno, that of the gluttonous. Their shades are prostrated in fetid mud where hail, dirty rain, and snow fall upon them with unvarying intensity. They are deafened by the continual howling of Cerberus, the three-headed monster, who also tears them apart and flays them with his claw-like hands. There is little that seems human in this circle: only one shade speaks, and he lacks individuality. The damned here are what their gross appetites have made them – subhuman, almost sub-bestial.

The one shade who is interested enough in the visitors to speak to them is Ciacco: he recognises Dante as a fellow Florentine. In response to Dante's questions, he discusses the troubles in their native city, and hints at Dante's coming exile. It is noteworthy that he attributes all the discord in Florence to the moral faults of the citizens, and does not discuss policies at all. We have here the start of one of the great themes of the *Comedy* – the history of Florence.

As the companions continue to walk through this circle, they discuss the life to come, and Virgil explains what the state of the damned will be after the Last Judgement.

They then descend to the fourth circle, which is dominated by Pluto, god of wealth.

Al tornar della mente, che si chiuse   I
    dinanzi alla pietà de' due cognati,
    che di trestizia tutto mi confuse,
novi tormenti e novi tormentati
    mi veggio intorno, come ch'io mi mova
    e ch'io mi volga, e come che io guati.
Io sono al terzo cerchio, della piova
    etterna, maladetta, fredda e greve:
    regola e qualità mai non l'è nova.
Grandine grossa, acqua tinta e neve   10
    per l'aere tenebroso si riversa –
    pute la terra che questo riceve.
Cerbero, fiera crudele e diversa,
    con tre gole caninamente latra
    sopra la gente che quivi è sommersa.
Li occhi ha vermigli, la barba unta e atra,
    e 'l ventre largo, e unghiate le mani:
    graffia li spiriti, iscoia ed isquatra.
Urlar li fa la pioggia come cani:
    dell'un de' lati fanno all'altro schermo;   20
    volgonsi spesso i miseri profani.
Quando ci scorse Cerbero, il gran vermo[a],
    le bocche aperse e mostrocci le sanne –
    non avea membro che tenesse fermo.
E 'l duca mio distese le sue spanne,
    prese la terra, e con piene le pugna
    la gittò dentro alle bramose canne.
Qual è quel cane ch'abbaiando agugna,
    e si racqueta poi che 'l pasto morde,
    ché solo a divorarlo intende e pugna,   30
cotai si fecer quelle facce lorde
    dello demonio Cerbero, che 'ntrona
    l'anime sì ch'esser vorrebber sorde.
Noi passavam su per l'ombre che adona
    la greve pioggia, e ponavam le piante
    sopra lor vanità che par persona.

---

a. 'Worm', both in the archaic English sense of 'monster' and also connoting a filthy grovelling creature. The word is used of Lucifer in XXXIV: 108.

On coming to my senses, lost when faced   1
    With all the wretchedness of those in-laws
    Whose sad plight left me totally confused,
I see new torments, new tormented shades
    Rising around me as I move around,
    Wherever I turn myself, wherever I gaze.
I've come to the third circle[1], that of heavy
    Rain which goes on for ever, coldly cursed,
    Whose nature and whose volume never vary.
Huge hail, with water of a filthy texture   10
    And snow, comes pouring down through murky air –
    The earth is stinking that receives this mixture.
And Cerberus[2], a strange and cruel beast,
    Is growling like a dog through all three gullets
    Over the people who lie here immersed.
He has red eyes, a black and greasy beard,
    A swollen belly, and great claws for hands,
    By which the shades are rent apart and flayed.
The spirits howl like hounds under the rain:
    They have to shelter one flank with the other,   20
    And so the sinners turn and turn again.
When Cerberus perceived us, the great worm,
    He opened all his mouths, and bared his fangs.
    There was no part of him that did not squirm.
And then my leader spreads his hands out, tears
    Up earth until his fists are overflowing,
    And thrusts it in those gaping apertures.[3]
Then like a dog that, barking for a bone,
    Calms down immediately it gnaws its food,
    Solely intent on gobbling it all down,   30
Just so did the three filthy faces there
    Of Cerberus, the demon dog who stuns
    The spirits till they wish they could not hear.
We walked across those shades the constant flood
    Goes beating down upon, placing our feet
    On nothingness which seems like flesh and blood.

1. That of the gluttonous.

2. The classical poets represent Cerberus, the guardian of their underworld, as a three-headed dog. So does Dante, but he adds grotesque details of his own.

3. A parody of the feeding of Cerberus in the *Aeneid* with a sop of honey and drugged meal to soothe him, so that he may allow Aeneas to enter the underworld.

Elle giacean per terra tutte quante,
    fuor d'una ch'a seder si levò, ratto
    ch'ella ci vide passarsi davante.
'O tu che se' per questo inferno tratto,'   40
    mi disse, 'riconoscimi, se sai:
    tu fosti, prima ch'io disfatto, fatto.'
E io a lui: 'L'angoscia che tu hai
    forse ti tira fuor della mia mente,
    sì che non par ch'i' ti vedessi mai.
Ma dimmi chi tu se' che 'n sì dolente
    loco se' messo e hai sì fatta pena,
    che, s'altra è maggio, nulla è sì spiacente.'
Ed elli a me: 'La tua città, ch'è piena
    d'invidia sì che già trabocca il sacco,   50
    seco mi tenne in la vita serena.
Voi cittadini mi chiamaste Ciacco:
    per la dannosa colpa della gola,
    come tu vedi, alla pioggia mi fiacco.
E io anima trista non son sola,
    ché tutte queste a simil pena stanno
    per simil colpa.' E più non fe' parola.
Io li rispuosi: 'Ciacco, il tuo affanno
    mi pesa sì ch'a lagrimar mi 'nvita;
    ma dimmi, se tu sai, a che verranno   60
li cittadin della città partita –
    s'alcun v'è giusto, e dimmi la cagione
    per che l'ha tanta discordia assalita.'
Ed elli a me: 'Dopo lunga tencione
    verranno al sangue, e la parte selvaggia
    caccerà l'altra con molta offensione.
Poi appresso convien che questa caggia
    infra tre soli, e che l'altra sormonti
    con la forza di tal che testé piaggia.
Alte terrà lungo tempo le fronti,   70
    tenendo l'altra sotto gravi pesi,
    come che di ciò pianga o che n'adonti.

They went on lying prostrate, all of them
    Except for one who sat up suddenly
    The instant that he saw us passing him.
'O you,' he called, 'who are now being led   40
    Through this Inferno, please call me to mind,
    For you were born a while before I died.'
And I to him: 'The torment that you suffer
    Appears to drive you from my memory,
    So that it seems we never knew each other.
But tell me who you are, you who are placed
    In such a spot, with such a penalty
    That if there's worse, none rouses more disgust.'
And he replied: 'While I lived in the sun,
    That city[4], overflowing with its envy,   50
    Which is your city still, was also mine.
Ciacco[5] was what you citizens called me.
    You see me here, a broken man in rain,
    And ruined by the sin of gluttony.
And, sad soul that I am, I'm not alone,
    Since all these suffer the same penalty
    For the same sin.' He did not carry on,
And so I said: 'Ciacco, your wretched state
    So weighs upon me that it makes me weep.
    But tell me, if you can, the future fate   60
Of the divided city's citizens.[6]
    Is there one man who's just? Tell me the reason
    Why it's a prey to so much dissidence.'
And then he answered: 'After much dispute
    There will be bloodshed, and the rural party[7]
    Will use brute force to drive the other out.
Then this party will lose its dominance
    Inside three years, and the other party[8] triumph
    With help from him who's sitting on the fence.[9]
This party then will hold the other down,   70
    And hold its own head high, with gross inflictions[10]
    For many years, however they complain.

4. Florence.
5. Possibly a nickname meaning 'swine'.
6. Divided politically into Guelphs and Ghibellines, and subdivided, as we learn in the next few lines,
   into White Guelphs (of whom Dante is one) and Black Guelphs.
7. White Guelphs.
8. Black Guelphs.
9. Probably Pope Boniface VIII, a *bête noire* of Dante's. See especially XIX: 52–7.
10. Including Dante's banishment from his native city.

Giusti son due, e non vi sono intesi:
    superbia, invidia e avarizia sono
    le tre faville c'hanno i cuori accesi.'
Qui puose fine al lacrimabil sono;
    e io a lui: 'Ancor vo' che m'insegni,
    e che di più parlar mi facci dono.
Farinata e 'l Tegghiaio[b], che fuor sì degni,
    Iacopo Rusticucci, Arrigo e 'l Mosca   80
    e li altri ch'a ben far puoser li 'ngegni,
dimmi ove sono e fa ch'io li conosca,
    ché gran disio mi stringe di savere
    se 'l ciel li addolcia, o lo 'nferno li attosca.'
E quelli: 'Ei son tra l'anime più nere:
    diverse colpe giù li grava al fondo:
    se tanto scendi, là i potrai vedere.
Ma quando tu sarai nel dolce mondo,
    priegoti ch'alla mente altrui mi rechi:
    più non ti dico e più non ti rispondo.'   90
Li diritti occhi torse allora in biechi,
    guardommi un poco, e poi chinò la testa:
    cadde con essa a par delli altri ciechi.
E 'l duca disse a me: 'Più non si desta
    di qua dal suon dell'angelica tromba,
    quando verrà la nimica podèsta:
ciascun rivederà la trista tomba,
    ripiglierà sua carne e sua figura,
    udirà quel ch'in etterno rimbomba.'
Sì trapassammo per sozza mistura   100
    dell'ombre e della pioggia, a passi lenti,
    toccando un poco la vita futura;
per ch'io dissi: 'Maestro, esti tormenti
    crescerann'ei dopo la gran sentenza,
    o fier minori, o saran sì cocenti?'
Ed elli a me: 'Ritorna a tua scienza,
    che vuol, quanto la cosa è più perfetta,
    più senta il bene, e così la doglienza.

b. Pronounced as two syllables (in Dante's time, the 'iaio' diphthong was pronounced as one syllable).

There are two just men,[11] but they're never heard.
    For three sparks only have set hearts on fire:
    Envy I mean, and avarice, and pride.'
And so he ended on a cheerless note.
    But I said: 'I would like more information.
    Therefore I beg you, tell me more than that.
Farinata, Tegghiaio – men of honour –
    Jacopo Rusticucci, Arrigo, Mosca,   80
    And all who set their hearts on right behaviour –
Say where they are that we may come together.
    I have a longing to be told if Heaven
    Comforts them, or the Inferno makes them bitter.'
'Among the blackest souls is where they are,
    For different sins have sent them to the depths.[12]
    You'll see them there, if you go down so far.
But when you're back in the sweet world again,
    I beg you to remember me to people.
    I'll say no more to you. You'll ask in vain.'   90
With that he turned aside his steady glance,
    And looked at me a while, then bent his head,
    And fell down with the other blinded ones.[13]
'He will not rise,' my leader said to me,
    'Until the blast of the angelic trumpet
    Heralds the inimical authority,[14]
When all will reassume their flesh and figure[15]
    (Once they have found the place where they are buried)
    And hear the sentence that resounds for ever.'
And so we passed across the squalid slime,   100
    A mix of shades and mud – and we walked slowly,
    Touching a little on the life to come.
And so I asked him: 'Master, these torments,
    Will they grow greater from the Judgement Day,
    Or lessen, or be simply as intense?'
Then he to me: 'Your learning makes it plain:
    The nearer something comes to its perfection,
    The greater is its pleasure and its pain.

11. We are left to guess who they may be. Possibly all that is intended is an indefinite small number.
12. Of these five prominent Florentines, Farinata is mentioned again, in X, Tegghiaio and
    Rusticucci in XVI, and Mosca in XXVIII. No more is heard of Arrigo.
13. Face-down in mud, of course, but spiritually blind also.
14. Christ.
15. A reference to the dogma of the resurrection of the body.

Tutto che questa gente maladetta
   in vera perfezion già mai non vada,   110
   di là più che di qua essere aspetta.'
Noi aggirammo a tondo quella strada,
   parlando più assai ch'io non ridico;
   venimmo al punto dove si digrada:
quivi trovammo Pluto, il gran nemico.

And these accursèd people here, although
    They'll never ever reach their true perfection,   110
    Expect to be much nearer then than now.'[16]
We went on walking that circumference,
    Talking of more things than I care to say,
    And came at last to where the road descends.[17]
Here we found Pluto[18], the great enemy.

16. They cannot, since they are damned, ever be perfect. But they will be nearer to perfection when
    their souls are reunited with their bodies at the Last Judgement.
17. From the third to the fourth circle.
18. The classical god of wealth. He is 'the great enemy' because 'the love of money is the root of all evil'
    (2 Timothy 6: 10).

CANTO VII

At the entrance to the fourth circle is Pluto, the mythical god of the underworld, personifying wealth, the love of which is 'the root of all evil'. He is angry at Dante's arrival, but Virgil immediately takes the wind out of his sails, and the travellers are able to descend into the fourth circle.

Here are the souls of misers and spendthrifts, guilty of sins which at first sight seem opposite, and yet are very similar because they both involve a lack of judgement in the use of riches. They are in two groups, rolling great weights towards each other with their chests, upbraiding each other as they do so. When the two groups have clashed together, they turn back to where they started from, describe a semicircle, and then once more roll their weights towards each other, to clash again in the middle. It is a striking image of futile effort. Dante wishes to see if he can recognise any of them, but they are so disfigured by their sins that they are unrecognisable.

In answer to Dante's question, Virgil explains the function of Fortune, seen here as an angel appointed by God to move this world's wealth about. Virgil stresses that the reasons for her actions are quite beyond human comprehension.

Following a watercourse which runs from the fourth circle, Dante and Virgil arrive at a marsh, the Styx. The wrathful are here, naked and covered in mud, and attacking each other savagely with their teeth and every other part of their bodies.

Submerged in the marsh – their presence revealed by bubbles which rise to the surface – are the souls of the sullen, whose anger is turned inward on themselves. They cannot speak properly, because of the mud in their throats, but Virgil explains to Dante what they are trying to say: they wilfully lived in gloom.

As Dante and Virgil continue to walk round the circle, they come across a tower.

'*Papé Satàn, papé Satàn aleppe!*'[a]   1
    cominciò Pluto con la voce chioccia;
    e quel savio gentil, che tutto seppe,
disse per confortarmi: 'Non ti noccia
    la tua paura, ché, poder ch'elli abbia,
    non ci torrà lo scender questa roccia.'
Poi si rivolse a quella infiata labbia,
    e disse: 'Taci, maladetto lupo –
    consuma dentro te con la tua rabbia.
Non è sanza cagion l'andare al cupo: 10
    vuolsi nell'alto, là dove Michele
    fe' la vendetta del superbo strupo.'
Quali dal vento le gonfiate vele
    caggiono avvolte poi che l'alber fiacca,
    tal cadde a terra la fiera crudele.
Così scendemmo nella quarta lacca
    pigliando più della dolente ripa
    che 'l mal dell'universo tutto insacca.
Ahi giustizia di Dio! tante chi stipa
    nove travaglie e pene quant'io viddi?   20
    e perché nostra colpa sì ne scipa?
Come fa l'onda là sovra Cariddi,
    che si frange con quella in cui s'intoppa,
    così convien che qui la gente riddi.
Qui vidi gente più ch'altrove troppa,
    e d'una parte e d'altra, con grand'urli,
    voltando pesi per forza di poppa.
Percoteansi incontro, e poscia pur lì
    si rivolgea ciascun, voltando a retro,
    gridando: 'Perché tieni?' e 'Perché burli?'   30
Così tornavan per lo cerchio tetro
    da ogni mano all'opposito punto,
    gridandosi anche loro ontoso metro;
poi si volgea ciascun, quand'era giunto,
    per lo suo mezzo cerchio all'altra giostra.
    E io, ch'avea lo cor quasi compunto,

---

a. 'Papé' seems to express wonder, and 'aleppe' perhaps refers to Satan. The line is analogous to
Nimrod's speech in XXXI: 67 in its obscurity. However, its general trend is obvious from Virgil's reaction
and Dante's.

'*Papé Satàn, papé Satàn, aleppe!*'[1]   1
  That is what Pluto rasped in raucous tones.
  But that all-knowing sage, keeping me happy,
Said: 'Never let the sound of him perplex
  Or frighten you. Whatever power he has,
  He cannot stop us climbing down these rocks.'
He turned back to that bloated face, and said:
  'Silence, cursed wolf! If you must be consumed
  With anger, let it gobble you inside.
This is no pointless journey into dark.   10
  It is decided there on high, where Michael
  Left arrogant rebellion thunderstruck.'[2]
As sails, once proudly swollen in the wind,
  Slump in a tangle with the snapping mast,
  So that outrageous beast dropped to the ground.
We went to the fourth level, and ahead
  Along the edge of the abyss where all
  The evils of the world are pocketed.
Justice of God! Who's ever seen amassed
  So many uncouth torments as I saw?   20
  Why does this guilt of ours so lay us waste?
As near Charybdis[3], where the waters, once
  They batter the opposing waters, shatter,
  The people here are led a merry dance.
Here I saw shades more numerous than ever,
  Rolling great weights by pushing with their chests,
  Howling out loud, from one side to the other.
They struck against each other, and then they
  All turned around and rolled the weights back shouting:
  'Why do you hoard?' and 'Why d'you throw away?'[4]   30
Describing a half-circle in the gloom,
  They went from each side to the opposite,
  Once more repeating their opprobrium.
Then each lot turned, when they had reached the spot
  Half round the circle, for another joust.
  And I, who felt so very sick at heart,

1. Like others with posts of responsibility in the Inferno (e.g. Charon and Minos), Pluto is annoyed at Dante's arrival. He seems to be addressing his chief, Satan.
2. 'And there was war in heaven: Michael and his angels fought against the dragon; and the dragon fought and his angels, and prevailed not; neither was their place found any more in heaven. And the great dragon was cast out, that old serpent, called the Devil, and Satan, which deceiveth the whole world: he was cast out into the earth, and his angels were cast out with him.' (Revelation 12: 7–9)
3. The whirlpool in the Straits of Messina.
4. Misers and spendthrifts are punished together and in the same way, because both have failed to observe moderation in their use of wealth.

dissi: 'Maestro mio, or mi dimostra
   che gente è questa, e se tutti fuor cherci
   questi chercuti alla sinistra nostra.'
Ed elli a me: 'Tutti quanti fuor guerci   40
   sì della mente in la vita primaia
   che con misura nullo spendio ferci.
Assai la voce lor chiaro l'abbaia
   quando vegnono a' due punti del cerchio
   dove colpa contraria li dispaia.
Questi fuor cherci, che non han coperchio
   piloso al capo, e papi e cardinali,
   in cui usa avarizia il suo soperchio.'
E io: 'Maestro, tra questi cotali
   dovre' io ben riconoscere alcuni   50
   che furo immondi di cotesti mali.'
Ed elli a me: 'Vano pensiero aduni:
   la sconoscente vita che i fe' sozzi
   ad ogni conoscenza or li fa bruni.
In etterno verranno alli due cozzi:
   questi resurgeranno del sepulcro
   col pugno chiuso, e questi coi crin mozzi.
Mal dare e mal tener lo mondo pulcro
   ha tolto loro, e posti a questa zuffa:
   qual ella sia, parole non ci appulcro.   60
Or puoi veder, figliuol, la corta buffa
   de' ben che son commessi alla Fortuna,
   per che l'umana gente si rabbuffa;
ché tutto l'oro ch'è sotto la luna
   e che già fu, di quest'anime stanche
   non poterebbe farne posare una.'
'Maestro,' diss'io lui, 'or mi di' anche:
   questa Fortuna di che tu mi tocche,
   che è, che i ben del mondo ha sì tra branche?'
Ed elli a me: 'Oh creature sciocche,   70
   quanta ignoranza è quella che v'offende!
   Or vo' che tu mia sentenza ne 'mbocche.

Said: 'Master, I would like all this explained.
   Who are these people here? Were they all clerics,
   These here, the tonsured ones on our left hand?'
And he to me: 'All of them used to squint –   40
   Squint mentally I mean – while they were living:
   There was no golden mean in how they spent.
Their own loud voices bark this clearly out
   Whenever they reach those two points on the circle
   Where their opposing faults show them apart.
Those on the left were clerics (those with less
   Hair on the top), and popes and cardinals,
   Among whom there is endless avarice.'
And then I said: 'Master, among all these,
   Who fouled themselves with either of the sins,   50
   There should be some whom I can recognise.'
And he replied: 'You think such thoughts in vain.
   The undiscerning life that made them filthy
   Now makes their features harder to discern.
To all eternity these weights are rolled.
   This lot will one day leave their sepulchres
   With fists clenched tight,[5] and those with heads quite bald.[6]
Ill-giving and ill-keeping took away
   The bright world from them, leaving them these clashes
   I will not scrat around to beautify.   60
And now, my son, you see the brief illusion
   Of this world's wealth, which is in Fortune's hands,
   And brings the human race to such confusion.
For all the gold that is beneath the moon,
   Or ever was, could never pacify,
   Among these weary spirits, even one.'[7]
'Master,' I asked him then, 'tell me, who is
   This so-called Fortune you have touched upon,
   Who has all this world's riches in her claws?'
And he replied: 'How much sheer ignorance   70
   Are foolish human beings the victims of!
   Now, as I feed it you, digest my sense.

5. The misers, on the Day of Judgement.
6. The spendthrifts. The idea is that they are so wasteful that they have thrown away even the hair from their heads.
7. No amount of wealth could pacify them in Hell, any more than it could in life.

Colui lo cui saver tutto trascende
   fece li cieli e diè lor chi conduce,
      sì ch'ogni parte ad ogni parte splende,
distribuendo igualmente la luce:
   similemente alli splendor mondani
      ordinò general ministra e duce
che permutasse a tempo li ben vani
   di gente in gente e d'uno in altro sangue,   80
      oltre la difension di senni umani;
per ch'una gente impera ed altra langue,
   seguendo lo giudicio di costei,
      che è occulto come in erba l'angue.
Vostro saver non ha contasto a lei:
   questa provede, giudica, e persegue
      suo regno come il loro li altri dei.
Le sue permutazion non hanno triegue –
   necessità la fa esser veloce –
      sì spesso vien chi vicenda consegue.   90
Quest'è colei ch'è tanto posta in croce
   pur da color che le dovrien dar lode,
      dandole biasmo a torto e mala voce;
ma ella s'è beata, e ciò non ode:
   con l'altre prime creature lieta
      volve sua spera e beata si gode.
Or discendiamo omai a maggior pièta –
   già ogni stella cade che saliva
      quand'io mi mossi, e 'l troppo star si vieta.'
Noi ricidemmo il cerchio all'altra riva   100
   sovr'una fonte che bolle e riversa
      per un fossato che da lei deriva.
L'acqua era buia assai più che persa,
   e noi, in compagnia dell'onde bige,
      entrammo giù per una via diversa.
In la palude va c'ha nome Stige
   questo tristo ruscel, quand'è disceso
      al piè delle maligne piagge grige.

He whose wisdom is utterly transcendent
    Made the heavens, and gave them guides[8] so that
    Each part to every other was resplendent,
With all the light apportioned equally.
    And he ordained a guide and minister
    For worldly wealth and fame in the same way,
To move these empty goods, when time was right,
    From race to race, and over families,   80
    Beyond the influence of human wit.
So, while one people rules, another's weak,
    Exactly as that minister decides,
    Whose judgement's hidden in long grass, a snake.
Your wisdom cannot come to grips with hers.
    For she foresees, and judges, and maintains
    Her kingdom as the other gods[9] do theirs.
Her permutations never know a truce.
    Necessity compels her to be swift,
    So often do men have to change their place.   90
So this is she who is reviled and cursed,
    Even by those who ought to give her praise,
    And blamed without being guilty, and traduced.
But she is blessèd, and she does not hear:
    With the other primal creatures[10] she is happy –
    Rejoicing in her bliss, she turns her sphere.[11]
Now let's descend to greater misery,
    For every star is setting that was rising
    When I set out, and we must not delay.'
We crossed onto the further bank, from which   100
    There is a spring that gurgles and pours out
    Into a sort of effluential ditch.
The water was obscure rather than black.
    And we, together with those murky waves,
    Went down along a rough, uneven track.
This melancholy stream descends, and makes –
    Beyond the foot of that accursèd slope –
    Its way into a swamp known as the Styx[12].

8. The angelic intelligences who rule the heavenly spheres.
9. Virgil is using the term a pagan would use to refer to the angelic intelligences.
10. The angels, the first beings to be created.
11. As other angelic intelligences guide the heavenly spheres, so Fortune regulates those things
(worldly wealth and status) which are within her sphere of influence. There is also a hint of the
traditional notion of Fortune's wheel.
12. One of the rivers of the classical underworld.

E io, che di mirare stava inteso,
    vidi genti fangose in quel pantano,   110
    ignude tutte, con sembiante offeso.
Queste si percotean non pur con mano,
    ma con la testa e col petto e coi piedi,
    troncandosi co' denti a brano a brano.
Lo buon maestro disse: 'Figlio, or vedi
    l'anime di color cui vinse l'ira;
    e anche vo' che tu per certo credi
che sotto l'acqua ha gente che sospira,
    e fanno pullular quest'acqua al summo,
    come l'occhio ti dice, u' che s'aggira.   120
Fitti nel limo, dicon: "Tristi fummo
    nell'aere dolce che dal sol s'allegra,
    portando dentro accidioso fummo:
or ci attristiam nella belletta negra."
    Quest'inno si gorgoglian nella strozza,
    ché dir nol posson con parola integra.'
Così girammo della lorda pozza
    grand'arco tra la ripa secca e 'l mézzo[b],
    con li occhi vòlti a chi del fango ingozza:
venimmo al piè d'una torre al da sezzo.   130

b. 'Wetness'.

And I, who'd come to a halt to stand and gaze,
    Saw muddied people wallowing in the mire,   110
    All of them naked, all with looks of rage.
And these, not only did they beat and beat
    Each other with their fists, heads, breasts, and feet,
    But tore each other piecemeal with their teeth.[13]
My kindly teacher said: 'My son, you see
    The souls of those whom anger overmastered.
    And what is more – I hope you'll credit me –
Beneath the surface many people sigh,
    With lots of little bubbles rising up,
    As you can see, wherever you cast your eye.   120
They say, stuck in the mud: "Our minds stayed dark
    In the sweet air enlightened by the sun.
    Inside us was a sort of sluggish smoke.
Now we are sullen in the gloomy mud."[14]
    This is the hymn they're gurgling in their gullets,
    Because they can't sing words out as they should.'[15]
So, in a wide arc round the mire, we came –
    Between the dry bank and the filthy moist,
    Our eyes upon the gulpers-down of slime –
Right to the foot of a lofty tower at last.   130

13. The wrathful act in the Inferno as they did on earth, but in the Inferno there is no disguising
    the essential nature of their actions.
14. They, like the other souls in this circle, are wrathful, but their wrath turns inward on themselves.
15. Because of the mud in their throats.

CANTO VIII

Here, in the fifth circle (that of the wrathful, the proud, and the sullen), Dante goes back in his account to the time before he and Virgil reached the tower. They could see two fires burning at the top of the tower, and another fire in the distance apparently answering them.

A boat arrives, guided by the angry demon Phlegyas. When Dante steps into the boat, it sinks lower in the water because of his body's weight.

A figure rears up out of the water, demanding to know who they are. Dante brusquely retorts with the same question and then reveals he knew him all along. Virgil praises Dante for his harshness towards the shade, who to Dante's delight is attacked by his fellow-sufferers in the swamp. He is Filippo Argenti, a proud and foul-tempered Florentine.

Dante is here showing himself full of a righteous indignation at evil, which is sharply distinguished from unwarranted and excessive anger. Virgil certainly approves of his attitude.

The sound of lamentation is heard, and then we are back to the moment when Dante and Virgil arrived beneath the high tower. This is the city of Dis, named after a classical god of the underworld. Virgil explains that the towers of the city look red because of the fires always burning inside them.

On the city walls are more than a thousand devils. They say that Virgil may proceed, but Dante must go back. Virgil attempts to encourage Dante, and goes forward to speak with the devils alone. Their conversation does not last long. The devils run back into the city and shut its gates in Virgil's face. Virgil walks slowly back to where Dante is waiting in trepidation. Virgil, although he is clearly not so confident as he was, again tries to encourage Dante by describing how the gates of the Inferno were broken at Christ's Harrowing of Hell, and by saying that help is on its way.

Io dico, seguitando, ch'assai prima   1
    che noi fossimo al piè dell'alta torre,
    li occhi nostri n'andar suso alla cima
per due fiammette che i' vedemmo porre,
    e un'altra da lungi render cenno
    tanto ch'a pena il potea l'occhio tòrre.
E io mi volsi al mar di tutto 'l senno:
    dissi: 'Questo che dice? e che risponde
    quell'altro foco? e chi son quei che 'l fenno?'
Ed elli a me: 'Su per le sucide onde   10
    già scorgere puoi quello che s'aspetta,
    se 'l fummo del pantan nol ti nasconde.'
Corda non pinse mai da sé saetta
    che sì corresse via per l'aere snella,
    com'io vidi una nave piccioletta
venir per l'acqua verso noi in quella,
    sotto il governo d'un sol galeoto,
    che gridava: 'Or se' giunta, anima fella!'
'Flegiàs, Flegiàs, tu gridi a vòto,'
    disse lo mio signore, 'a questa volta: 20
    più non ci avrai che sol passando il loto.'
Qual è colui che grande inganno ascolta
    che li sia fatto, e poi se ne rammarca,
    fecesi Flegiàs nell'ira accolta.
Lo duca mio discese nella barca,
    e poi mi fece intrare appresso lui,
    e sol quand'io fui dentro parve carca.
Tosto che 'l duca e io nel legno fui,
    segando se ne va l'antica prora
    dell'acqua più che non suol con altrui.   30
Mentre noi corravam la morta gora,
    dinanzi mi si fece un pien di fango,
    e disse: 'Chi se' tu che vieni anzi ora?'
E io a lui: 'S'i' vegno, non rimango –
    ma tu chi se', che sì se' fatto brutto?'
    Rispuose: 'Vedi che son un che piango.'

To go back quite a way – when we'd not yet   I
     Come to the high tower's foot, as I have mentioned,
     Our eyes were drawn up to the top of it
By two small flames which somebody placed there,
     And yet another answering their signal,
     So far away it seemed much tinier.[1]
And I turned to the ocean of good sense:
     'What does this mean? What does that other fire
     Reply? And who are they who send the signs?'
And he replied: 'Over these muddy waves   10
     You can already see what to expect,
     Unless the marsh mist hides it from your eyes.'
No arrow from a bowstring ever shot
     Away so rapidly through yielding air
     As I could see a very little boat
Coming towards us through the waves meanwhile,
     Under the guidance of a single boatman.
     'I've got you now,' he shrieked, 'you wicked soul!'[2]
'O Phlegyas[3], O Phlegyas, you waste
     Your breath,' my master said, 'on this occasion: 20
     You've only got us till the marsh is crossed.'
Like one who has uncovered some foul plot
     He's been the victim of, which makes him angry,
     Just so was Phlegyas, choking in defeat.
My leader stepped into the little boat,
     And made me follow after. Only then
     Did it sink lower, underneath my weight.[4]
And once we two were in the boat together,
     The ancient prow went cutting through the waves,
     Plunging more deeply than it had done ever.   30
While we were moving through the stagnant slime
     There rose before me someone caked in mud
     Who asked: 'Who are you, here before your time?'[5]
'I'm here,' I said, 'but I shall not remain.
     And who are you, who've made yourself so filthy?'
     His answer was: 'You see me weep for sin.'

1. In Dante's day such signals suggested military activity.
2. The boatman presumes that Dante is a damned soul.
3. A character from Greek myth who, to avenge his daughter's death at the hands of Apollo, set fire to Apollo's temple at Delphi. He is therefore included here as an embodiment of impious and uncontrolled rage.
4. Virgil, who went into the boat before Dante, is a weightless shade.
5. This shade is more perceptive than Phlegyas, since he realises Dante is still alive.

E io a lui: 'Con piangere e con lutto,
   spirito maladetto, ti rimani –
   ch'i' ti conosco, ancor sie lordo tutto.'
Allor distese al legno ambo le mani,   40
   per che 'l maestro accorto lo sospinse,
   dicendo: 'Via costà con li altri cani!'
Lo collo poi con le braccia mi cinse,
   baciommi il volto e disse: 'Alma sdegnosa,
   benedetta colei che in te s'incinse!
Quei fu al mondo persona orgogliosa –
   bontà non è che sua memoria fregi:
   così s'è l'ombra sua qui furiosa.
Quanti si tengon or là su gran regi
   che qui staranno come porci in brago,   50
   di sé lasciando orribili dispregi!'
E io: 'Maestro, molto sarei vago
   di vederlo attuffare in questa broda
   prima che noi uscissimo dal lago.'
Ed elli a me: 'Avante che la proda
   ti si lasci veder, tu sarai sazio:
   di tal disio convien che tu goda.'
Dopo ciò poco vid'io quello strazio
   far di costui alle fangose genti,
   che Dio ancor ne lodo e ne ringrazio.   60
Tutti gridavano: 'A Filippo Argenti!'
   e 'l fiorentino spirito bizzarro
   in sé medesmo si volvea co' denti.
Quivi il lasciammo, che più non ne narro,
   ma nell'orecchio mi percosse un duolo,
   per ch'io avante l'occhio intento sbarro.
Lo buon maestro disse: 'Omai, figliuolo,
   s'appressa la città c'ha nome Dite,
   coi gravi cittadin, col grande stuolo.'
E io: 'Maestro, già le sue meschite   70
   là entro certe nella valle cerno,
   vermiglie come se di foco uscite

Then I to him: 'With weeping and regret,
    Accursèd spirit, you're here and must remain.
    For I know who you are, despite the dirt.'
He stretched up both his hands to grip the boat –   40
    At this, my wary master pushed him off,
    And said: 'Back to the other dogs! Off! Out!'
My lord then threw his arms around my neck,
    Kissed me, and said: 'Indignant soul, how blessed
    The womb that bore, the paps that gave you suck![6]
That man was, in the world, presumptuous;
    No kindly acts adorn his memory:
    Therefore down here his shade is furious.
How many now up there are full of pride,
    Who will one day be here like pigs in mud,   50
    Leaving behind but scorn for what they did!'
I answered: 'Master, I would really like
    To see this fellow drenched in this pigswill
    Before we end our voyage on the lake.'
And he: 'Before the shore comes into sight
    That aspiration will be satisfied:
    To grant you such a wish is only right.'
I saw that spirit grabbed, soon after that,
    As I had wanted, by more muddy people,
    And I'm still giving thanks to God for it.   60
'Filippo Argenti! Grab him!'[7] they all cried,
    At which the shade of the waspish Florentine
    Tore at himself, being eaten up inside.
We left him then, with no more to be said,
    But sudden lamentation strikes my ears,
    And I, my eyes wide open, peer ahead.
My kindly master told me: 'Now, my son,
    We're getting near that city known as Dis[8],
    With its grave citizens and garrison.'
'Master,' I said, 'already I discern   70
    Its mosques[9] down in the valley quite distinctly,
    Bright red, as though they'd recently been drawn

6. An echo of Luke 11: 27: 'Blessed is the womb that bare thee, and the paps which thou hast sucked.'
   In the gospel these words are addressed to Christ.
7. A Florentine, contemporary with Dante, easily aroused to anger. He was said to have been so proud
   that he had his horse shod with silver, and his surname (from *argento*, silver) seems to allude to this.
8. On several occasions in the Inferno Dante uses this name for Satan.
9. These are the city's towers, which rise above its walls. Dante and his contemporaries considered
   Islam a Christian heresy.

fossero.' Ed ei mi disse: 'Il foco etterno
    ch'entro l'affoca[a] le dimostra rosse,
    come tu vedi in questo basso inferno.'
Noi pur giugnemmo dentro all'alte fosse
    che vallan quella terra sconsolata:
    le mura mi parean che ferro fosse.
Non sanza prima far grande aggirata,
    venimmo in parte dove il nocchier forte   80
    'Usciteci,' gridò, 'qui è l'entrata.'
Io vidi più di mille in su le porte
    da ciel piovuti, che stizzosamente
    dicean: 'Chi è costui che sanza morte
va per lo regno della morta gente?'
    E 'l savio mio maestro fece segno
    di voler lor parlar secretamente.
Allor chiusero un poco il gran disdegno,
    e disser: 'Vien tu solo, e quei sen vada,
    che sì ardito intrò per questo regno.   90
Sol si ritorni per la folle strada:
    pruovi, se sa, ché tu qui rimarrai
    che li ha' iscorta sì buia contrada.'
Pensa, lettor, se io mi sconfortai
    nel suon delle parole maladette,
    ché non credetti ritornarci mai.
'O caro duca mio, che più di sette
    volte m'hai sicurtà renduta e tratto
    d'alto periglio che 'ncontra mi stette,
non mi lasciar,' diss'io, 'così disfatto;   100
    e se 'l passar più oltre ci è negato,
    ritroviam l'orme nostre insieme ratto.'
E quel signor che lì m'avea menato,
    mi disse: 'Non temer, ché 'l nostro passo
    non ci può tòrre alcun: da tal n'è dato.
Ma qui m'attendi, e lo spirito lasso
    conforta e ciba di speranza bona,
    ch'i' non ti lascerò nel mondo basso.'

---

a. Lit. 'the eternal fire which makes them red-hot'. Another example of *traductio*: see note to I: 36.

From fire.' He answered: 'Fire eternally
    Glowing, red-hot within them, turns them red
    Down in these nether regions, as you see.'
At last we came to where deep trenches made
    A ring of moats round this despondent city:
    Its walls were built of iron, it appeared.
Not without ranging first in a wide turn,
    We came to somewhere where the blatant boatman   80
    Shouted: 'Get out! This is where you go in.'
I saw a thousand or more, all ranged above,[10]
    Poured down like rain from heaven,[11] angrily
    Wanting to know: 'Who is this, still alive,
Who's coming through the kingdom of the dead?'
    My master made a sign to show his wish
    To speak with them, a little to one side.
Then they clamped down somewhat on their disdain,
    And said: 'Come by yourself, and let him go.
    He's over-bold, to enter this domain.   90
Let him retrace his steps on his mad road –
    That's if he can! For you are staying here,
    You who have been, through this dark realm, his guide.'
Imagine, Reader, if you can, my fear,
    Hearing them saying those accursèd words.
    I thought I'd never find my way back here.
'O my dear leader, who have frequently
    Given me confidence, and snatched me safe
    Out of the dangers that stood in my way,
Don't leave me in this plight,' I tried to say,   100
    'And, if we are forbidden to go further,
    Then let's go back together, straight away!'
He who had guided me so far replied:
    'You need not fear. None can prevent our passage:
    Consider him by whom it's guaranteed![12]
Wait for me here, and let your heart be filled
    And nourished with good hope and comfort. I
    Shall not forsake you in this nether world.'

10. On the walls of the city.
11. The rebel angels, who were cast out of heaven, became devils.
12. God.

Così sen va, e quivi m'abbandona
    lo dolce padre, e io rimango in forse,   110
    che no e sì nel capo mi tenciona.
Udir non potti quello ch'a lor porse;
    ma ei non stette là con essi guari,
    che ciascun dentro a pruova si ricorse.
Chiuser le porte que' nostri avversari
    nel petto al mio segnor, che fuor rimase,
    e rivolsesi a me con passi rari.
Li occhi alla terra e le ciglia avea rase
    d'ogni baldanza, e dicea ne' sospiri:
    'Chi m'ha negate le dolenti case!'   120
E a me disse: 'Tu, perch'io m'adiri,
    non sbigottir, ch'io vincerò la prova,
    qual ch'alla difension dentro s'aggiri.
Questa lor tracotanza non è nova,
    ché già l'usaro a men secreta porta,
    la qual sanza serrame ancor si trova.
Sopr'essa vedestù la scritta morta:
    e già di qua da lei discende l'erta,
    passando per li cerchi sanza scorta,
tal che per lui ne fia la terra aperta.'   130

He leaves me there, while he goes on ahead,
     My kindly guide leaves me in dreadful doubt,   110
     With yes and no contending in my head.
I could not make out what it was he said,
     But he had not been with them very long
     Before they all went running back inside.
They slammed the city gates, our enemies,
     Full in my master's face. He, left outside,
     Turned back, and walked towards me by degrees.
His eyes cast down, no sign left on his face
     Of former confidence, he sighed and said:
     'And these have barred me from this mournful place!'   120
Then turned to me: 'Because I seem dismayed,
     Don't be cast down, for I shall win this battle,
     Whatever defence is organised inside.
This insolence of theirs is nothing new.
     They showed it at a less secluded gate,[13]
     Which stays unbarred since it was broken through.[14]
You saw that gate and saw its deadly word.[15]
     Already inside it, coming down the abyss,
     Through circle after circle with no guide,
Is one who'll open up the way for us.'[16]   130

13. The entrance to the Inferno. See the beginning of III.
14. By Christ, at the Harrowing of Hell. See IV: 46–63 and notes.
15. The inscription on the gate at the entrance to the Inferno.
16. There has been repeated emphasis on the difficulty of the way by which Dante and Virgil have travelled. The ease with which this new arrival moves is therefore all the more mysterious and significant. His identity and purpose are not made clear until halfway through the next canto.

CANTO IX

Dante and Virgil are left in suspense outside the City of Dis and, despite Virgil's suggestion in the previous canto that help is on the way, their consternation increases. Virgil, the embodiment of human reason unaided by divine grace, remains baffled in the face of unmotivated malevolence, and his bewilderment is communicated to Dante.

In reply to Dante's fearful question, Virgil says that he has been right down to the lowest depth of the Inferno once before, and he therefore knows the way. However, any comfort this might have brought to Dante is cancelled by the appearance on the city walls of the three Furies, grotesque and terrifying personifications of the spirit of vengeance.

Even more frightening is the appearance of the Gorgon Medusa who has the power to turn people to stone. Virgil warns Dante to turn his back on her, and adds his own hands to Dante's to cover Dante's eyes. The terror caused by all this is converted to awe when, heralded by a great wind, a figure is seen moving without effort across the marsh. The shades of the damned in the marsh scuttle away at this angel's approach. The angel then opens the gates of the City of Dis by the mere touch of a little wand, rebukes the devils, and goes away. Divine grace has achieved effortlessly what no human endeavours could.

Dante and Virgil are now able to enter the city un-opposed. Inside it they see a large stretch of countryside (the sixth circle) covered with monumental tombs. The lids of the tombs are propped open, and wailing is heard from within them. The tombs are heated by flames scattered among them. Inside the tombs are heretics, punished by greater or less heat according to the gravity of the heresy of which they were guilty.

Quel color che viltà di fuor mi pinse   1
    veggendo il duca mio tornare in volta,
    più tosto dentro il suo novo[a] ristrinse.
Attento si fermò com'uom ch'ascolta,
    ché l'occhio nol potea menare a lunga
    per l'aere nero e per la nebbia folta.
'Pur a noi converrà vincer la punga,'
    cominciò el, 'se non... Tal ne s'offerse –
    oh quanto tarda a me ch'altri qui giunga!'
I' vidi ben sì com'ei ricoperse   10
    lo cominciar con l'altro che poi venne,
    che fur parole alle prime diverse;
ma nondimen paura il suo dir dienne,
    perch'io traeva la parola tronca
    forse a peggior sentenzia che non tenne.
'In questo fondo della trista conca
    discende mai alcun del primo grado,
    che sol per pena ha la speranza cionca?'
Questa question fec'io; e quei: 'Di rado
    incontra,' mi rispuose, 'che di noi   20
    faccia 'l cammino alcun per qual io vado.
Vero è ch'altra fiata qua giù fui,
    congiurato da quella Eritón cruda
    che richiamava l'ombre a' corpi sui.
Di poco era di me la carne nuda,
    ch'ella mi fece intrar dentr'a quel muro,
    per trarne un spirto del cerchio di Giuda.
Quell'è 'l più basso loco e 'l più oscuro,
    e 'l più lontan dal ciel che tutto gira:
    ben so il cammin – però ti fa sicuro.   30
Questa palude che 'l gran puzzo spira
    cigne dintorno la città dolente,
    u' non potemo intrare omai sanz'ira.'
E altro disse, ma non l'ho a mente,
    però che l'occhio m'avea tutto tratto
    ver l'alta torre alla cima rovente,

a. 'New' in the sense of 'unusual' and therefore 'striking'.

That I through cowardice had lost my colour,   1
    Seeing my leader turning slowly back,
    Made him dissemble his unwonted pallor.
He paused like an attentive listener,
    Because he could not see into the distance
    Through the dense fog and the benighted air.
'There is no question: we must win this fight,'
    He said. 'If not... But think who's interceded...
    I can't but fear it's being left too late!'
I saw quite clearly how he tried to hide   10
    What he'd begun to say with further words
    Of different meaning from the first he said.
That hardly stopped his words from rousing fear,
    Because I gave the sentence he'd cut short
    A meaning worse perhaps than it could bear.
'Does anybody ever come so deep
    Into this hollow from the highest circle,
    Whose only torment is his lack of hope?'[1]
That was my question, and he said, 'Although
    It seldom happens any one of us   20
    Goes on the road on which I'm going now,
The truth is that I have been here before,
    Under the spell of pitiless Erichtho[2]
    Who called shades back to where their bodies were.
My flesh had not been parted from my soul
    For long when she sent me inside this city
    To draw a spirit from the depth of Hell.[3]
I mean the lowest, darkest place of all,
    Furthest from the all-motivating sphere.[4]
    Be reassured: I know the way there well.   30
This swamp which breathes out such a stinking mist
    Goes all the way around the cheerless city
    Which now we cannot enter unopposed.'
Though he said more, I don't remember it,
    Because my eyes directed my attention
    Towards the high tower where it glowed red-hot,

1. Dante's question reveals his uncertainty as to Virgil's knowledge of the way.
2. A mythical Thessalian witch.
3. Judecca, where Judas Iscariot is.
4. The Primum Mobile, so called because it is the first of the heavenly spheres to be set in motion
   (by God). It surrounds all the other moving spheres and itself sets them in motion.

dove in un punto furon dritte ratto
    tre furie infernal di sangue tinte,
    che membra femminine avìeno e atto,
e con idre verdissime eran cinte;   40
    serpentelli e ceraste avìen per crine,
    onde le fiere tempie erano avvinte.
E quei, che ben conobbe le meschine
    della regina dell'etterno pianto,
    'Guarda,' mi disse, 'le feroci Erine.
Quest'è Megera dal sinistro canto –
    quella che piange dal destro è Aletto –
    Tesifone è nel mezzo,' e tacque a tanto.
Con l'unghie si fendea ciascuna il petto,
    battìensi a palme, e gridavan sì alto   50
    ch'i' mi strinsi al poeta per sospetto.
'Vegna Medusa: sì 'l farem di smalto,'
    dicevan tutte riguardando in giuso:
    'mal non vengiammo in Teseo l'assalto.'
'Volgiti in dietro e tien lo viso chiuso,
    ché se il Gorgón si mostra e tu 'l vedessi,
    nulla sarebbe del tornar mai suso.'
Così disse 'l maestro, ed elli stessi
    mi volse, e non si tenne alle mie mani,
    che con le sue ancor non mi chiudessi.   60
O voi ch'avete li 'ntelletti sani,
    mirate la dottrina che s'asconde
    sotto 'l velame delli versi strani.
E già venìa su per le torbide onde
    un fracasso d'un suon, pien di spavento,
    per che tremavano amendue le sponde,
non altrimenti fatto che d'un vento
    impetuoso per li avversi ardori,
    che fier la selva e sanz'alcun rattento
li rami schianta, abbatte e porta fori: 70
    dinanzi polveroso va superbo,
    e fa fuggir le fiere e li pastori.

Where, on a sudden, there before my eyes
    Stood three infernal Furies stained with blood.
    They looked like women and had women's ways,
With bright green hydras twisted round the waist,   40
    With thin serpents and two-horned snakes for hair,
    Bound round their savage heads and interlaced.
And he, so cognisant of old of these
    Slaves of the queen of eternal lamentation,
    Said to me: 'Look! The fierce Erinyes[5]!
That is Megaera on the left; the one
    Who's weeping on our right hand is Alecto;
    Tisiphone's between.' Then he was done.
They tore their breasts with fingernails – they clawed
    And slapped themselves – their shrieking was so loud   50
    I clutched the poet: I was terrified.
'When Medusa[6] is here, he'll turn to stone,'
    They all three said, as they looked down at us.
    'When Theseus challenged, we were too humane.'[7]
'Now turn right round, and keep your eyes shut tight,
    For if the Gorgon comes and you see her,
    There'll be no way back to the world of light.'
My master said this, and he made me turn,
    And, not content that I should use my hands,
    He covered up my eyes with both his own.   60
O you, whose minds are sound and full of sense,
    Notice the deeper meaning hidden here,
    Veiled by these lines that speak of strange events.
And now a noise across the muddy water
    Rang out, re-bellowed – and so terribly
    It caused the river banks to shake and shudder.
Exactly like the sound made by a wind
    Enticed and driven wild by adverse warmth;
    It strikes a forest – nothing can withstand
It – breaking boughs, and bearing them away,   70
    It proudly sweeps along a cloud of dust,
    And makes wild beasts and shepherds turn and flee.

5. Classical embodiments of the spirit of vengeance, and often, to those who saw them, of remorse.
6. One of the three Gorgons, monsters who petrified whoever looked at them. Possibly she is here
  a symbol of despair, the worst sin of all.
7. When Theseus entered the underworld, in an attempt to abduct Proserpine, he was captured,
  but not killed. He had to be rescued by Hercules.

Li occhi mi sciolse e disse: 'Or drizza il nerbo
   del viso su per quella schiuma antica
   per indi ove quel fummo è più acerbo.'
Come le rane innanzi alla nimica
   biscia per l'acqua si dileguan tutte,
   fin ch'alla terra ciascuna s'abbica[b],
vid'io più di mille anime distrutte
   fuggir così dinanzi ad un ch'al passo   80
   passava Stige con le piante asciutte.
Dal volto rimovea quell'aere grasso,
   menando la sinistra innanzi spesso,
   e sol di quell'angoscia parea lasso.
Ben m'accorsi ch'elli era da ciel messo,
   e volsimi al maestro, e quei fe' segno
   ch'i' stessi queto ed inchinassi ad esso.
Ahi quanto mi parea pien di disdegno!
   Venne alla porta, e con una verghetta
   l'aperse, che non v'ebbe alcun ritegno.   90
'O cacciati del ciel, gente dispetta,'
   cominciò elli in su l'orribil soglia,
   'ond'esta oltracotanza in voi s'alletta?
Perché recalcitrate a quella voglia
   a cui non puote il fin mai esser mozzo,
   e che più volte v'ha cresciuta doglia?
Che giova nelle fata dar di cozzo?
   Cerbero vostro, se ben vi ricorda,
   ne porta ancor pelato il mento e 'l gozzo.'
Poi si rivolse per la strada lorda,   100
   e non fe' motto a noi, ma fe' sembiante
   d'omo cui altra cura stringa e morda
che quella di colui che li è davante;
   e noi movemmo i piedi inver la terra,
   sicuri appresso le parole sante.
Dentro li entrammo sanz'alcuna guerra;
   e io, ch'avea di riguardar disio
   la condizion che tal fortezza serra,

---

b. A hapax legomenon in this poem. The term is probably derived from 'bica' (a sheaf, e.g. of corn): the frogs form themselves into a heap.

He took his hands away: 'Now look your fill
    Across that prehistoric foam or scum,
    There where the mist is thickest and most foul.'
Like frogs, scared by their enemy the snake,
    Retreating rapidly across the water,
    To pile up on the land in one great stack,
So I saw hordes of the ruined people flee
    In front of one[8] who passed over the marsh,   80
    And crossed the Styx, keeping his feet quite dry.
He brushed the viscid atmosphere from time
    To time out of his face with his left hand,
    And that was all that seemed to trouble him.
I had no doubt at all that he was one
    Sent down from heaven, and turned towards my master,
    Who signed me to be silent and bow down.
How magisterial he seemed to me!
    He reached the gate, and with a little wand
    He opened it, and none stood in his way.   90
'O you, outcasts of heaven, wretched race,'
    He said, when he was standing on the threshold,
    'What is it in you breeds such arrogance?
Why do you kick against the pricks again?
    That will is not diverted from its end,
    And more than once it has increased your pain.[9]
Why bang your heads against the wall of fate?
    That Cerberus of yours, if you remember,
    Still has the flesh scraped off his chin and throat.'[10]
Then he turned back upon the filthy road,   100
    And said no word to us, but had the look
    Of someone whom some other care devoured[11]
Than that of those who stood before him there.
    And so we turned our steps towards the city:
    After his holy speech we were secure.
We went inside, and there was no dispute.
    And I, who had a longing to discover
    What kind of things were locked in such a fort,

8. An angel.
9. An allusion to the descent into the underworld of Theseus and Hercules and, more importantly, Christ's Harrowing of Hell.
10. When Cerberus opposed him, Hercules tied him with a chain and dragged him away. It was this chain's attrition which removed the flesh from his chin and throat.
11. His wish to return to Heaven? The thought of his next task?

com'io fui dentro, l'occhio intorno invio,
    e veggio ad ogne man grande campagna   110
    piena di duolo e di tormento rio.
Sì come ad Arli, ove Rodano stagna,
    sì com'a Pola, presso del Carnaro
    ch'Italia chiude e suoi termini bagna,
fanno i sepulcri tutt'il loco varo,
    così facevan quivi d'ogni parte,
    salvo che 'l modo v'era più amaro:
ché tra gli avelli fiamme erano sparte,
    per le quali eran sì del tutto accesi,
    che ferro più non chiede verun'arte.   120
Tutti li lor coperchi eran sospesi,
    e fuor n'uscivan sì duri lamenti
    che ben parean di miseri e d'offesi.
E io: 'Maestro, quai son quelle genti
    che, seppellite dentro da quell'arche,
    si fan sentir con li sospir dolenti?'
Ed elli a me: 'Qui son li eresiarche
    co' lor seguaci, d'ogni setta, e molto
    più che non credi son le tombe carche.
Simile qui con simile è sepolto,   130
    e i monimenti son più o men caldi.'
    E poi ch'alla man destra si fu vòlto,
passammo tra i martìri e li alti spaldi.

Cast my eyes round it, once I was within,
    And saw, on every side, a rural region   110
    Of lamentation and of cruel pain.
And as at Arles, there where the Rhone stagnates,
    Or as at Pola, near to where Quarnero
    Washes that Italy it demarcates,
Sepulchres make the ground irregular,
    So they did here on every hand, except
    The circumstances were much crueller.
For here and there among the tombs a scatter
    Of fire and flame made every tomb so hot
    No smith would need his iron to be hotter.   120
All of the lids were open and upended,
    And from them came such direful lamentation
    As only from the grievously tormented.
I asked him: 'Master, tell me, who are these
    Who, laid to rest in monumental tombs,
    Make themselves heard with lamentable sighs?'
He said: 'Heresiarchs, and their followers
    Of every sect, are here. And many more
    Than you might think are in these sepulchres.
Of all the sects, like is entombed with like,   130
    With heat that varies through the monuments.'[12]
    We went on then and, turning to the right,
Passed between torments and high battlements.

12. The heat is greater or less according to the gravity of the particular heresy. In Dante's day a
    common punishment for heresy was to be burnt alive.

CANTO X

Virgil and Dante are now in the area reserved for those heretics who insisted that the soul died with the body.

One of the shades, realising from his speech that Dante is a fellow-citizen of Florence, wishes to talk with him. This is Farinata degli Uberti, onetime leader of the Ghibelline faction: Dante's family were Guelphs. The feud is continued in Hell, as Farinata boasts of twice routing the Guelphs, and Dante retorts that his party recovered, whereas Farinata's did not.

They are interrupted by the shade of Cavalcante dei Cavalcanti, who cannot understand – if Dante can visit the Inferno by the power of his intellect – why his son Guido, Dante's friend, is not with him. Cavalcante fears that his son is dead and, when Dante hesitates to reply to his questions, Cavalcante falls back into his tomb, and is not seen or heard again.

Farinata alludes to Dante's future exile from Florence. He asks why the Florentines are so set against his family, and Dante recalls the rout of the Guelph forces at Montaperti. Farinata insists that it was he alone who prevented the destruction of Florence after that battle.

Farinata explains that the damned can see the future, but not the present: at the end of time they will know nothing.

Dante asks Farinata to explain to Cavalcante that his son is still alive; but there is no indication that Farinata even tries to do this.

With Virgil impatient to continue their journey, Dante pauses only long enough to learn from Farinata that his tomb contains also the shades of the Emperor Frederick II and 'the Cardinal'.

Virgil, told by Dante of his worries over his own future, advises him to wait until he meets Beatrice, when the course and purpose of his life will be revealed.

Virgil and Dante now move away from the walls of Dis towards the centre of the sixth circle. Their path leads to a valley which will take them down to the seventh circle. The stench from this valley is already rising to meet them.

Ora sen va per un secreto calle,   I
    tra 'l muro della terra e li martìri,
    lo mio maestro, e io dopo le spalle.
'O virtù somma, che per li empi giri
    mi volvi,' cominciai, 'com'a te piace,
    parlami, e sodisfammi a' miei disiri.
La gente che per li sepolcri giace
    potrebbesi veder? Già son levati
    tutt'i coperchi, e nessun guardia face.'
Ed elli a me: 'Tutti saran serrati   10
    quando di Iosafàt qui torneranno
    coi corpi che là su hanno lasciati.
Suo cimitero da questa parte hanno
    con Epicuro tutt'i suoi seguaci,
    che l'anima col corpo morta fanno.
Però alla dimanda che mi faci
    quinc'entro satisfatto sarà tosto,
    e al disio ancor che tu mi taci.'
E io: 'Buon duca, non tegno riposto
    a te mio cuor se non per dicer poco,   20
    e tu m'hai non pur mo a ciò disposto.'
'O Tosco[a] che per la città del foco
    vivo ten vai così parlando onesto,
    piacciati di restare in questo loco.
La tua loquela ti fa manifesto
    di quella nobil patria natio
    alla qual forse fui troppo molesto.'
Subitamente questo suono uscìo
    d'una dell'arche – però m'accostai,
    temendo, un poco più al duca mio.   30
Ed el mi disse: 'Volgiti, che fai?
    Vedi là Farinata che s'è dritto:
    dalla cintola in su tutto 'l vedrai.'
Io avea già il mio viso nel suo fitto,
    ed el s'ergea col petto e con la fronte
    com'avesse l'inferno in gran dispitto.

a. 'Tuscan', the usual form in this poem for 'Toscano'.

We passed along a narrow, hidden track   1
    Between the tortured people and the wall,
    My master first, and I behind his back.
'O you, most virtuous man, bringing me through
    These sacrilegious gyres, as you think best,
    Please speak, and tell me what I long to know.
Are any visible, of all those laid
    Within these sepulchres? I see the lids
    Are lifted, and there's nobody on guard.'
He said: 'The sepulchres will all be sealed   10
    When these[1] return here from Jehoshaphat
    Bringing their bodies from the upper world.[2]
This region is the burial ground of those –
    Epicurus[3] and all his followers –
    Who say the soul dies when the body does.
And now the question you have asked of me
    Will quickly find its answer in this circle,
    As will the longing which you hide away.'[4]
I answered: 'My kind guide, this reticence
    Comes simply from a wish to guard my tongue,   20
    As you've admonished me – and more than once.'
'O Tuscan walking through this land of fire,
    While still alive, and with such courteous speech,
    May it please you, pause and linger here.
To me your way of speaking makes it clear
    That you're a native of that noble city
    Where I perhaps was too unpopular.'
This sound came all of a sudden from inside
    One of the sepulchres, and in my fear
    I crept a little closer to my guide.   30
He said to me: 'Turn round! Why be distressed?
    Look there: it's Farinata who has risen;
    You will see all of him above the waist.'[5]
I had already caught his eye, meanwhile
    He held his chest and held his head up high,
    As though he had a huge contempt for Hell.

1. The shades of the dead.
2. On the Day of Judgement all the souls of the dead will be reunited with their bodies. See Joel
   3: 2: 'I will also gather all nations, and bring them down into the valley of Jehoshaphat...'
3. A Greek philosopher (341–270 BC). His philosophy was essentially materialist.
4. Dante's wish to see Farinata.
5. Farinata degli Uberti (who died about a year before Dante's birth) was a leader of the Ghibelline
   faction in Florence.

E l'animose man del duca e pronte
   mi pinser tra le sepulture a lui,
   dicendo: 'Le parole tue sien conte.'
Com'io al piè della sua tomba fui,   40
   guardommi un poco, e poi, quasi sdegnoso,
   mi dimandò: 'Chi fuor li maggior tui?'
Io, ch'era d'ubidir disideroso,
   non lil celai, ma tutto lil'apersi,
   ond'ei levò le ciglia un poco in soso;
poi disse: 'Fieramente furo avversi
   a me e a miei primi e a mia parte,
   sì che per due fiate li dispersi.'
'S'ei fur cacciati, ei tornar d'ogni parte,'
   rispuosi lui, 'l'una e l'altra fiata –   50
   ma i vostri non appreser ben quell'arte.'
Allor surse alla vista scoperchiata
   un'ombra, lungo questa, infino al mento:
   credo che s'era in ginocchie levata.
Dintorno mi guardò, come talento
   avesse di veder s'altri era meco;
   e poi che il sospecciar fu tutto spento,
piangendo disse: 'Se per questo cieco
   carcere vai per altezza d'ingegno,
   mio figlio ov'è? E perché non è teco?'   60
E io a lui: 'Da me stesso non vegno:
   colui ch'attende là, per qui mi mena
   forse[b] cui Guido vostro ebbe a disdegno.'
Le sue parole e 'l modo della pena
   m'avean di costui già letto il nome,
   però fu la risposta così piena.
Di subito drizzato gridò: 'Come
   dicesti? Elli ebbe? Non viv'elli ancora?
   Non fiere li occhi suoi il dolce lume?'
Quando s'accorse d'alcuna dimora   70
   ch'io facea dinanzi alla risposta,
   supin ricadde e più non parve fora.

---

b. This probably refers to 'mena', to express uncertainty as to the outcome of their journey. It might refer to 'ebbe a disdegno', and so express doubt as to Guido's disdain.

And my leader, whose hands were prompt and quick,
    Pushed me to Farinata through the tombs,
    And said: 'Think carefully before you speak.'
When I was at his sepulchre then he   40
    Looked at me for a while. Then, with some pride,
    He wished to know: 'What is your ancestry?'
I, who was all too keen to answer that,
    Hid nothing from him, but made all quite clear.
    Which when he heard, he raised his brows somewhat,
And said: 'They were so savagely adverse
    To me and to my forebears and my party,
    I had to scatter them – and do it twice!'[6]
'Yes, they were scattered, but they all returned
    From all around,' I said, 'and did that twice –   50
    A skill your party never really learned!'[7]
And then nearby another shade arose[8]
    Till it was visible down to the chin:
    I think he must have got up on his knees.
He looked all round, as if he really wanted
    To find somebody in my company;
    And when he was completely disappointed,
He said in tears: 'If you can tread this blind
    Prison by virtue of your intellect,
    Where is my son? Why is he not at hand?'   60
I answered him: 'My strength is not my own:
    He who is waiting there, perhaps will guide me
    To one[9] for whom your Guido felt disdain.'
What he said, and the way he was tormented,
    Immediately informed me who this was;
    And that was why my answer was so pointed.
He started up, and cried: 'What? Did you say
    He "*felt* disdain"? Is he not still alive?
    Does he no longer see the light of day?'[10]
When he perceived there was a pause before   70
    I found the words in answer to his question,
    He fell back; and he failed to reappear.

6. The Guelphs were driven from Florence in 1248 and 1260.
7. The Ghibellines were ultimately defeated.
8. That of Cavalcante dei Cavalcanti, a Florentine Guelph, father of Dante's great friend, the poet Guido Cavalcanti. Both father and son had the reputation of being heretics.
9. Probably Beatrice, as a representative of the Christian faith, but this could equally refer to Virgil or to God.
10. As Dante explains later, Guido Cavalcanti was alive at the date given to Dante's vision (the spring of 1300). He died in August of that year.

Ma quell'altro magnanimo a cui posta
    restato m'era, non mutò aspetto,
    né mosse collo, né piegò sua costa;
e sé continuando al primo detto,
    'S'elli han quell'arte,' disse, 'male appresa,
    ciò mi tormenta più che questo letto.
Ma non cinquanta volte fia raccesa
    la faccia della donna che qui regge,   80
    che tu saprai quanto quell'arte pesa.
E se tu mai nel dolce mondo regge,
    dimmi: perché quel popolo è sì empio
    incontr'a' miei in ciascuna sua legge?'
Ond'io a lui: 'Lo strazio e 'l grande scempio
    che fece l'Arbia colorata in rosso,
    tal orazion fa far nel nostro tempio.'
Poi ch'ebbe sospirando il capo mosso,
    'A ciò non fu' io sol,' disse, 'né certo
    sanza cagion con li altri sarei mosso.   90
Ma fu' io solo, là dove sofferto
    fu per ciascun di tòrre via Fiorenza,
    colui che la difesi a viso aperto.'
'Deh, se riposi mai vostra semenza,'
    prega' io lui, 'solvetemi quel nodo
    che qui ha inviluppata mia sentenza.
El par che voi veggiate, se ben odo,
    dinanzi quel che 'l tempo seco adduce,
    e nel presente tenete altro modo.'
'Noi veggiam come quei c'ha mala luce   100
    le cose,' disse, 'che ne son lontano –
    cotanto ancor ne splende il sommo duce.
Quando s'appressano o son, tutto è vano
    nostro intelletto, e s'altri non ci apporta,
    nulla sapem di vostro stato umano.
Però comprender puoi che tutta morta
    fia nostra conoscenza da quel punto
    che del futuro fia chiusa la porta.'

But that other great soul, at whose demand
    I'd stopped to speak, did not change his expression,
    Or turn his face, or any way unbend,
Adding to what he had already said:
    'If they have failed to learn that skill correctly,
    That is a greater torment than this bed.
And yet, before the fiftieth time the queen
    Who rules down here has found her face rekindled,[11]   80
    You'll know how hard a skill that is to learn.[12]
And – may you get back to the world – tell me:
    Why are that city's citizens so savage
    In all their laws against my family?'[13]
I answered him: 'The slaughter at the rout
    Which left the River Arbia running red[14]
    Is what brought all such orisons[15] about.'
He sighed and shook his head: 'You know I was
    Hardly alone in that. Nor certainly
    Would I have joined the others without cause.   90
Yet there at Empoli[16] I was the one –
    When all agreed on Florence's destruction –
    Who set his face against it, I alone.'
'So may your seed eventually have rest,'
    I begged him, 'please undo a tangled knot,
    This doubt which keeps my mind in such a twist.
You see beforehand, if I hear aright,
    Those things which time brings with it in its course,
    But with things present it is not like that.'
'We see, as people do who have long sight,   100
    Things,' he replied, 'that are remote from us:
    The supreme lord still gives us that much light.
When things are near, or here, our minds are quite
    Empty; and, if there's none to bring us word,
    Then we know nothing of your human state.
Therefore we shall be utterly without
    Knowledge or understanding from the moment
    The gate into the future has been shut.'[17]

11. Proserpine, the wife of Pluto, is identified with the moon. Farinata is saying his prophecy will
    come true before there have been fifty more full moons (i.e. months).
12. A hint of Dante's exile from Florence, which is often referred to later in the *Comedy*.
13. The Uberti were excluded from all amnesties.
14. The Battle of Montaperti (1260) at which the Guelphs were utterly defeated by the Ghibellines.
15. The measures against the Uberti family are spoken of as prayers, such as would be offered in times
    of crisis.
16. A town some twenty miles from Florence where, after their victory at Montaperti, the Tuscan
    Ghibellines met to decide the fate of Florence.
17. At the Day of Judgement, when time will give way to eternity.

Allor, come di mia colpa compunto,
    dissi: 'Or direte dunque a quel caduto   110
    che 'l suo nato è co' vivi ancor congiunto;
e s'i' fui, dianzi, alla risposta muto,
    fate i saper che 'l feci che pensava
    già nell'error che m'avete soluto.'
E già il maestro mio mi richiamava,
    per ch'i' pregai lo spirto più avaccio
    che mi dicesse chi con lu' istava.
Dissemi: 'Qui con più di mille giaccio:
    qua dentro è 'l secondo Federico,
    e 'l Cardinale – e delli altri mi taccio.'   120
Indi s'ascose, ed io inver l'antico
    poeta volsi i passi, ripensando
    a quel parlar che mi parea nemico.
Elli si mosse, e poi, così andando,
    mi disse: 'Perché se' tu sì smarrito?'
    E io li sodisfeci al suo dimando.
'La mente[c] tua conservi quel ch'udito
    hai contra te,' mi comandò quel saggio.
    'E ora attendi qui,' e drizzò 'l dito:
'quando sarai dinanzi al dolce raggio   130
    di quella il cui bell'occhio tutto vede,
    da lei saprai di tua vita il viaggio.'
Appresso mosse a man sinistra il piede:
    lasciammo il muro e gimmo inver lo mezzo
    per un sentier ch'a una valle fiede
che 'nfin là su facea spiacer suo lezzo.

---

c. As often in Dante, 'memory'.

I then said, feeling guilty for not giving
    This answer earlier, 'Tell the stricken shade[18]   110
    That son of his[19] is still among the living.
And if I was, before, slow to reply,
    Tell him that I was busy thinking over
    That problem which you have resolved for me.'
My master was now wanting me to come;
    And therefore I was quick to beg that spirit
    To name, and quickly, those entombed with him.
He said: 'I'm lying here with thousands more.
    In my tomb is the second Frederick[20], and
    The Cardinal[21]: other names I forbear.'   120
With that he hid himself – I turned to walk
    Back to the ancient poet, thinking over
    Words that had seemed to prophesy ill-luck.[22]
He started off and, as he walked, he said:
    'I want to know why you are so confused.'
    And I made quite sure that he understood.
'Remember everything that you have heard
    To your distress,' that wise man recommended.
    'Now mark my words!' He raised his finger, said:
'When you are standing in the radiance   130
    Of her[23] whose lovely eyes see everything,
    You'll know from her the course of your life hence.'
With that he turned his feet to the left hand,
    Towards the circle's centre, from the wall,
    Along a path with a valley at the end.
Even up there, that valley's stench was foul.

18. Cavalcante dei Cavalcanti.
19. Guido Cavalcanti.
20. The Holy Roman Emperor Frederick II (1194–1250), who was reputed to be a heretic. He engaged in a long political struggle with the Papacy.
21. Cardinal Ottaviano degli Ubaldini (died 1272), generally credited with the remark: 'I can say that, if there is a soul, I have lost mine for the Ghibellines.'
22. See ll. 79–81 above.
23. Beatrice.

CANTO XI

Virgil and Dante look down into the abyss, where they see more shades heaped up. The stench rising from this abyss makes them draw back behind the tomb of Pope Anastasius II, who reputedly had heretical tendencies.

Virgil suggests that they pause awhile, to accustom themselves to the stench, before they descend. So that their time may not be wasted, he will spend it describing what sort of sinners they will find below and, indeed, outlining the plan of the Inferno as a whole.

There are three main divisions of the Inferno: that of incontinence (above and outside the City of Dis, and already visited by Dante), that of violence, and that of fraud. One important distinction here is that those who sin through incontinence are less culpable than those whose sin necessarily involves a clear decision. Throughout the Inferno, the worse the sin the lower the sinner is placed, and so violence and fraud are inside the City of Dis.

The violent are in the first circle immediately below Dante and Virgil, which is the seventh of the circles in the Inferno as a whole. Those guilty of defrauding people who have no particular reason to trust them are in the second circle below, the eighth from the beginning. Finally, those who defraud, or betray, people who have good reason to trust them, are in the last circle below, the lowest place of all. There are many subdivisions also.

In this almost entirely didactic canto Dante relies very much, for his classification of the sins, on pagan authorities, particularly Aristotle. This has the effect of implying that the world is, and always has been, essentially a moral system, the basic understanding of whose nature does not depend on Christian faith.

Finally, Virgil mentions the present position of the stars which indicates that it is nearly dawn in the world above, where those stars may be seen. It is therefore time for them to move on and down.

In su l'estremità d'un'alta ripa   1
   che facevan gran pietre rotte in cerchio
   venimmo sopra più crudele stipa;
e quivi per l'orribile soperchio
   del puzzo che 'l profondo abisso gitta,
   ci raccostammo, in dietro, ad un coperchio
d'un grand'avello, ov'io vidi una scritta
   che dicea: 'ANASTASIO PAPA GUARDO,
   LO QUAL TRASSE FOTIN DELLA VIA DRITTA'.
'Lo nostro scender conviene esser tardo,   10
   sì che s'ausi un poco in prima il senso
   al tristo fiato, e poi no i fia riguardo.'
Così 'l maestro; e io: 'Alcun compenso,'
   dissi lui, 'trova, che 'l tempo non passi
   perduto.' Ed elli: 'Vedi ch'a ciò penso.
Figliuol mio, dentro da cotesti sassi,'
   cominciò poi a dir, 'son tre cerchietti
   di grado in grado, come que' che lassi.
Tutti son pien di spirti maladetti:
   ma perché poi ti basti pur la vista,   20
   intendi come e perché son costretti.
D'ogni malizia ch'odio in cielo acquista
   ingiuria è 'l fine, ed ogni fin cotale
   o con forza o con frode altrui contrista.
Ma perché frode è dell'uom proprio male,
   più spiace a Dio – e però stan di sotto
   li frodolenti e più dolor li assale.
De' violenti il primo cerchio è tutto,
   ma perché si fa forza a tre persone,
   in tre gironi è distinto e costrutto.   30
A Dio, a sé, al prossimo si pòne[a]
   far forza, dico in loro ed in lor cose,
   come udirai con aperta ragione.
Morte per forza e ferute dogliose
   nel prossimo si danno, e nel suo avere
   ruine, incendi e tollette dannose;

a. The enclitic particle 'ne', which is semantically redundant, is still very common in many Italian dialects. Here, for 'pòne', read 'può'.

We – from the very edge of a high steep,   1
    Made by a circle of huge broken rocks –
    Looked down at shades more cruelly heaped up.
And here, because of the extremely bad
    Odour arising from the deep abyss,
    We drew together, back behind the lid
Of a great tomb, where I saw words which say:
    'HERE LIES POPE ANASTASIUS, WHOM PHOTINUS
    PERSUADED FROM THE STRAIGHT AND NARROW WAY'.[1]
'Before going down we must delay somewhat,   10
    So that our nostrils may grow more accustomed
    To the foul breath, which then we can forget.'
So said my master. And I said: 'Then find
    Some compensation, lest our time be wasted.'
    And he: 'Something's already in my mind.
My son, within this band of broken stone,'
    So he began, 'there are three smaller circles,[2]
    Like those you've left, and always going down.
They are all full of spirits that are cursed;
    And for your understanding when you see them,   20
    Hear for what cause and whereabouts they're placed.
Of every sin that earns the hate of God
    The end's injustice, and all such injustice
    Harms somebody, either by force or fraud.
But, since fraud is peculiar to man,
    It grieves God more; and so the fraudulent
    Are lower down, subject to greater pain.
And the first circle under us belongs
    To the violent; but since force is threefold,
    The circle's made of three concentric rings.   30
On God, oneself, one's neighbour one may use
    Force – on them or on what they own, I mean –
    As I intend more fully to disclose.
A violent death or grievous wounds may be
    Inflicted on a neighbour; on his goods
    Ruin, arson, extortion, and robbery.

1. Pope Anastasius, who reigned 496–8, was said to have been led by Photinus, a deacon from
   Thessalonica, into denying the divine origin of Christ.
2. The Inferno consists of nine circles, one below the other, which – since the Inferno is shaped like
   an inverted cone – become smaller the lower one goes. See illustration on p.3.

onde omicide e ciascun che mal fiere,
   guastatori e predon, tutti tormenta
   lo giron primo per diverse schiere.
Puote omo avere in sé man violenta   40
   e ne' suoi beni – e però nel secondo
   giron convien che sanza pro si penta
qualunque priva sé del vostro mondo,
   biscazza e fonde la sua facultade,
   e piange là dov'esser de' giocondo.
Puossi far forza nella deitade,
   col cor negando e bestemmiando quella,
   e spregiando natura e sua bontade;
e però lo minor giron suggella
   del segno suo e Soddoma e Caorsa   50
   e chi, spregiando Dio col cor, favella.
La frode, ond'ogni coscienza è morsa,
   può l'uomo usare in colui che 'n lui fida
   ed in quel che fidanza non imborsa.
Questo modo di retro par ch'uccida
   pur lo vinco d'amor che fa natura;
   onde nel cerchio secondo s'annida
ipocrisia, lusinghe e chi affattura,
   falsità, ladroneccio e simonia,
   ruffian, baratti, e simile lordura.   60
Per l'altro modo quell'amor s'oblia
   che fa natura, e quel ch'è poi aggiunto,
   di che la fede spezial si cria;
onde nel cerchio minore, ov'è 'l punto
   dell'universo in su che Dite siede,
   qualunque trade in etterno è consunto.'
E io: 'Maestro, assai chiara procede
   la tua ragione, ed assai ben distingue
   questo baratro e 'l popol ch'e' possiede.
Ma dimmi: quei della palude pingue,   70
   che mena il vento, e che batte la pioggia,
   e che s'incontran con sì aspre lingue,

Killers, and all who use force sinfully,
　　Looters and pillagers, are all tormented
　　In the first ring, but punished differently.
A man may raise his hand in violence　　　　　　　　40
　　Against himself or his own goods. Therefore
　　In the next ring, in pointless penitence,
Lie those who up in your world did away
　　With themselves, or dissipated wealth in gambling
　　Till lamentation took the place of joy.
One may use force, and use it against God,
　　Denying him in secret, or blaspheming,
　　Or scorning nature and her plenitude;
And so the smallest of the rings has set
　　Its seal on Sodom[3], Cahors[4], and everyone　　　　50
　　Who blasphemes, scorning God within his heart.
Now fraud, by which the conscience *must* be pierced,[5]
　　May be practised on one who trusts the trickster,
　　Or else on one who has no call to trust.
Clearly this latter merely cuts across
　　The bonds by which we're bound by nature.[6] So
　　Down in the second circle under us[7]
Hypocrites, flatterers, and sorcery
　　Must nestle, forgers, thieves, simoniacs,
　　Pimps, barrators, and suchlike blackguardry.　　　60
But, by the other kind of fraud,[8] not just
　　Love formed by nature is forgotten, but
　　That added love which makes for special trust.
So in the smallest circle,[9] at the centre
　　Of all the universe, the seat of Dis,
　　All who are traitors are consumed for ever.'
And I: 'Master, your reasoning is precise,
　　And it distinguishes most carefully
　　Among the people held in this abyss.
But tell me now: those in the slimy marsh,　　　　　70
　　Or blown on the wind, or beaten by the rain,
　　Or those whose altercations are so harsh[10] –

3. One of the 'cities of the plain' (Genesis 19: 29) destroyed by God. It gave its name to sodomy.
4. Cahors, a city in southern France, proverbial for usury.
5. Those who practise fraud are bound by the nature of their actions to be conscious of what they do, since it requires the concurrence of their reason. Their sin is therefore the more grievous.
6. The love for each other which is inborn in human beings, since man is by nature a social creature.
7. That is, the eighth circle in the Inferno as a whole.
8. That practised against those who have a particular reason (e.g. a close relationship) to trust us.
9. The ninth and last.
10. In the last tercet, Virgil refers to, respectively, the wrathful (VII and VIII), the lustful (V), the gluttonous (VI), the avaricious and prodigals (VII).

perché non dentro dalla città roggia
    sono ei puniti, se Dio li ha in ira?
    E se non li ha, perché sono a tal foggia?'
Ed elli a me 'Perché tanto delira,'
    disse, 'lo 'ngegno tuo da quel che sòle?
    O ver la mente dove altrove mira?
Non ti rimembra di quelle parole
    con le quai la tua Etica pertratta   80
    le tre disposizion che 'l ciel non vole –
incontinenza, malizia e la matta
    bestialitade? – e come incontinenza
    men Dio offende e men biasimo accatta?
Se tu riguardi ben questa sentenza,
    e rechiti alla mente chi son quelli
    che su di fuor sostegnon penitenza,
tu vedrai ben perché da questi felli
    sien dipartiti, e perché men crucciata
    la divina vendetta li martelli.'   90
'O sol che sani ogni vista turbata,
    tu mi contenti sì quando tu solvi
    che, non men che saver, dubbiar m'aggrata.
Ancora in dietro un poco ti rivolvi,'
    diss'io, 'là dove di' ch'usura offende
    la divina bontade, e 'l groppo solvi.'
'Filosofia,' mi disse, 'a chi la 'ntende,
    nota non pur in una sola parte,
    come natura lo suo corso prende
dal divino intelletto e da sua arte;   100
    e se tu ben la tua Fisica note,
    tu troverai, non dopo molte carte,
che l'arte vostra quella, quanto pote,
    segue, come 'l maestro fa il discente,
    sì che vostr'arte a Dio quasi è nepote.
Da queste due, se tu ti rechi a mente
    lo Genesì dal principio, convene
    prender sua vita ed avanzar la gente;

Whyever in this city's[14] conflagration
    Are they not punished too, if loathed by God?
    If not, why are they plagued in such a fashion?'
Then he replied: 'Why does your reasoning take,
    So unaccustomedly, this deviant course?
    Or are you off upon a different tack?[15]
Are you oblivious then of what is said
    In detail in your *Ethics*[16] of the three   80
    Dispositions which are opposed to God –
Incontinence, and malice, and insane
    Brutality? And how incontinence
    Offends God less and so incurs less blame?
If you consider well what has been said,
    And if you then remember who they are
    Who suffer punishment above outside,[17]
You will see clearly why they're kept away
    From evil souls like these, and why God's anger
    Strikes them indeed, but much less heavily.'   90
'O sun, clearing the clouds from troubled sight,
    You make me so contented with your answers
    That, much as knowledge pleases, so does doubt.
Go back,' I said, 'a little way, to that
    Point where you said that usury was offensive
    To God's own goodness, and undo the knot.'
'For one who understands, philosophy
    Points out,' he said, 'not only in one passage,
    How nature, in her working, makes her way
After divine intelligence and art.   100
    Then, if you've read your *Physics*[18] with some care,
    You'll find this noted, and quite near the start:
Human skill works, as closely as it may,
    Following nature, as a child his teacher;
    So your skill is God's grandchild, one might say.
So from these two – remember the beginning
    Of *Genesis*[19] – it follows that mankind
    Should make its way in the world and make a living.

14. The City of Dis.
15. Virgil suggests that Dante is either foolishly forgetting here to distinguish between degrees of
    culpability in sinning, or else deliberately adopting the Stoic view that all faults are equally culpable.
16. Aristotle's *Nicomachean Ethics*, which Virgil implies is one of Dante's favourite books.
17. In the first five circles, which lie above and outside the City of Dis.
18. Aristotle's *Physics*.
19. For example, 'And the Lord God took the man, and put him into the garden of Eden to dress and
    keep it' (Genesis 2: 15), and 'In the sweat of thy face shalt thou eat bread..' (Genesis 3: 19).

e perché l'usuriere altra via tene,
 per sé natura e per la sua seguace   110
 dispregia, poi ch'in altro pon la spene.
Ma seguimi oramai, che 'l gir mi piace,
 ché i Pesci guizzan su per l'orizzonta,
 e 'l Carro tutto sovra 'l Coro giace,
e 'l balzo via là oltra si dismonta.'

That's not the method of the usurer,
    For he must slight both nature and her pupil,   110
    Hard human work, placing his hopes elsewhere.[20]
Follow me now, because I think it best.
    The Fish[21] flash up on the horizon, and
    The Wain[22] is lying over the north-west.
Further on is the place where we descend.[23]

20. The argument against usury here is essentially that the usurer does not produce anything by working, as he should, in co-operation with God and God's creation. Instead, he uses money (which is not wealth in itself but merely a means of exchange, a token of wealth) to take for himself, in Shakespeare's words, 'a breed for barren metal'.
21. The constellation Pisces.
22. The constellation Ursa Major, the Great Bear.
23. To the seventh circle.

CANTO XII

Dante and Virgil scramble down a mass of fallen rocks into the seventh circle, that of the violent, and into the first ring of this circle, reserved for those who were violent against their neighbour. Virgil explains that the landslip was caused by the earthquake at the time of the Crucifixion. The Minotaur, the guardian of this circle, is angry at their arrival, but Virgil provokes the monster to a blind frenzy which enables them to evade it.

Around the circle runs a river of boiling blood. This is the Phlegethon, the fiery river of the classical underworld, although Dante does not name it until Canto XIV. The banks of the river are patrolled by centaurs armed with bows and arrows, who shoot any of the damned who rise too far out of it, for the violent are immersed in it to a greater or less depth according to the gravity of their sin.

The centaurs are at first suspicious of Virgil and Dante, but their leader, Chiron, obeys Virgil's orders and gives them Nessus to be their guide and to carry Dante on his back when they ford the river. Nessus explains the way the damned are punished here, and points many of them out. Then Nessus goes back across the ford.

This canto is a good example of how Dante develops imaginatively what are basically very simple, even obvious, images. The centaurs, who have both human and animal attributes, clearly symbolise the state of those human beings who have acted bestially. Then the river of boiling blood is a development of the common metaphor we use when we say something like, 'It makes my blood boil' (a metaphor also used in Italian of course). The grotesque features of this circle mirror the grotesque nature of the sins involved, the 'blind cupidity and senseless anger' which cause us to sin in our short lives and so merit a punishment which lasts for ever.

Era lo loco ov'a scender la riva   1
    venimmo alpestro e, per quel che v'er'anco,
    tal ch'ogni vista ne sarebbe schiva.
Qual è quella ruina che nel fianco
    di qua da Trento l'Adice percosse,
    o per tremoto o per sostegno manco,
che da cima del monte, onde si mosse,
    al piano è sì la roccia discoscesa,
    ch'alcuna via darebbe a chi su fosse;
cotal di quel burrato era la scesa,   10
    e 'n su la punta della rotta lacca
    l'infamia di Creti era distesa
che fu concetta nella falsa vacca –
    e quando vide noi, sé stesso morse,
    sì come quei cui l'ira dentro fiacca.
Lo savio mio inver lui gridò: 'Forse
    tu credi che qui sia 'l duca d'Atene,
    che su nel mondo la morte ti porse?
Partiti, bestia, ché questi non vène
    ammaestrato dalla tua sorella,   20
    ma vassi per veder le vostre pene.'
Qual è quel toro che si slaccia in quella
    c'ha ricevuto già 'l colpo mortale,
    che gir non sa, ma qua e là saltella,
vid'io lo Minotauro far cotale;
    e quello accorto gridò: 'Corri al varco:
    mentre ch'è in furia, è buon che tu ti cale.'
Così prendemmo via giù per lo scarco
    di quelle pietre, che spesso moviènsi
    sotto i miei piedi per lo novo carco.   30
Io gìa pensando, e quei disse: 'Tu pensi,
    forse, in questa ruina ch'è guardata
    da quell'ira bestial ch'i' ora spensi.
Or vo' che sappi che l'altra fiata
    ch'i' discesi qua giù nel basso inferno,
    questa roccia non era ancor cascata;

The place we came to, for our journey down,
    Was strewn with rocks; and there was something else,
    And such as anybody's eyes would shun.[1]
Like that landslip, this side of Trent, which struck
    The River Adige on its left bank –
    Whether through faulty shoring or earthquake –
Where from the mountain-top down to the plain
    The rocks are shattered and all heaped up so
    They give some footing to one climbing down –
Such was the way to get into that pit.   10
    And, on the broken chasm's very brink,
    Spreadeagled, lay the infamy of Crete,
Who was conceived inside a cow-like cage;[2]
    And catching sight of us, he bit himself,
    Like somebody consumed with inward rage.
My sage called out to him: 'Could it be said
    That you believe this is the Duke of Athens[3]
    At whose hands, in the world above, you died?
But no! Be off! This man has not come here
    Under your sister's artful tutelage,[4]   20
    But to observe the torments you endure.'
Now like a bull that breaks its bondage at
    The instant it receives the fatal blow,
    And cannot walk, but goes plunging about –
That's how I saw the Minotaur behave.
    Quickly my guide cried out: 'Make for the pass –
    You'd best descend while he is in this rage.'
And so we made our way: under my feet
    Rocks and stones were frequently dislodged,
    Because of all the unaccustomed weight.[5]   30
I went on, lost in thought. He said: 'You will
    Be thinking of that fall of rocks watched over
    By the brute wrath I managed to control.
Now I would have you know, the first time when
    I came down here and into nether hell[6]
    This mass of rocks had not yet fallen down.

---

1. What this 'something else' is becomes clear only in ll. 11–13.
2. The Minotaur, half man and half bull, the offspring of Pasiphae (wife of King Minos of Crete) and a bull. Pasiphae ordered the construction of a wooden cow, into which she placed herself to receive the bull.
3. Theseus.
4. Theseus was provided by Ariadne, the Minotaur's half-sister, with a sword to kill the monster, and a ball of thread by which to retrace his steps out of the labyrinth where the monster was kept.
5. One of several reminders in the Inferno that Dante, being still alive, is not a shade.
6. See IX: 22–7.

ma certo poco pria, se ben discerno,
   che venisse colui che la gran preda
   levò a Dite del cerchio superno,
da tutte parti l'alta valle feda   40
   tremò sì ch'i' pensai che l'universo
   sentisse amor, per lo qual è chi creda
più volte il mondo in caòs converso;
   ed in quel punto questa vecchia roccia
   qui e altrove tal fece riverso.
Ma ficca li occhi a valle, ché s'approccia
   la riviera del sangue in la qual bolle
   qual che per violenza in altrui noccià.'
Oh cieca cupidigia e ira folle,
   che sì ci sproni nella vita corta,   50
   e nell'etterna poi sì mal c'immolle!
Io vidi un'ampia fossa in arco torta,
   come quella che tutto 'l piano abbraccia,
   secondo ch'avea detto la mia scorta;
e, tra 'l piè della ripa ed essa, in traccia
   corrìen Centauri, armati di saette,
   come solìen nel mondo andare a caccia.
Veggendoci calar, ciascun ristette,
   e della schiera tre si dipartiro
   con archi e asticciuole prima elette;   60
e l'un gridò da lungi: 'A qual martiro
   venite voi che scendete la costa?
   Ditel costinci – se non, l'arco tiro.'
Lo mio maestro disse: 'La risposta
   farem noi a Chiron costà di presso:
   mal fu la voglia tua sempre sì tosta.'
Poi mi tentò, e disse: 'Quelli è Nesso,
   che morì per la bella Deianira
   e fe' di sé la vendetta elli stesso.
E quel di mezzo, ch'al petto si mira,   70
   è il gran Chiron, il qual nodrì Achille –
   quell'altro è Folo, che fu sì pien d'ira.

But, if I'm not mistaken, a short while
    Before *He* came, who took away from Dis,
    And from the highest circle, glorious spoil,[7]
This deep and dirty hollow all around   40
    Shuddered so much I think the universe
    Felt love, by which it has been often turned,
As some believe, to chaos once again.
    And at that point this ancient mass of rocks,
    Both here, and elsewhere like this, tumbled down.[8]
But look down there, and look intently: we'll
    Soon be beside the stream of blood, where those
    Who in their violence injure others boil.'
O blind cupidity and senseless anger,
    Which goad us on throughout our little life,   50
    Then soak us in such anguish, and for ever!
I saw a ditch bent in a curve and broad,
    Encircling as it went the entire level,
    Just as my guide, some time before, had said.
Between it and the scarp I saw some running:
    A file of centaurs[9], armed with bows and arrows,
    As, in the world above, they went out hunting.
As we came down, they stopped and stood there steady,
    And three of them broke ranks and stared at us,
    Holding their bows and arrows at the ready.   60
One shouted from far off: 'Tell me to what
    Punishment you are coming down the slope.
    Tell me from where you are. If not, I'll shoot.'
My master said: 'Our answer will be made
    To Chiron, when we get to where he is:
    You always were too quick for your own good.'
Then he nudged me, 'That was Nessus,' he said,
    'Who died for the lovely Deianira, and
    Took vengeance for himself when he was dead.[10]
That big one in the middle, with bowed head,   70
    Is the great Chiron, guardian of Achilles.
    The other's Pholus, known for his bad blood.[11]

---

7. A reference to Christ's Harrowing of Hell after the Crucifixion, His rescue of the souls of patriarchs and prophets from Limbo ('the highest circle').

8. A reference to the earthquake which accompanied the Crucifixion. Virgil, a pagan, tries to understand this in the light of the Empedoclean idea that the supervention of harmony, or love, in creation results in disorder. Virgil speaks more truly than he realises, in that the Crucifixion is love in action.

9. Mythological beings, with a human torso joined to the body of a horse. As creatures with both human and bestial attributes they are well placed in the circle of the violent.

10. He tried to rape Deianira, and was killed by her husband, Heracles. Before he died Nessus told Deianira to take his shirt covered with his blood to use as a love charm. She gave it to Heracles, and when he put it on, it turned out to be poisonous and he was killed.

11. He provoked the famous fight, at a wedding feast, between the centaurs and Lapiths.

Dintorno al fosso vanno a mille a mille,
    saettando qual anima si svelle
    del sangue più che sua colpa sortille.'
Noi ci appressammo a quelle fiere snelle:
    Chiron prese uno strale, e con la cocca
    fece la barba in dietro alle mascelle.
Quando s'ebbe scoperta la gran bocca,
    disse a' compagni: 'Siete voi accorti   80
    che quel di retro move ciò ch'el tocca?
Così non soglion far li piè de' morti.'
    E 'l mio buon duca, che già li era al petto,
    dove le due nature son consorti,
rispuose: 'Ben è vivo, e sì soletto
    mostrar li mi convien la valle buia:
    necessità 'l ci 'nduce, e non diletto.
Tal si partì da cantare alleluia
    che mi commise quest'officio novo:
    non è ladron, né io anima fuia.   90
Ma per quella virtù per cu' io movo
    li passi miei per sì selvaggia strada,
    danne un de' tuoi, a cui noi siamo a provo,
e che ne mostri là dove si guada
    e che porti costui in su la groppa,
    ché non è spirto che per l'aere vada.'
Chiron si volse in su la destra poppa
    e disse a Nesso: 'Torna, e sì li guida,
    e fa cansar s'altra schiera v'intoppa.'
Or ci movemmo con la scorta fida   100
    lungo la proda del bollor vermiglio,
    dove i bolliti facìeno alte strida.
Io vidi gente sotto infino al ciglio,
    e 'l gran Centauro disse: 'E' son tiranni
    che dier nel sangue e nell'aver di piglio.
Quivi si piangon li spietati danni –
    quivi è Alessandro, e Dionisio fero,
    che fe' Cicilia aver dolorosi anni.

They run in thousands by the stream, and shoot
    At any guilty soul who lifts himself
    Out of the blood beyond what is his lot.'[12]
And now, as we were getting near to those
    Quick creatures, Chiron, with an arrow's nock,
    Brushed back his beard on both sides from his jaws.
And when his big mouth was disclosed for speech,
    He said to his companions: 'Have you noticed   80
    The one behind moving what his feet touch?
Feet of the dead don't usually do that.'
    And my good guide, already at that breast
    Where the two natures of the creature meet,
Answered: 'He's certainly alive, and he
    Comes here that I may show him this dark valley.
    Not pleasure brings him, but necessity.
She[13] came from singing songs of praise who laid
    This charge upon me, novel as it was:
    He is no robber, I'm no thieving shade.   90
But by that power through which I am allowed
    To go on such a rugged journey, give us
    One of your band whom we may stay beside,
And, following the stream, let him show where
    To ford it, bearing this man on his crupper:
    He is no spirit to fly through the air.'
Then Chiron turned and wheeled to the right hand,
    Commanding Nessus: 'Come, and be their guide,
    And clear the way of any other band.'[14]
And so, together with our faithful guide,   100
    We went beside the boiling, crimson river;
    I heard the high-pitched shrieks of those being boiled.
I saw some there up to their eyebrows under;
    And the huge centaur told us: 'They are tyrants
    Who liked to soak their hands in blood and plunder.
They pay for pitiless brutality –
    Alexander[15], and fierce Dionysius[16]
    Who gave such years of grief to Sicily.

12. The depth to which the violent are immersed in the boiling blood varies according to the gravity
    of their sin.
13. Beatrice.
14. These centaurs are frequently referred to in military terms. They are reminiscent of the roving bands
    of mercenaries and brigands who troubled Italy in Dante's day.
15 Presumably, since the name lacks any qualification, Alexander the Great.
16. Dionysius the Elder, who died in 367 BC, after a tyrannous reign of thirty-eight years.

E quella fronte c'ha 'l pel così nero
    è Azzolino, e quell'altro ch'è biondo,   110
    è Opizzo da Esti, il qual per vero
fu spento dal figliastro su nel mondo.'
    Allor mi volsi al poeta, e quei disse:
    'Questi ti sia or primo, e io secondo.'
Poco più oltre il Centauro s'affisse
    sovr'una gente che 'nfino alla gola
    parea che di quel bulicame uscisse.
Mostrocci un'ombra dall'un canto sola,
    dicendo: 'Colui fesse in grembo a Dio
    lo cor che 'n su Tamici ancor si cola[a].'   120
Poi vidi gente che di fuor del rio
    tenean la testa ed ancor tutto il casso,
    e di costoro assai riconobb'io.
Così a più a più si facea basso
    quel sangue, sì che cocea pur li piedi,
    e quindi fu del fosso il nostro passo.
'Sì come tu da questa parte vedi
    lo bulicame che sempre si scema,'
    disse 'l Centauro, 'voglio che tu credi
che da quest'altra a più a più giù prema   130
    lo fondo suo, infin ch'el si raggiunge
    ove la tirannia convien che gema.
La divina giustizia di qua punge
    quell'Attila che fu flagello in terra,
    e Pirro e Sesto – ed in etterno munge
le lagrime, che col bollor diserra,
    a Rinier da Corneto, a Rinier Pazzo,
    che fecero alle strade tanta guerra.'
Poi si rivolse, e ripassossi 'l guazzo.

---

a. Usually taken as 'is honoured' ('si cole'), but can also mean 'drips blood' (a sign that the murder was unavenged).

That brow on which the hair is very black
    Is Ezzelino[17]; and the other, fair,   110
    Obizzo da Este[18], who indeed was struck
Down by the hand of his unnatural son.'[19]
    I then turned to the poet, and he said:
    'Listen to him now, and me later on.'
A little further and the centaur stood
    Beside a group that even to their necks
    Appeared to rise above the boiling blood.
He pointed to one separated shade,
    Saying: 'That man, within God's bosom, pierced
    The heart that by the Thames still drips with blood.'[20] 120
Then I saw people keeping their heads raised,
    And even their whole chests, above the river;
    And quite a few of these I recognised.
So bit by bit I saw the boiling blood
    Go shallower, until it scalded feet
    And nothing else; and here we crossed the ford.
'Just as on this side, as you must have seen,
    The stream goes shallower and shallower,'
    The centaur said, 'so now I must explain
That on the other side its bed sinks down   130
    Deeper and deeper, till we come once more
    To there where tyranny is made to groan.
And so God's justice on the far side stings
    That Attila[21] who was a scourge on earth,
    Pyrrhus[22], and Sextus[23]; and forever wrings
Tears out from those being boiled – Rinier de' Pazzi
    And Rinier da Corneto,[24] two who made
    Our roads the scene of action in their wars.'
Then he turned round, and back across the ford.

17. Ezzelino III da Romano, 1194–1259.
18. Obizzo da Este, 1264–93.
19. The centaur confirms the rumour that Obizzo was killed by his son.
20. Guy de Montfort, son of the famous Simon de Montfort, in 1271 murdered his first cousin in a church. The heart of his victim was kept in a reliquary in London: it is said to be still bleeding because the death went unavenged. He is set apart from the other shades because of the peculiar horror of his sin.
21. King of the Huns (406–53), known as 'the scourge of God'.
22. Probably the son of Achilles, whose cruelty after the fall of Troy is described by Virgil in his *Aeneid*.
23. Probably the son of Pompey the Great, a pirate who was put to death in 35 BC.
24. Rinieri de' Pazzi, a notorious highway robber, died before 1280; Rinieri da Corneto, a contemporary of Dante, was a bandit chief who operated on the roads leading into Rome.

CANTO XIII

Virgil and Dante make their way through a tangled wood of gnarled and twisted bushes – the wood of the suicides and profligates. This wood is inhabited by harpies – eerie birds with the faces of women. Virgil explains that they are now in the second ring of the seventh circle, reserved for those who used violence against themselves – either their own bodies or their own goods.

Around them is the sound of groaning, but nobody seems to be there to make the sound. Acting on Virgil's suggestion, Dante plucks a twig from a thornbush and hears the bush complaining of that ill-treatment. The bush, speaking through the wound left by its mutilation, says that it is the shade of the poet Pier della Vigna, who died by his own hand after his political disgrace. He insists he was innocent of the charges made against him, but admits he sinned in killing himself. He explains that, when a soul deliberately separates itself from its body, it is condemned to the seventh circle of the Inferno, where it falls into this wood like a seed, and sprouts and becomes a bush. It is tormented by the Harpies, who eat its leaves, thereby leaving wounds through which the bush groans. On the Day of Judgement these souls will regain their bodies, but they will not put them on again. Instead, the bodies will hang on the bushes which are their souls. It would not be right for body and soul to be reunited when the human being they formed has deliberately willed their separation.

Suddenly there is the noise of hunting, and two naked and lacerated shades run through the wood, chased by hounds which catch them and tear them. These shades are the spendthrifts, who are now laid waste as their goods were once.

One of these shades explains that he was a Florentine, and he attributes the troubles of that city to its change of patron from Mars to John the Baptist. He says he hanged himself in his own home.

Non era ancor di là Nesso arrivato,   1
   quando noi ci mettemmo per un bosco
   che da nessun sentiero era segnato.
Non fronda verde, ma di color fosco –
   non rami schietti, ma nodosi e 'nvolti –
   non pomi v'eran, ma stecchi con tosco:
non han sì aspri sterpi né sì folti
   quelle fiere selvagge che in odio hanno
   tra Cecina e Corneto i luoghi colti.
Quivi le brutte Arpìe lor nidi fanno,   10
   che cacciar delle Strofade i Troiani
   con tristo annunzio di futuro danno.
Ali hanno late, e colli e visi umani,
   piè con artigli, e pennuto il gran ventre –
   fanno lamenti in su li alberi strani[a].
E 'l buon maestro, 'Prima che più entre,
   sappi che se' nel secondo girone,'
   mi cominciò a dire, 'e sarai mentre
che tu verrai nell'orribil sabbione:
   però riguarda ben – sì vederai   20
   cose che torrien fede al mio sermone.'
Io sentìa d'ogni parte trarre guai,
   e non vedea persona che 'l facesse,
   per ch'io tutto smarrito m'arrestai.
Cred'io ch'ei credette ch'io credesse
   che tante voci uscisser tra quei bronchi
   da gente che per noi si nascondesse.
Però disse 'l maestro: 'Se tu tronchi
   qualche fraschetta d'una d'este piante,
   li pensier c'hai si faran tutti monchi.'   30
Allor porsi la mano un poco avante,
   e colsi un ramicel da un gran pruno,
   e 'l tronco suo gridò: 'Perché mi schiante?'
Da che fatto fu poi di sangue bruno,
   ricominciò a dir: 'Perché mi scerpi?
   non hai tu spirto di pietà alcuno?

a. The adjective 'strani', which can refer either to 'lamenti' or 'alberi', is best taken as referring to both, to increase the sense of strangeness here.

Nessus has not yet reached the other side,   1
   And we've already started on our way
   Through what's apparently a trackless wood.[1]
No fresh green leaves, but only sable ones;
   No smooth, straight boughs, but only gnarled and twisted;
   And no fruit either, only poison thorns:
Wild creatures loathing cultivated earth,
   Living near Cecina and Corneto, never
   Come across such unyielding, tangled growth.
And here the filthy Harpies make their home,   10
   Who drove the Trojans from the Strophades
   With dark announcements of their future doom.[2]
They have broad wings; their faces are of women;
   Their feet have talons, their big bellies feathers;
   Their wailing in the trees seems less than human.
My master said: 'Before you penetrate
   The wood much further, know that you're within
   The second ring,[3] and will remain in it
Until you come upon the sand of dread.[4]
   So study all you see: you will see things   20
   For which I know you'd never take my word.'
I could hear groaning coming from all round,
   Which stopped me in my tracks and in confusion,
   Because I saw nobody make the sound.
I think that he was thinking that I thought
   That all those voices in among the trunks
   Issued from people hidden from our sight.
Therefore my master told me: 'Tear a bit,
   A little twig, from any of these branches:
   You'll find your thoughts will also be cut short.'   30
I stretched my hand a short way out before me,
   And snapped a tiny branch from off a thorn;
   And then the trunk screamed out: 'Why do you tear me?'
And when a stream of blood had blackened it,
   It started off again: 'Why do you rend me?'
   Have you no drop of pity in your heart?

1. The wood of the suicides. Dante and Virgil are still in the seventh circle, but now the second ring of it, where those who were violent against themselves are punished.
2. In his *Aeneid* (III: 209 ff.) Virgil describes how Aeneas and his companions, when they came to the islands of the Strophades, were unable to eat because Harpies swooped down, snatched food from the table, and fouled everything with their droppings. One of the Harpies, Celaeno, also prophesied further trouble for the Trojans.
3. Of the seventh circle. See XI: 28 ff. for the significance of the three rings in this circle.
4. In the third ring of the seventh circle, which Virgil and Dante reach in the next canto.

Uomini fummo, e or siam fatti sterpi:
  ben dovrebb'esser la tua man più pia,
  se state fossimo anime di serpi.'
Come d'un stizzo verde ch'arso sia   40
  dall'un de' càpi, che dall'altro geme
  e cigola per vento che va via,
sì della scheggia rotta usciva insieme
  parole e sangue – ond'io lasciai la cima
  cadere, e stetti come l'uom che teme.
'S'elli avesse potuto creder prima,'
  rispuose 'l savio mio, 'anima lesa,
  ciò c'ha veduto pur con la mia rima,
non averebbe in te la man distesa,
  ma la cosa incredibile mi fece   50
  indurlo ad ovra ch'a me stesso pesa.
Ma dilli chi tu fosti, sì che 'n vece
  d'alcun'ammenda tua fama rinfreschi
  nel mondo su, dove tornar li lece.'
E 'l tronco: 'Sì col dolce dir m'adeschi,
  ch'i' non posso tacere, e voi non gravi
  perch'io un poco a ragionar m'inveschi.
Io son colui che tenni ambo le chiavi
  del cor di Federigo, e che le volsi,
  serrando e diserrando, sì soavi   60
che dal secreto suo quasi ogn'uom tolsi:
  fede portai al glorioso offizio,
  tanto ch'i' ne perde' li sonni e' polsi.
La meretrice che mai dall'ospizio
  di Cesare non torse li occhi putti –
  morte comune e delle corti vizio –
infiammò contra me li animi tutti,
  e li 'nfiammati infiammar sì Augusto
  che' lieti onor tornaro in tristi lutti.
L'animo mio, per disdegnoso gusto,   70
  credendo col morir fuggir disdegno,
  ingiusto fece me contra me giusto.

Once we were men, and now we're stumps and stocks:
    Your hand might well have shown us greater mercy,
    If we'd turned out to be the souls of snakes.'
As from a firebrand, at one end on fire –   40
    While from the other, since it is still green,
    It drips and hisses with the escaping air –
So, from the stump that I had injured, blood
    Came out mixed up with words. I let the twig
    Drop, and I stood like somebody afraid.
'If he'd been able to believe at first,
    O damaged soul,' my sage replied to him,
    'What he'd seen only as he found it versed,[5]
He never would have laid his hand on you;
    But such a thing, so incredible, required   50
    Persuasion to this deed which hurts me too.
Say who you were. He will, in recompense,
    Restore you to your worldly reputation,
    Once he, who is allowed up there, returns.'
The trunk replied: 'Your words to me are such
    I can't keep silent; but I beg indulgence,
    If for a while I'm tempted into speech.
I am the man who used to hold both keys
    Of Emperor Frederick's heart,[6] and used to turn them,
    Locking, unlocking, with such practised ease   60
That I kept almost all men from his thought,
    And was so conscientious in that office
    I lost both sleep and health because of it.
That whore[7] who never turned her harlot's eyes
    Away from Caesar's household[8] – always fatal
    Throughout the world, in courts a special vice –
Inflamed men's minds against me and my state,
    And all those so inflamed inflamed Augustus,[9]
    And joyful honour turned to foul despite.
For all of this my mind had such disgust   70
    It hoped by death to flee distaste, and made me
    Unjust against myself, though I was just.

5. In the *Aeneid* (III: 19–68) there is a comparable episode, which Dante used as his source.
6. This is the poet Pier della Vigna (*c*.1190–1249) who, after being chief adviser to the Emperor
    Frederick II, was disgraced and imprisoned. His death in prison was attributed to suicide.
7. Envy.
8. A flattering way of referring to Frederick II's court.
9. It is a compliment to Frederick II to equate him with Augustus, the first Roman Emperor.

Per le nove radici d'esto legno,
  vi giuro che già mai non ruppi fede
  al mio signor, che fu d'onor sì degno.
E se di voi alcun nel mondo riede,
  conforti la memoria mia, che giace
  ancor del colpo che 'nvidia le diede.'
Un poco attese, e poi: 'Da ch'el si tace,'
  disse 'l poeta a me, 'non perder l'ora,   80
  ma parla, e chiedi a lui, se più ti piace.'
Ond'io a lui: 'Domandal tu ancora
  di quel che credi ch'a me satisfaccia,
  ch'i' non potrei, tanta pietà m'accora!'
Perciò ricominciò: 'Se l'uom ti faccia
  liberamente ciò che 'l tuo dir priega,
  spirito incarcerato, ancor ti piaccia
di dirne come l'anima si lega
  in questi nocchi – e dinne, se tu puoi,
  s'alcuna mai di tai membra si spiega.'   90
Allor soffiò il tronco forte, e poi
  si convertì quel vento in cotal voce:
  'Brievemente sarà risposto a voi.
Quando si parte l'anima feroce
  dal corpo ond'ella stessa s'è disvelta,
  Minòs la manda alla settima foce.
Cade in la selva, e non l'è parte scelta,
  ma là dove fortuna la balestra,
  quivi germoglia come gran di spelta.
Surge in vermena ed in pianta silvestra: 100
  l'Arpìe, pascendo poi delle sue foglie,
  fanno dolore, ed al dolor fenestra.
Come l'altre verrem per nostre spoglie,
  ma non però ch'alcuna sen rivesta,
  ché non è giusto aver ciò ch'om si toglie.
Qui le strascineremo, e per la mesta
  selva saranno i nostri corpi appesi,
  ciascuno al prun dell'ombra sua molesta.'

Now, by the roots of this abnormal timber
    I swear to you I never broke my faith
    To my great lord, so worthy of all honour.
If one of you gets back into the world,
    Let him revive my glorious memory,
    Still prostrate from the darts that envy hurled.'
My poet waited, and, 'Since he's not speaking,'
    He said to me, 'then do not waste your time,   80
    But question him according to your liking.'
To this I answered: 'Please go on with it,
    And ask him what you think I need to know;
    I cannot, there's such anguish in my heart!'
So he began once more: 'All will be done,
    And willingly, that you have begged of us,
    Imprisoned spirit, if you speak again,
And tell us how the soul comes to be tied
    In knots like these; and tell us, if you can,
    If there was ever anybody freed.'   90
And then the hapless trunk hissed very hard
    Until its wheezing breath became a voice:
    'To that you'll have your answer in a word.
The cruel soul – when it has torn itself
    Out of its body, which it leaves behind,
    And Minos sends it to the seventh gulf[10] –
Falls in the wood, in no particular part;
    Merely where random fortune slings or flings it,
    It sprouts and springs up like a grain of spelt.
It rises as a tender woodland plant: 100
    The Harpies, who are feeding on its foliage,
    Cause pain, and for the pain provide a vent.[11]
We'll come for our remains, like everyone,
    But not that we may put them on once more:
    What men renounce they cannot have again.[12]
No, we shall drag them here; throughout the sad
    Wood all our bodies will be left to hang,
    Each on the thornbush of its harmful shade.'

10. The seventh circle, reserved for the violent.

11. The bushes are able to speak through the wounds left in them by their mutilation.

12. On the Day of Judgement these souls, like all the others, will assemble in the valley of Jehoshaphat
with their bodies (see X: 10–12). They alone, however, will not be allowed to put their bodies
on once more, since they chose to separate their souls from their bodies.

Noi eravamo ancora al tronco attesi,
    credendo ch'altro ne volesse dire,   110
    quando noi fummo d'un rumor sorpresi,
similemente a colui che venire
    sente il porco e la caccia alla sua posta,
    ch'ode le bestie, e le frasche stormire.
Ed ecco due dalla sinistra costa,
    nudi e graffiati, fuggendo sì forte,
    che della selva rompìeno ogni rosta.
Quel dinanzi: 'Or accorri, accorri, morte!'
    E l'altro, cui pareva tardar troppo,
    gridava: 'Lano, sì non furo accorte   120
le gambe tue alle giostre dal Toppo!'
    E poi che forse li fallìa la lena,
    di sé e d'un cespuglio fece un groppo.
Di retro a loro era la selva piena
    di nere cagne, bramose e correnti
    come veltri ch'uscisser di catena.
In quel che s'appiattò miser li denti,
    e quel dilaceraro a brano a brano,
    poi sen portar quelle membra dolenti.
Presemi allor la mia scorta per mano,   130
    e menommi al cespuglio che piangea,
    per le rotture sanguinenti, in vano.
'O Giacomo,' dicea, 'da Santo Andrea,
    che t'è giovato di me fare schermo?
    Che colpa ho io della tua vita rea?'
Quando 'l maestro fu sovr'esso fermo,
    disse: 'Chi fosti, che per tante punte
    soffi con sangue doloroso sermo?'
Ed elli a noi: 'O anime che giunte
    siete a veder lo strazio disonesto   140
    c'ha le mie fronde sì da me disgiunte,
raccoglietele al piè del tristo cesto.
    I' fui della città che nel Batista
    mutò 'l primo padrone – ond'e' per questo

We were all eyes and ears, waiting upon
    The trunk, believing he had more to say,   110
    When straight we were distracted by a din,[13]
Like somebody made all at once aware,
    From where he stands, of wild boar being hunted,
    Who hears the hounds, and hears the bushes stir.
And suddenly, upon our left, there went
    Two beings, scratched and naked, through the wood,
    So fast they broke through all entanglement.
The one in front cried out: 'O death, come quick!'
    The other one, who seemed to lag behind,
    Shouted out: 'Lano, you were not so slick   120
When jousting near the Toppo!'[14] and at that,
    Perhaps because his breath was coming short,
    Melted into a bush and made one knot.
Behind them, and throughout the wood, there rushed
    A horde of sable bitches, hungry, rapid,
    Like greyhounds that are suddenly unleashed.
They, where he crouched, got their teeth into him,
    And mangled all his body inch by inch,
    Then carried off each lacerated limb.
And now my guide has grasped my hand, and taken   130
    Me to the blackthorn bush that is lamenting
    Uselessly through the bleeding where it's broken.
'O Jacopo da Santo Andrea[15],' said
    The thornbush, 'Did I make a helpful shelter?
    Am I to blame because your life was bad?'
My master came, stood over it, and said:
    'Who were you once, who through so many wounds
    Breathe out such grievous language with your blood?'[16]
And he to us: 'O souls who've made your way
    To look upon this horrifying havoc,   140
    And see my leaves have all been torn away,
Gather them at the wretched bush's foot.
    I'm from the city which for John the Baptist
    Changed its first patron,[17] who, because of that,

13. We now see those who did violence to themselves, not by suicide, but by squandering their wealth. Dante also gives examples of conspicuous consumption and deliberate waste in XXIX: 121–32.
14. Lano was a Sienese spendthrift killed in battle near the River Toppo in 1288. The reference to the battle as 'jousting' is ironical. Lano is thought to have belonged to the 'brigata spendereccia' (brotherhood of big spenders) whose aim in life was to waste as much as possible.
15. Died 1239. Notorious for wasting his inheritance. For example, he is said to have sailed on the River Brenta, dropping coins into the water.
16. This soul says many things, but not his name. We are left to speculate why this should be so. Perhaps Dante includes him as a representative of all those suicides not famous enough to be remembered.
17. It is said that the first patron of Florence was Mars, who resented the change of patron. His 'skill' was of course in warfare, and the Florentines were notoriously quarrelsome.

sempre con l'arte sua la farà trista.
    E se non fosse che 'n sul passo d'Arno
    rimane ancor di lui alcuna vista,
que' cittadin che poi la rifondarno
    sovra 'l cener che d'Attila rimase,
    avrebber fatto lavorare indarno.   150
Io fei gibetto a me delle mie case.'

Now uses all his skill to make her mourn;
 And if, close by the bridge across the Arno,
 Some semblance of that god did not remain,[18]
Those citizens who laboured to refound
 The town on ash Attila left for them[19]
 Would certainly have laboured to no end.   150
I made myself a scaffold in my home.'

18. In Dante's time part of a statue of Mars still survived near the Ponte Vecchio.
19. Attila the Hun, according to legend, sacked Florence. See XII: 134.

CANTO XIV

Dante gathers up the leaves which have fallen from the bush which was his fellow-citizen, and places them at the foot of the bush. Then the two travellers move from the second ring of the seventh circle into the third ring.

This is a bare sandy plain onto which flakes of fire are falling continually. Some damned souls (those who have been violent against God) are lying there supine, some (the usurers, violent against art or industry) are crouching, and some (the sodomites, who have done violence to nature) are continually in motion.

The pilgrims see the shade of Capaneus, one of the seven kings against Thebes, who is still unrepentantly cursing God. Virgil explains to him, and to Dante, that his anger is its own punishment. (The god whom Capaneus blasphemes is, of course, Jove. It is characteristic of Dante's all-embracing vision that this does not stop him using Capaneus as a symbol of the person who sins by refusing to accept the nature of things.)

A red stream issues from the wood of the suicides and runs across the burning sand. This is Phlegethon, which the travellers have seen before. Virgil explains how all the rivers of the Inferno originate in a fissure in a giant statue of an old man in Crete, composed of various metals, except for one of his feet which is of baked clay. The interpretation of this image – even if we realise its biblical origin and know the interpretation offered there – is difficult. It may be contrasted with the boiling blood of Phlegethon whose interpretation is obvious.

The stream protects the air above and the margins alongside it from the rain of fire. Virgil now tells Dante to move away from the wood and onto the edge of the stream, where they may walk safely.

Poi che la carità del natio loco   1
   mi strinse, raunai le fronde sparte,
   e rende'le a colui ch'era già fioco.
Indi venimmo al fine ove si parte
   lo secondo giron dal terzo e dove
   si vede di giustizia orribil arte.
A ben manifestar le cose nove,
   dico che arrivammo ad una landa
   che dal suo letto ogni pianta rimove.
La dolorosa selva l'è ghirlanda   10
   intorno, come 'l fosso tristo ad essa:
   quivi fermammo i passi a randa a randa.
Lo spazzo era una rena arida e spessa,
   non d'altra foggia fatta che colei
   che fu da' piè di Caton già soppressa.
O vendetta di Dio, quanto tu dei
   esser temuta da ciascun che legge
   ciò che fu manifesto alli occhi miei!
D'anime nude vidi molte gregge
   che piangean tutte assai miseramente,   20
   e parea posta lor diversa legge.
Supin giacea in terra alcuna gente,
   alcuna si sedea tutta raccolta,
   e altra andava continuamente.
Quella che giva intorno era più molta,
   e quella men che giacea al tormento,
   ma più al duolo aveva la lingua sciolta.
Sovra tutto 'l sabbion, d'un cader lento,
   piovean di foco dilatate falde,
   come di neve in alpe sanza vento.   30
Quali Alessandro in quelle parti calde
   d'India vide sopra 'l suo stuolo
   fiamme cadere infino a terra salde –
per ch'ei provide a scalpitar lo suolo
   con le sue schiere, acciò che lo vapore
   mei si stingueva mentre ch'era solo –

Only affection for my native place   1
    Urged me to gather up the scattered leaves
    For him who had already lost his voice.
From there we came at last to the division
    Between the second and third rings, there where
    Justice is seen in fearful operation.
To bring to light a scene unseen as yet,
    I say that we had come upon a plain
    Which gives no green thing leave to grow on it.
The wood of sorrow[1] garlands it about,   10
    Like the grim stream[2] around the wood itself:
    We paused upon the very edge of it.
The ground was dry, compacted sand, like that
    Which on his journey through the Libyan desert
    Cato of Utica trod underfoot.[3]
Vengeance of God, how greatly you should be
    Dreaded by all who merely read about
    What was here made so manifest to me!
Here I saw many herds of naked souls,
    All weeping, and all weeping wretchedly,   20
    All subject, so it seemed, to different rules;
For some were lying supine on the ground,[4]
    Some sitting all bent up within themselves,[5]
    And some of them were moving round and round.[6]
Those who were moving were most numerous;
    Those least who took their torment lying down,
    And yet these were the ones whose tongues were loose.
Over that stretch of sand, a gentle fall
    Of fire in broadest flakes was drifting down,
    Like snow in mountains with no wind at all.   30
As Alexander[7] in hot India once
    Saw unextinguished flames of fire descending
    Onto the earth and his battalions,
And therefore told his men to trample on
    The ground, so that the flaming flakes of fire
    Would be extinguished swiftly one by one –

1. The wood of the suicides (XIII).
2. Phlegethon, the river of boiling water.
3. 95–46 BC A Roman renowned for his integrity, he appears later in the *Comedy* as the guardian
   of the entrance to Purgatory.
4. The violent against God, the blasphemers.
5. The usurers.
6. The sodomites.
7. Alexander the Great.

tale scendeva l'etternale ardore,
    onde la rena s'accendea, com'esca
    sotto focile, a doppiar lo dolore.
Sanza riposo mai era la tresca   40
    delle misere mani, or quindi or quinci
    escotendo da sé l'arsura fresca.
I' cominciai: 'Maestro, tu che vinci
    tutte le cose, fuor che' demon duri
    ch'all'entrar della porta incontra uscinci,
chi è quel grande che non par che curi
    lo 'ncendio e giace dispettoso e torto,
    sì che la pioggia non par che 'l maturi?'
E quel medesmo, che si fu accorto
    ch'io domandava il mio duca di lui,   50
    gridò: 'Qual io fui vivo, tal son morto.
Se Giove stanchi 'l suo fabbro da cui
    crucciato prese la folgore aguta
    onde l'ultimo dì percosso fui –
o s'elli stanchi li altri a muta a muta
    in Mongibello alla focina negra,
    chiamando "Buon Vulcano, aiuta, aiuta!"
sì com'el fece alla pugna di Flegra,
    e me saetti di tutta sua forza –
    non ne potrebbe aver vendetta allegra.'   60
Allora il duca mio parlò di forza
    tanto ch'i' non l'avea sì forte udito:
    'O Capaneo, in ciò che non s'ammorza
la tua superbia se' tu più punito:
    nullo martiro, fuor che la tua rabbia,
    sarebbe al tuo furor dolor compito.'
Poi si rivolse a me con miglior labbia
    dicendo: 'Quei fu l'un de' sette regi
    ch'assiser Tebe – ed ebbe e par ch'elli abbia
Dio in disdegno, e poco par che 'l pregi,   70
    ma, com'io dissi a lui, li suoi dispetti
    sono al suo petto assai debiti fregi.

Just so the everlasting heat came down;
    And so the sand was set on fire, like tinder
    Under the flint, to give them double pain.
No let-up in the twisting and the turning   40
    Of the poor hands, on this side and on that,
    Trying to beat away the freshest burning.
I said: 'O master, able to defeat
    All enemies except those stubborn devils
    Who came against us at the city gate,[8]
Who is that giant who seems not to care
    About the burning, but lies scornful, scowling,
    As though not tortured by the rain of fire?'
And he who lay there, knowing what I said
    Referred to him, forestalled my guide, and shouted: 50
    'What I was when alive, such am I dead!
Though Jove tire out that smith[9] from whom he took
    In his great rage the piercing flash of lightning
    Whence I, on my last day, was thunderstruck;
Or if he tire the others[10] taking turns
    In Mongibello[11] at the filthy forge,
    Crying out, "Help me, Vulcan, just this once!",
Just as he did upon the field of Phlegra[12],
    And hurled his bolts at me with all his strength –
    His vengeance would not give him any pleasure.'   60
And then my leader, with such vehemence
    As I had never heard before, spoke out:
    'You are, Capaneus, since your arrogance
Is unextinguished, punished all the more:
    No torment but this ranting and this raving
    Could be commensurate with your own ire.'
And then, turning to me, my master said,
    More gently now: 'This man was of the seven
    Besieging Thebes.[13] He held, and still holds, God
In high disdain, and not of much account;   70
    But, as I told him, such scorn only makes,
    For breasts like his, a fitting ornament.

8. The entrance to Dis (VIII: 82 ff.).
9. Vulcan, the blacksmith of the classical gods.
10. The cyclopes, who worked for Vulcan in his forge.
11. Beneath Mount Etna.
12. Where Jove fought with the Titans who were trying to scale Mount Olympus.
13. This siege is the subject of a tragedy by Aeschylus. According to the myth, Capaneus was struck
    dead by a thunderbolt when he was in the act of scaling the city walls.

Or mi vien dietro, e guarda che non metti,
    ancor, li piedi nella rena arsiccia,
    ma sempre al bosco tien li piedi stretti.'
Tacendo divenimmo là 've spiccia
    fuor della selva un picciol fiumicello,
    lo cui rossore ancor mi raccapriccia.
Quale del Bulicame esce ruscello
    che parton poi tra lor le pettatrici[a],   80
    tal per la rena giù sen giva quello.
Lo fondo suo ed ambo le pendici
    fatt'era 'n pietra, e' margini da lato,
    per ch'io m'accorsi che 'l passo era lici.
'Tra tutto l'altro ch'i' t'ho dimostrato,
    poscia che noi entrammo per la porta
    lo cui sogliare a nessuno è negato,
cosa non fu dalli tuoi occhi scorta
    notabile com'è 'l presente rio,
    che sovra sé tutte fiammelle ammorta.'   90
Queste parole fuor del duca mio,
    per ch'io 'l pregai che mi largisse il pasto
    di cui largito m'avea il disio.
'In mezzo mar siede un paese guasto,'
    diss'elli allora, 'che s'appella Creta,
    sotto 'l cui rege fu già il mondo casto.
Una montagna v'è che già fu lieta
    d'acqua e di fronde, che si chiamò Ida:
    or è diserta come cosa vieta.
Rea la scelse già per cuna fida   100
    del suo figliuolo, e per celarlo meglio,
    quando piangea, vi facea far le grida.
Dentro dal monte sta dritto un gran veglio,
    che tien volte le spalle inver Damiata
    e Roma guarda come suo speglio.
La sua testa è di fino oro formata,
    e puro argento son le braccia e il petto,
    poi è di rame infino alla forcata;

---

a. 'pettatrici' were, presumably, workers hackling flax or hemp (Dante in *Eclogues*, I: 42 uses 'pexare capillos', i.e. 'to comb hair'). An alternative reading, 'peccatrici', suggests that some waters flowing from Bulicame were reserved for prostitutes to wash themselves and their clothing.

Now come behind me. Take care not to tread,
    At this stage even, on the burning sand;
    But always keep your feet close to the wood.'
We came in silence where there gushes out
    A very tiny streamlet from the wood,
    A stream whose redness makes me shudder yet.
As from the spring of Bulicame runs
    A watercourse carders have to themselves,[14]   80
    So did this stream run down across the sands.
The stream's bed and its sloping banks were made
    Of stone, as were the margins running by them;
    And so I saw that as the place to tread.
'Of all the other things that I have shown
    Since first we came together through that gate
    Whose threshold's crossing is denied to none,[15]
Nothing has ever been exhibited
    To you as striking as this present river
    Quenching the conflagration overhead.'   90
These words were spoken by my guide. At that
    I begged him to be generous with the feast[16]
    For which he had aroused my appetite.
'Mid-sea there lies an island, now a waste,'
    He answered me, 'an island known as Crete,
    Under whose King the world was onetime chaste.[17]
There is a mountain there that was well covered
    With leaves and running water, known as Ida,
    Abandoned now, like something old and withered.
Rhea once chose this place, as a safe cot   100
    For her young son and, to disguise his presence
    When he was crying, used to raise a shout.[18]
A huge old man stands in the mountain's mass,
    Holding his shoulders turned towards Damietta,[19]
    Gazing at Rome as on his looking glass.
The finest gold has gone to form his head;
    His arms and breast are fashioned from pure silver;
    Then all is brass to where his legs divide;

14. Bulicame is a hot sulphurous spring near Viterbo, about 80 km north of Rome, whose waters were used by carders of flax and hemp.
15. The entrance to the Inferno. See the beginning of III.
16. A 'feast' of explanation.
17. This refers to the fabled Golden Age, during the reign of Saturn.
18. Rhea, to save her son Jove from Saturn (who was accustomed to eat his children), hid him on Mount Ida and ordered her priests to make a noise to drown the infant's cries.
19. In Egypt. The statue is therefore looking east.

da indi in giuso è tutto ferro eletto,
    salvo che 'l destro piede è terracotta –   110
    e sta 'n su quel più che 'n su l'altro eretto.
Ciascuna parte, fuor che l'oro, è rotta
    d'una fessura che lagrime goccia,
    le quali, accolte, foran quella grotta.
Lor corso in questa valle si diroccia:
    fanno Acheronte, Stige e Flegetonta;
    poi sen van giù per questa stretta doccia
infin là ove più non si dismonta:
    fanno Cocito – e qual sia quello stagno,
    tu lo vedrai, però qui non si conta.'   120
E io a lui: 'Se 'l presente rigagno
    si diriva così dal nostro mondo,
    perché ci appar pur a questo vivagno?'
Ed elli a me: 'Tu sai 'l luogo è tondo,
    e tutto che tu sie venuto molto
    pur a sinistra, giù calando al fondo,
non se' ancor per tutto il cerchio vòlto:
    per che, se cosa n'apparisce nova,
    non de' addur maraviglia al tuo volto.'
E io ancor: 'Maestro, ove si trova   130
    Flegetonta e Letè? ché dell'un taci,
    e l'altro di' che si fa d'esta piova.'
'In tutte tue question certo mi piaci,'
    rispuose; 'ma 'l bollor dell'acqua rossa
    dovea ben solver l'una che tu faci.
Letè vedrai, ma fuor di questa fossa,
    là dove vanno l'anime a lavarsi
    quando la colpa pentuta è rimossa.'
Poi disse: 'Ormai è tempo da scostarsi
    dal bosco – fa' che di retro a me vegne: 140
    li margini fan via, che non son arsi,
e sopra loro ogni vapor si spegne.'

All's iron unalloyed from that point down,
    Except his right foot, made of terracotta,   110
    On which he rests more than the other one.[20]
Through all, except the gold, there runs a crack,
    And tears are always dripping down that fissure
    To gather at his feet and pierce the rock,
Dropping down crags till they turn out to be
    The Acheron, the Styx, the Phlegethon;
    Then, through this narrow gap, till finally
They come to where there is no going down.[21]
    That is Cocytus – what that pool is like
    You'll shortly see, and so I'll not explain.'   120
And I to him: 'Why, if the course is such
    That this stream follows, coming from our world,
    Is it not seen until this utmost verge?'
He said: 'You know this place is circular;
    And, even though you've come in a great arc
    Towards the left, descending more and more,
You have not yet completed the whole round.
    So, if we come on something that is new,
    That surely is not something to astound.'
I questioned him again: 'Master, where is   130
    Lethe? Where Phlegethon? You ignore the first,
    And say that Phlegethon's a rain of tears.'
'I'm pleased you ask these questions, certainly,'
    He answered; 'but the stream of boiling blood
    Should have solved one that you've just put to me.
You will see Lethe, not in this abyss,
    But where souls go to purify themselves
    When all their guilt's repented and dismissed.'[22]
Then he went on: 'It's time that we were turning
    Out of the wood – now follow where I lead: 140
    The margins make a road, for they're not burning:
The flames are all extinguished overhead.'

20. The image of the old man of Crete – open to apparently endless allegorical interpretation, particularly in its details – is primarily an image of the progressive deterioration of mankind. Its source is biblical – Nebuchadnezzar's dream in the second chapter of the Book of Daniel. In that chapter Daniel interprets the King's dream; but his interpretation is not necessarily to be taken to coincide with Dante's intention.
21. The lowest part of the Inferno, at the centre of the world.
22. The River Lethe is in the Earthly Paradise (*Purgatory* XXVIII: 25–33).

CANTO XV

As Dante and Virgil move along the river's margin, they encounter a group of shades running towards them on the burning sand, one of whom plucks at the hem of Dante's robe.

This is Brunetto Latini, once Dante's mentor and friend, but now damned for the sin of sodomy. The meeting is joyful, but distressing also in that their situations are now so different. It is forbidden for these shades to pause, but Brunetto walks along with Dante for a while.

Brunetto regrets that he cannot now help Dante in his work. Like Farinata in the circle of the heretics, Brunetto prophesies, in a rather vague way, future trouble for Dante. Dante says that he hopes for some explication of these prophecies when he meets Beatrice. Brunetto says his group is made up entirely of clerics, all famous men of letters, and all guilty of the one sin. (Very many, perhaps most, educated men in Dante's day were in minor orders at least, and not all of these 'clerics' performed religious duties. So far as is known, Brunetto himself did not.)

As they see another group of sinners approaching, Brunetto, fearful of the punishment he will incur if he does not rejoin his group, races away.

This canto, a striking rebuttal of any notion that Dante merely 'put his enemies in hell', arouses many, apparently contradictory, reactions. The love and respect on both sides is clear, but so is the gulf between the old friends; worldly fame is valued, but it is seen to be nothing compared to one's eternal fate; Brunetto's intellectual and artistic qualities are stressed, but so is the foulness of his sin. The final image of Brunetto racing away 'like the winning, not the losing, runner', with the sad undertone of the literal reason for his speed – one of the most famous images in the *Comedy* – summarises implicitly much that has gone before.

Ora cen porta l'un de' duri margini;   1
    e 'l fummo del ruscel di sopra aduggia,
    sì che dal foco salva l'acqua e li argini[a].
Quale i Fiamminghi tra Guizzante e Bruggia,
    temendo il fiotto che 'nver lor s'avventa,
    fanno lo schermo perché 'l mar si fuggia,
e quale i Padoan lungo la Brenta,
    per difender lor ville e lor castelli,
    anzi che Chiarentana il caldo senta,
a tale imagine eran fatti quelli,   10
    tutto che né sì alti né sì grossi,
    qual che si fosse, lo maestro felli.
Già eravam dalla selva rimossi
    tanto, ch'i' non avrei visto dov'era,
    perch'io in dietro rivolto mi fossi,
quando incontrammo d'anime una schiera
    che venìan lungo l'argine, e ciascuna
    ci riguardava come suol da sera
guardare uno altro sotto nuova luna –
    e sì ver noi aguzzavan le ciglia   20
    come 'l vecchio sartor fa nella cruna.
Così adocchiato da cotal famiglia,
    fui conosciuto da un che mi prese
    per lo lembo e gridò: 'Qual maraviglia!'
E io, quando 'l suo braccio a me distese,
    ficca' li occhi per[b] lo cotto aspetto,
    sì che 'l viso abbruciato non difese
la conoscenza sua al mio intelletto,
    e chinando la mia alla sua faccia,
    rispuosi: 'Siete voi qui, ser Brunetto?'   30
E quelli: 'O figliuol mio, non ti dispiaccia
    se Brunetto Latino un poco teco
    ritorna in dietro e lascia andar la traccia.'
I' dissi lui: 'Quanto posso, ven preco –
    e se volete che con voi m'asseggia,
    faròl, se piace a costui che vo seco.'

a. The precious rhymes in '-argini' and '-uggia' stress the strangeness of the situation.
b. 'Through', suggesting the difficulty Dante had in recognising him.

Now the hard margin takes us on from there: 1
    Steam from the river darkens overhead,
    Shielding the shores and water from the fire.
As the Flemings, from Wissant up to Bruges,
    Fearing the ocean rushing in on them,
    Have built a dyke along the water's edge;
And like the Paduans where the Brenta flows,
    In order to defend their towns and castles,
    Before warm weather melts Carinthia's snows,
In the same fashion were these margins made –   10
    Whoever was the builder who designed them –
    Except not raised so high and not so broad.[1]
We had already left the wood behind
    So far that I could not have any longer
    Seen where it was, if I had turned around;
We met up with a company of shades
    Coming along the riverside,[2] who all
    Stared hard at us as, when the daylight fades,
Men stare if there is no moon in the sky;
    They knit their brows and squinnied up at us   20
    Like an old tailor at a needle's eye.
Then, as the group of shades stared up like this,
    One recognised me, and caught hold of me
    By my gown's hem and cried: 'What a surprise!'
And I, as he was stretching out his hand
    Towards me, fixed my eyes on his baked features,
    Till the scorched face could not prevent my mind
Recalling him, and all became quite clear;
    And, as I bent my face towards his face,
    I said: 'O Ser Brunetto, are you here?'[3]   30
And he replied: 'Don't be displeased, my son,
    If Brunetto Latini for a while
    Turns back to you, and lets the rest pass on.'
I said: 'With all my heart, I beg of you!
    And should you wish that I should pause, I will,
    If he with whom I've come allows me to.'

1. We gather during the course of this canto that the margins are about the height of a man.
2. These shades are moving in the opposite direction to Dante and Virgil.
3. As the title 'Ser' suggests, Brunetto Latini (c.1210–94) was a notary. He was a Florentine Guelph who, as he was returning from an embassy to Castile, learnt of the defeat of his party at Montaperti (1260) and their expulsion from Florence. He remained in France until after the Battle of Benevento (1265), when he returned to Florence and resumed his important part in public affairs. His most famous literary works were *Li Livres dou Tresor* ('The Treasury', an encyclopedia written in French), and *Il Tesoretto* ('The Little Treasury', an unfinished narrative poem written in Italian). He was almost certainly not an offical teacher of Dante, but rather a well-loved mentor; he was, of course, much older than Dante.

'O figliuol,' disse, 'qual di questa greggia
   s'arresta punto, giace poi cent'anni
   sanz'arrostarsi quando 'l foco il feggia.
Però va' oltre: i' ti verrò a' panni,   40
   e poi rigiugnerò la mia masnada,
   che va piangendo i suoi etterni danni.'
I' non osava scender della strada
   per andar par di lui; ma 'l capo chino
   tenea com'uom che reverente vada.
El cominciò: 'Qual fortuna o destino
   anzi l'ultimo dì qua giù ti mena?
   e chi è questi che mostra 'l cammino?'
'Là su di sopra, in la vita serena,'
   rispuos'io lui, 'mi smarri' in una valle,   50
   avanti che l'età mia fosse piena.
Pur ier mattina le volsi le spalle:
   questi m'apparve, tornand'io in quella,
   e reducemi a ca per questo calle.'
Ed elli a me: 'Se tu segui tua stella,
   non puoi fallire a glorioso porto,
   se ben m'accorsi nella vita bella;
e s'io non fossi sì per tempo morto,
   veggendo il cielo a te così benigno,
   dato t'avrei all'opera conforto.   60
Ma quello ingrato popolo maligno
   che discese di Fiesole ab antico,
   e tiene ancor del monte e del macigno,
ti si farà, per tuo ben far, nemico:
   ed è ragion, ché tra li lazzi sorbi
   si disconvien fruttare al dolce fico.
Vecchia fama nel mondo li chiama orbi –
   gent'è avara, invidiosa e superba:
   dai lor costumi fa' che tu ti forbi.
La tua fortuna tanto onor ti serba,   70
   che l'una parte e l'altra avranno fame
   di te – ma lungi fia dal becco l'erba.

'O son,' he said, 'whoever of this flock
    Pauses at all, must lie one hundred years
    Without defence as flakes of fire attack.
Therefore walk on; I'll keep close by your gown   40
    Down here; and then I must rejoin my troop
    Who go on mourning their eternal pain.'
I did not dare descend from off my road
    To where he walked; and yet, like somebody
    Who's full of reverence, I bowed my head.
Then he began: 'What chance or destiny
    Brings you down here before your final hour?
    And who is this who's showing you the way?'
'There, up above, in the world of living men,'
    I said, 'I strayed off in a gloomy valley,   50
    Before the midpoint of my life had come.
At dawn but yesterday I turned my back
    Upon it – then returned – this man appeared
    To put me once again on the right track.'
And he replied: 'If you follow your star,
    You cannot fail to reach a glorious haven,
    If my opinion while I lived was fair.
Had it not happened that I died too soon,
    Seeing that heaven was benign towards you,
    I would have helped in all that you took on.   60
But those ungrateful and malicious folk –
    Descending in the past from Fiesole,
    Still with some trace of mountain and of rock –
Will be, for your good works, your enemy:
    And with good reason: among bitter rowans
    Sweet fig trees were not meant to fructify.[4]
They are of old reputed to be blind –
    And they are greedy, envious, and presumptuous.
    Avoid the faults to which they are inclined!
Such honour is reserved for you by fate,   70
    That both sides[5] will be eager to devour you;
    But grass will be kept distant from the goat.[6]

---

4. According to old tradition the Romans conquered Fiesole and founded Florence on the plain below it, and the new city was inhabited first by a few Roman settlers and by refugees from Fiesole who brought their uncivilised ways with them. The vices of the Florentines, so often mentioned by Dante, are attributed by Brunetto to their Fiesolan ancestry.

5. Guelphs and Ghibellines.

6. This sounds like a proverb. Dante, a Guelph, incurred the enmity not only of the Ghibellines but of other Guelphs.

Faccian le bestie fiesolane strame
    di lor medesme, e non tocchin la pianta –
    s'alcuna surge ancora in lor letame –
in cui riviva la sementa santa
    di que' Roman che vi rimaser quando
    fu fatto il nido di malizia tanta.'
'Se fosse tutto pieno il mio dimando,'
    rispuosi lui, 'voi non sareste ancora   80
    dell'umana natura posto in bando,
ché 'n la mente m'è fitta, e or m'accora,
    la cara e buona imagine paterna
    di voi, quando nel mondo ad ora ad ora
m'insegnavate come l'uom s'etterna:
    e quant'io l'abbia in grado, mentr'io vivo
    convien che nella mia lingua si scerna.
Ciò che narrate di mio corso scrivo,
    e serbolo a chiosar con altro testo
    a donna che saprà, s'a lei arrivo.   90
Tanto vogl'io che vi sia manifesto,
    pur che mia coscienza non mi garra,
    che alla Fortuna, come vuol, son presto.
Non è nuova alli orecchi miei tal arra:
    però giri Fortuna la sua rota
    come le piace, e 'l villan la sua marra.'
Lo mio maestro allora in su la gota
    destra si volse in dietro, e riguardommi;
    poi disse: 'Bene ascolta chi la nota.'
Né per tanto di men parlando vommi   100
    con ser Brunetto, e dimando chi sono
    li suoi compagni più noti e più sommi.
Ed elli a me: 'Saper d'alcuno è bono,
    delli altri fia laudabile tacerci,
    ché 'l tempo saria corto a tanto sòno.
Insomma sappi che tutti fur cherci
    e litterati grandi e di gran fama,
    d'un peccato medesmo al mondo lerci.

Let beasts of Fiesole forage among
    Themselves, and leave untouched the family tree –
    If any still arises from their dung –
In which there lives once more the sacred seed
    Of those first Romans who remained there when
    It turned into a nest of such bad blood.'
'If all my prayers were answered utterly,'
    I said in my reply, 'you would not yet   80
    Have been excluded from humanity;
For still I have in mind, to my great pain,
    The dear, the kindly, the paternal image
    Of you who, in the world, time and again
Taught me how man becomes eternal:[7] while
    There's breath in me, my gratitude for that
    Is something that my language must reveal.
What you say of my future I shall store
    Beside another text,[8] to be expounded
    By one[9] who will know how, if I reach her.   90
This much I'd have you understand quite clearly –
    Provided that my conscience does not chide –
    Whatever Fortune brings me, I am ready.
Such prophecies to me are nothing new:
    And so I say, let Fortune turn her wheel
    As she thinks best, the peasant wield his hoe.'[10]
My master turned his head towards the right
    At this, and then right round to look at me,
    And said: 'He listens well who takes good note.'
Nevertheless I wished to talk some more   100
    With Ser Brunetto; so I asked about
    Those in his flock most famed and with most power.
And he replied: 'It's well to know of some;
    As for the others, we had best be silent:
    There is not time enough to talk of them.
In short, know they were clerics, one and all,
    Great men of letters, and men of renown,
    Whom in the world above one sin[11] made foul.

---

7. Lives on after death because of his renown. Dante was not indifferent to worldly fame, and Brunetto is still very anxious for it even in the Inferno (see ll. 119–20 below).

8. Farinata's prophecy in X: 79–81.

9. Beatrice.

10. Fortune's wheel is a traditional image of the uncertainty of worldly affairs; the peasant wielding his hoe has the ring of a proverb; together they suggest that nothing will affect Dante's state of mind.

11. The 'one sin' is sodomy. This seems clear from what Virgil has said at XI: 49–51. However, there is no other known independent evidence that Brunetto was guilty of this sin, and Dante strangely does not name it in this present canto. Other suggestions have therefore been made, but unpersuasively.

Priscian sen va con quella turba grama,
 e Francesco d'Accorso – anche vedervi,   110
 s'avessi avuto di tal tigna brama,
colui potéi che dal servo de' servi
 fu trasmutato d'Arno in Bacchiglione,
 dove lasciò li mal protesi nervi.
Di più direi, ma 'l venire e 'l sermone
 più lungo esser non può, però ch'i' veggio
 là surger novo fummo del sabbione.
Gente vien con la quale esser non deggio:
 sieti raccomandato il mio *Tesoro*,
 nel qual io vivo ancora, e più non cheggio.'   120
Poi si rivolse, e parve di coloro
 che corrono a Verona il drappo verde
 per la campagna – e parve di costoro
quelli che vince, non colui che perde.

You see there Priscian[12] running with that grim
    Crowd, and Francesco d'Accorso[13]; and also,   110
    If you had any wish to see such scum,
The bishop whom God's servant[14] ordered on,
    Who left the Arno for the Bacchiglione,
    Where he gave up that body strained by sin.[15]
I would say more – but not another word
    Am I allowed, another inch: I see
    A fresh cloud[16] rising from the sand of dread.
People are here with whom I must not be.
    I recommend to you my *Treasury*[17],
    In which I'm still alive: that's all I'll say.'   120
Then he turned round, and looked like one of those
    Who race, to win the green cloth at Verona,
    Across the fields; and looked, among all these,
Most like the winning, not the losing, runner.[18]

12. Probably the famous Latin grammarian (fl. *c*.500).
13. Francesco d'Accorso (1225–93) was a celebrated lawyer from Bologna; he lectured for some time at Oxford.
14. The Pope. The description *servus servorum Dei* (servant of the servants of God) is still used.
15. Andrea de' Mozzi, Bishop of Florence on the River Arno, was moved to Vicenza, on the River Bacchiglione, on account of his scandalous way of life. He died in 1296.
16. This probably refers to the cloud of sand raised by the shades running towards them.
17. See note 3 to line 30 above. The book mentioned here is probably Brunetto's large encyclopedia rather than his short narrative poem.
18. In this race the winner received a piece of green cloth, and the last runner a booby prize which exposed him to derision. The episode finishes on an apparently triumphant note: we may momentarily forget why he is racing back.

Dante hears falling water in the distance. Then three figures detach themselves from one of the bands of sinners: they have gathered from Dante's clothes that he is a Florentine, and they ask him to stop and talk.

Virgil warns Dante to show respect to these shades; but as they approach they form themselves into a ridiculous circle, and wheel round while still keeping their faces towards Dante. One of them, Jacopo Rusticucci, introduces the other two and then himself: they are all to be respected for the good qualities they showed in their lives. Only the thought of being tormented like them prevents Dante from rushing down to embrace the three, so great is his love and respect.

Jacopo Rusticucci is anxious for news of Florence, since a fellow-citizen, a new arrival in their circle of the Inferno, has come with disturbing reports. Dante replies by saying that newcomers into Florence and a sudden access of profits have brought about the city's moral decadence. Rusticucci asks Dante to keep the memory of him and his companions alive, if he should ever return to Florence. Then the shades rush away to rejoin their band of sinners.

The sound of falling water is now deafeningly near. Dante is wearing a cord around his waist, and he obeys Virgil's command by undoing it and handing it over. Virgil throws it down into the gulf beneath them, and they wait to see what will happen.

Dante explains to the reader that what is about to appear would tax anyone's credulity. A shape comes up from the depths of the Inferno, an eerie sight; but we have to wait until the next canto for a description.

Brunetto Latini in the previous canto was a representative of the clerisy, and now in this canto we see lay Florentines, like him justly famed and like him damned. In both cantos we see that there is a higher judgement than man's, but also that man's judgement is not to be despised.

Già era in loco onde s'udìa 'l rimbombo   1
    dell'acqua che cadea nell'altro giro,
    simile a quel che l'arnie fanno rombo,
quando tre ombre insieme si partiro,
    correndo, d'una torma che passava
    sotto la pioggia dell'aspro martiro.
Venìan ver noi, e ciascuna gridava:
    'Sostati tu ch'all'abito ne sembri
    esser alcun di nostra terra prava.'
Ahimè, che piaghe vidi ne' lor membri   10
    ricenti e vecchie, dalle fiamme incese!
    Ancor men duol pur ch'i' me ne rimembri.
Alle lor grida il mio dottor s'attese,
    volse 'l viso ver me e: 'Or aspetta,'
    disse, 'a costor si vuole esser cortese.
E se non fosse il foco che saetta
    la natura del loco, i' dicerei
    che meglio stesse a te che a lor la fretta.'
Ricominciar, come noi restammo, ei
    l'antico verso e, quando a noi fuor giunti,   20
    fenno una rota di sé tutti e trei:
qual sogliono i campion far nudi e unti,
    avvisando lor presa e lor vantaggio,
    prima che sien tra lor battuti e punti.
Così rotando, ciascuno il visaggio
    drizzava a me, sì che 'n contrario il collo
    faceva ai piè continuo viaggio.
E 'Se miseria d'esto loco sollo
    rende in dispetto noi e nostri prieghi,'
    cominciò l'uno, 'e 'l tinto aspetto e brollo,   30
la fama nostra il tuo animo pieghi
    a dirne chi tu se', che i vivi piedi
    così sicuro per lo 'nferno freghi.
Questi, l'orme di cui pestar mi vedi,
    tutto che nudo e dipelato vada,
    fu di grado maggior che tu non credi:

I was in earshot of re-echoing waves   1
    Cascading to the circle lying under,[1]
    Like the faint thunder of unnumbered hives,
When suddenly we saw three shades, that came
    Towards us, running from a crowd that passed
    Beneath the bitter torment of hot rain.
They raced to us, and shouted out as one:
    'Stop, you who by your clothing seem to be
    Someone who comes from our degenerate town[2]!'
What gaping wounds their bodies showed, alas,   10
    Old, or just opened by the excessive heat!
    It grieves me, merely to remember this.
My teacher listened carefully to their cries;
    Then turned to face me, and he said: 'Now wait.
    One must show courtesy to such as these.
Were it not for this fire that shoots down, through
    The nature of the place, I'd think it fitter
    For you to run to them than they to you.'
As soon as we stood still, their usual noises[3]
• Began again; when they arrived, the three   20
    Made up a wheel, a sort of ring o' roses.
As champions who are oiled and naked do,
    Looking for where to grasp and take advantage,
    Before it comes to kick, and punch, and blow,
So these wheeled round; and each one always bent
    His face towards me, and he turned his neck
    Contrariwise to how his footsteps went.
And 'If our plight upon this shifting sand
    Makes us and what we ask provoke disdain,'
    One said, 'and these our faces skinned and browned,   30
Then may our fame on earth incline you yet
    To tell us who you are, who go so safely
    Through the Inferno, and on living feet.
He, in whose footsteps now you see me walk,
    Although his skin is peeled and he goes naked,
    Was greater in degree than you'd have thought:

1. The eighth circle of the Inferno.
2. Florence.
3. Weeping and lamentation.

nepote fu della buona Gualdrada;
    Guido Guerra ebbe nome, ed in sua vita
    fece con senno assai e con la spada.
L'altro, ch'appresso me la rena trita,   40
    è Tegghiaio Aldobrandi, la cui voce
    nel mondo su dovrìa esser gradita[a].
E io, che posto son con loro in croce,
    Iacopo Rusticucci fui – e certo
    la fiera moglie più ch'altro mi nòce.'
S'i' fossi stato dal foco coperto,
    gittato mi sarei tra lor di sotto,
    e credo che 'l dottor l'avrìa sofferto;
ma perch'io mi sarei bruciato e cotto,
    vinse paura la mia buona voglia   50
    che di loro abbracciar mi facea ghiotto.
Poi cominciai: 'Non dispetto, ma doglia
    la vostra condizion dentro mi fisse,
    tanta che tardi tutta si dispoglia,
tosto che questo mio segnor mi disse
    parole per le quali i' mi pensai
    che qual voi siete, tal gente venisse.
Di vostra terra sono, e sempre mai
    l'ovra di voi e li onorati nomi
    con affezion ritrassi e ascoltai.   60
Lascio lo fele, e vo per dolci pomi,
    promessi a me per lo verace duca –
    ma infino al centro pria convien ch'i' tomi.'
'Se lungamente l'anima conduca
    le membra tue,' rispuose quelli ancora,
    'e se la fama tua dopo te luca,
cortesia e valor di' se dimora
    nella nostra città sì come sòle,
    o se del tutto se n'è gita fora,
ché Guiglielmo Borsiere, il qual si dole   70
    con noi per poco e va là coi compagni,
    assai ne cruccia con le sue parole.'

---

a. 'Welcomed' and 'listened to with more care'. If 'voce' in the previous line is taken to mean 'fame', then the meaning is that his fame should still be current.

He was a grandson of the good Gualdrada[4];
    His name was Guido Guerra[5]; all his life
    He was, with sword and thought, a worthy leader.
The other one who's with me, pounding sand,   40
    Is Tegghiaio Aldobrandi[6], whose opinion
    Ought to have been more often kept in mind.[7]
And I, who with them hang upon a cross,
    Was Jacopo Rusticucci; it was my
    Shrewish wife who brought me down to this.'
Now, were it not for fire and flames, I would
    Have thrown myself down there to be among them,
    Which I believe my guide might have allowed;
But, since that would have been to bake and burn,
    Sheer terror overcame my fine intention   50
    Of running to embrace them there and then.
'No, not disdain, but simple grief to see
    The state you're in,' I said, 'entered my heart –
    Grief that will take some time to fade away –
The instant that the words of my lord here
    Gave me good reason to believe that people
    Of such renown as yours were coming near.
Your fellow-citizen, I've never failed
    To dwell with great affection on your honoured
    Names and great deeds as I have heard them told.   60
I leave the bitter for the sweetest taste,[8]
    Just as my truthful guide has promised me;
    But I must drop down to the centre[9] first.'
'Now may your soul direct your body on
    For many years,' he spoke to me once more,
    'And may your fame shine out when you are gone!
Tell us if courtesy and valour still
    Live in our city as they used to do,
    Or if they've gone outside the city wall:
Guglielmo Borsiere[10] only recently   70
    Has felt our pains,[11] and goes there in our band,
    Disturbing us with what he has to say.'

4. Known for her domestic virtues.
5. c.1220–72. A leader of the Florentine Guelphs, he fought at Montaperti (1260), was exiled after that battle, fought at Benevento (1265), and returned to Florence.
6. A Florentine Guelph, who died before 1266. Dante has already inquired about him, and the present speaker (Jacopo Rusticucci) at V: 79–84.
7. He advised the Florentines against fighting at Montaperti, where they were defeated.
8. Dante is going to leave sin behind in the Inferno, and travel to Paradise.
9. The centre of the earth (pictured by Dante as a globe), and the uttermost depth of the Inferno.
10. Another Florentine with a good reputation.
11. He has died recently. He must therefore have died before the date (the spring of 1300) which Dante assigns to his journey.

'La gente nova e e' subiti guadagni
    orgoglio e dismisura han generata,
    Fiorenza, in te, sì che tu già ten piagni.'
Così gridai con la faccia levata,
    e i tre, che ciò inteser per risposta,
    guardar l'un l'altro com'al ver si guata.
'Se l'altre volte sì poco ti costa,'
    rispuoser tutti, 'il satisfare altrui,   80
    felice te se sì parli a tua posta!
Però, se campi d'esti luoghi bui
    e torni a riveder le belle stelle,
    quando ti gioverà dicere "I' fui",
fa' che di noi alla gente favelle.'
    Indi rupper la rota, ed a fuggirsi
    ali sembiar le gambe loro snelle.
Un amen non saria potuto dirsi
    tosto così com'e' furo spariti,
    per che al maestro parve di partirsi.   90
Io lo seguiva, e poco eravam iti,
    che 'l suon dell'acqua n'era sì vicino
    che per parlar saremmo a pena uditi.
Come quel fiume c'ha proprio cammino
    prima da Monte Veso inver levante,
    dalla sinistra costa d'Apennino,
che si chiama Acquaqueta suso, avante
    che si divalli giù nel basso letto,
    e a Forlì di quel nome è vacante,
rimbomba là sovra San Benedetto   100
    dell'Alpe per cadere ad una scesa
    ove dovria per mille esser recetto;
così, giù d'una ripa discoscesa,
    trovammo risonar quell'acqua tinta,
    sì che 'n poc'ora avria l'orecchia offesa.
Io avea una corda intorno cinta,
    e con essa pensai alcuna volta
    prender la lonza alla pelle dipinta.

'Newcomers and quick profits generate
    Such arrogance and such excess, O Florence,
    That you already have to weep for it.'
So I cried out, with my face elevated;[12]
    At this reply, they stared at one another,
    As men do when they hear the truth being stated.
'If you can offer such a free and full
    Answer on all occasions,' they replied,   80
    'Then happy you who speak out as you will!
And so, if you can but escape from here,
    And go from this dark land to see the stars,
    When you can say with pleasure, "I was there",
Please speak of us, that our renown may last.'
    They broke the wheel up then, and as they fled,
    Those legs of theirs seemed wings, they moved so fast.
No one could possibly have said 'Amen'
    In less time than they took to disappear:
    My master thought it time that we went on.   90
I follow him; and we have not gone far
    Before the sound of water[13] comes so close
    That any conversation's hard to hear.
Like that first river[14] which flows on its own[15]
    Down the left side of the high Appennines
    From Monte Viso to the east (and known
Up above as the Acquacheta first,
    Before it drops into its lower bed,
    Where at Forlí that former name is lost),
Making thunderous echoes near to San   100
    Benedetto in Alpe, where with one
    Fall, not a thousand, it goes hurtling down –
So from a rocky precipice we found
    That blackened water falling and resounding:
    We would have been, if we had stayed there, stunned.
Around my waist I had a knotted cord,
    With which onetime it had been my intention
    To catch the leopard with the speckled hide.[16]

12. To emphasise the importance of the generalised statement he is making. When speaking to shades
   in this circle Dante normally looks *down*, since they are below him.
13. The waterfall mentioned as at some distance from them at the beginning of this canto.
14. The Montone.
15. That is, it flows into the sea without joining another river.
16. The cord presumably represents some means Dante had used to combat the sins of incontinence
   (see I); but its allegorical significance here is uncertain.

Poscia che l'ebbi tutta da me sciolta,
    sì come 'l duca m'avea comandato,   110
    porsila a lui aggroppata e ravvolta.
Ond'ei si volse inver lo destro lato,
    e alquanto di lunge dalla sponda
    la gittò giuso in quell'alto burrato.
'Ei pur convien che novità risponda,'
    dicea fra me medesmo, 'al novo cenno
    che 'l maestro con l'occhio sì seconda.'
Ahi quanto cauti li uomini esser dienno
    presso a color che non veggion pur l'ovra,
    ma per entro i pensier miran col senno!   120
El disse a me: 'Tosto verrà di sovra
    ciò ch'io attendo e che il tuo pensier sogna:
    tosto convien ch'al tuo viso si scovra.'
Sempre a quel ver c'ha faccia di menzogna
    de' l'uom chiuder le labbra fin ch'el pote,
    però che sanza colpa fa vergogna –
ma qui tacer nol posso: e per le note
    di questa comedìa, lettor, ti giuro –
    s'elle non sien di lunga grazia vote –
ch'i' vidi per quell'aere grosso e scuro   130
    venir notando una figura in suso,
    maravigliosa ad ogni cor sicuro,
sì come torna colui che va giuso
    talora a solver l'ancora ch'aggrappa
    o scoglio o altro che nel mare è chiuso,
che 'n su si stende, e da piè si rattrappa.

As soon as I had got the cord undone,
    Just as my leader had commanded me,   110
    I gave it to him, in a hank or skein.
At that he turned away to his right hand,
    And at a certain distance[17] from the brink
    He flung it, down into the vast profound.
'Something that's very strange must make reply,'
    I told myself, 'to this unwonted signal
    Which my master is following with his eye.'
How cautious we should be who chance to find
    Ourselves with others who don't stop at actions,
    But have the wit to see inside the mind![18]   120
'Something,' he said to me, 'will soon emerge;
    Something I'm waiting for and you but dream of:
    Something will come in sight out of this gorge.'
Faced with that truth which seems to be a lie,
    A man should keep his mouth shut, if he can,
    Or he'll be brought to shame quite guiltlessly;
But here I can't be silent. By the verse
    Of this my comedy[19], I, Reader, swear –
    May it find favour over many years! –
That through that murky atmosphere I saw   130
    A shape swim up towards us – and a shape
    To strike the most self-confident with awe!
It moved most like a mariner, when he –
    Being down to free an anchor that was caught
    Upon a rock or something in the sea –
Shoots to the surface and draws in his feet.

17. To avoid its catching on the edge of the chasm.
18. As we see from the next tercet, and have seen previously, Virgil is often able to read Dante's thoughts.
19. Dante uses the word 'comedy' to denote poetry written in a humble style in the vernacular, which ends
    happily.

CANTO XVII

What turns out to be a strange composite beast comes to rest on the edge of the pit, after flying up from the depths of the Inferno. It is described in ways that make clear its nature as the embodiment of fraud. Virgil goes to speak with it, and he arranges for it to carry Dante and himself down into the eighth circle.

Meanwhile Dante walks among the usurers who are crouching in this third ring of the seventh circle. Each of them has hanging from his neck a purse which bears his family's coat of arms, and they are, as one might expect with usurers, feasting their eyes on their purses. When they were alive, they were all of high social rank, but they were guilty of what Dante clearly regards as a particularly low sin. One of them, a Paduan, takes pleasure in mentioning that all but himself in that place are Florentines, and says a few more unpleasant words to Dante. Dante's disgust at these sinners is such that he does not deign to reply.

Dante returns to where Virgil is already on the back of the monster, whose name we discover is Geryon. On Virgil's advice Dante, who is terrified, mounts in front of Virgil, who is then able to defend him from Geryon's harmful tail.

Their flight down is described. Geryon, on Virgil's orders, circles as he descends, which makes the descent more gradual and somewhat easier for Dante. Dante is so frightened that he has difficulty at first in gathering what is happening. Gradually, however, he becomes aware of the fires and lamentation below them. Geryon lands at the foot of some jagged rock and, once his passengers have disembarked, flies away like an arrow from a bow.

'Ecco la fiera con la coda aguzza,   1
   che passa i monti, e rompe i muri e l'armi –
   ecco colei che tutto 'l mondo appuzza!'
Sì cominciò lo mio duca a parlarmi,
   e accennolle che venisse a proda
   vicino al fin de' passeggiati marmi.
E quella sozza imagine di froda
   sen venne, ed arrivò la testa e 'l busto,
   ma 'n su la riva non trasse la coda.
La faccia sua era faccia d'uom giusto,   10
   tanto benigna avea di fuor la pelle,
   e d'un serpente tutto l'altro fusto;
due branche avea pilose infin l'ascelle –
   lo dosso e 'l petto e ambedue le coste
   dipinti avea di nodi e di rotelle:
con più color, sommesse e sovraposte
   non fer mai drappi Tartari né Turchi,
   né fuor tai tele per Aragne imposte.
Come tal volta stanno a riva i burchi,
   che parte sono in acqua e parte in terra,   20
   e come là tra li Tedeschi lurchi
lo bivero s'assetta a far sua guerra,
   così la fiera pessima si stava
   sull'orlo che, di pietra, il sabbion serra.
Nel vano tutta sua coda guizzava,
   torcendo in su la venenosa forca
   ch'a guisa di scorpion la punta armava.
Lo duca disse: 'Or convien che si torca
   la nostra via un poco insino a quella
   bestia malvagia che colà si corca.'   30
Però scendemmo alla destra mammella,
   e diece passi femmo in su lo stremo,
   per ben cessar la rena e la fiammella.
E quando noi a lei venuti semo,
   poco più oltre veggio in su la rena
   gente seder propinqua al luogo scemo.

'See there the monster with the stinging tail,   1
   That scales the heights, and shatters all defence!
   See there the beast that makes the whole world foul!'
That was an exclamation from my guide,
   Who beckoned to the beast to come ashore
   Close by the end of our hard stony road.
And that unclean embodiment of fraud
   Did draw up on the land his head and chest,
   But did not bring his tail up on the side.[1]
His countenance was of an honest man,   10
   Someone to all appearance well-disposed,
   And then the rest of him was serpentine;
He had two paws, with hair to the armpits –
   And back and breast and both his sides were painted
   With circles and with complicated knots:
Less colourful, less complex in design,
   Are fabrics from the Tartars and the Turks;
   Nor did Arachne weave such on her loom.[2]
As we sometimes see vessels left to lie
   Half drawn up on the shore and half in water,   20
   And as up there in gluttonous Germany[3]
The beaver sits to hunt, half on the land,[4]
   So did that worst of beasts stay on the margin
   Made out of stone enclosing the hot sand.
The whole tail in the void was quivering,
   And writhing upwards its envenomed pincers
   Which, like the scorpion's tail, contain a sting.
My leader said: 'It's necessary here
   To deviate somewhat to arrive at that
   Malevolent creature lying over there.'   30
So we went down a little to the right,
   And walked ten paces on the very edge,
   Avoiding carefully the sand and heat.
And, when we came to where the monster lay,
   I saw, a little further on the sand,
   People crouching, near where it falls away.

---

1. A notable example – one of many in the descriptions of Geryon – of how details are apt and realistic in the narrative and also allegorical: it is an essential characteristic of fraud to conceal its intended harm.
2. Arachne was an expert mythical weaver, who challenged Athena to a contest, was defeated, and was turned into a spider.
3. Northern Europeans were proverbially gluttonous.
4. The beaver was said, when hunting, to attract fish by waving its tail in the water.

Quivi 'l maestro: 'Acciò che tutta piena
    esperienza d'esto giron porti,'
    mi disse, 'va', e vedi la lor mena.
Li tuoi ragionamenti sian là corti: 40
    mentre che torni, parlerò con questa,
    che ne conceda i suoi omeri forti.'
Così ancor su per la strema testa
    di quel settimo cerchio tutto solo
    andai, dove sedea la gente mesta.
Per li occhi fora scoppiava lor duolo;
    di qua, di là soccorrìen con le mani
    quando a' vapori, e quando al caldo suolo:
non altrimenti fan di state i cani
    or col ceffo or col piè, quando son morsi   50
    o da pulci o da mosche o da tafani.
Poi che nel viso a certi li occhi porsi,
    ne' quali il doloroso foco casca,
    non ne conobbi alcun – ma io m'accorsi
che dal collo a ciascun pendea una tasca
    ch'avea certo colore e certo segno,
    e quindi par che 'l loro occhio si pasca.
E com'io riguardando tra lor vegno,
    in una borsa gialla vidi azzurro
    che d'un leone avea faccia e contegno.   60
Poi, procedendo di mio sguardo il curro,
    vidine un'altra come sangue rossa,
    mostrando un'oca bianca più che burro.
E un che d'una scrofa azzurra e grossa
    segnato avea lo suo sacchetto bianco,
    mi disse: 'Che fai tu in questa fossa?
Or te ne va' – e perché se' vivo anco,
    sappi che 'l mio vicin Vitaliano
    sederà qui dal mio sinistro fianco.
Con questi fiorentin son padovano: 70
    spesse fiate m'intronan li orecchi
    gridando: "Vegna il cavalier sovrano,

My master said: 'In order to obtain
    A perfect understanding of this ring[5],
    Go over there and see the state they're in.
Be sure to place a limit on your talk.   40
    Till you return I'll have some words with this
    Creature: he'll bear us both on his broad back.'
So further on, along the brink of that
    Unhappy seventh circle, all alone,
    I went to where the unhappy people sat.
Their pain gushed from their eyes; and with their hands
    They kept on trying to defend themselves
    Now from the flames, now from the burning sands:
Exactly as a dog in summer does,
    Now with its muzzle, now its paws, when bitten   50
    By irksome fleas or gnats, or by gadflies.
After I'd fixed my eyes on some of them
    On whom the painful fire is always falling,
    I recognised not one; but saw that from
The neck of each of them a purse was hanging,
    Each with its special colour and device,
    On which they seemed to feast their eyes with longing.[6]
And, as I walked around and kept my eye on
    Them all, I found a yellow purse with azure
    That had the face and bearing of a lion.[7]   60
Then, looking further as I saw things better,
    I saw another purse, as red as blood,
    That had on it a goose whiter than butter.[8]
And one, who had on his white reticule
    A pregnant sow depicted in bright blue,[9]
    Demanded: 'What's your purpose in this hole?
Just go away. And, since you're not yet dead,
    I'll let you know my neighbour Vitaliano[10]
    Will come and sit down here at my left side.
Among these Florentines I'm Paduan: 70
    I hear their voices ringing in my ears,
    Shouting: "We're waiting for that honoured man,

5. The third ring of the seventh circle.
6. Their heraldic devices reveal the high social rank of the usurers, while their attitude and the
    purses about their necks emphasise their depravity.
7. The arms of the Florentine Gianfigliazzi family, noted usurers.
8. The arms of the Obriachi family, also Florentines and noted usurers.
9. The arms of the Scrovegni family of Padua, to which several usurers belonged.
10. Obviously another Paduan, but not certainly identified.

che recherà la tasca con tre becchi!"' '
    Qui distorse la bocca e di fuor trasse
    la lingua come bue che 'l naso lecchi.
E io, temendo no 'l più star crucciasse
    lui che di poco star m'avea 'mmonito,
    torna'mi in dietro dall'anime lasse.
Trova' il duca mio ch'era salito
    già sulla groppa del fiero animale,   80
    e disse a me: 'Or sie forte e ardito.
Omai si scende per sì fatte scale:
    monta dinanzi, ch'i' voglio esser mezzo,
    sì che la coda non possa far male.'
Qual è colui che sì presso ha 'l riprezzo
    della quartana c'ha già l'unghie smorte,
    e triema tutto pur guardando il rezzo,
tal divenn'io alle parole porte,
    ma vergogna mi fe' le sue minacce,
    che innanzi a buon segnor fa servo forte.   90
I' m'assettai in su quelle spallacce:
    sì volli dir, ma la voce non venne
    com'io credetti: 'Fa' che tu m'abbracce.'
Ma esso, ch'altra volta mi sovvenne
    ad altro forse, tosto ch'io montai
    con le braccia m'avvinse e mi sostenne,
e disse: 'Gerïon, moviti omai:
    le rote larghe e lo scender sia poco –
    pensa la nova soma che tu hai.'
Come la navicella esce di loco   100
    in dietro in dietro, sì quindi si tolse;
    e poi ch'al tutto si sentì a gioco,
là 'v'era il petto la coda rivolse,
    e quella tesa, come anguilla, mosse,
    e con le branche l'aere a sé raccolse.
Maggior paura non credo che fosse
    quando Fetón abbandonò li freni,
    per che 'l ciel, come pare ancor, si cosse –

The knight who wears the purse that shows three goats!" '[11]
    At this he writhed his muzzle and stuck out
    His tongue, as oxen do to lick their snouts.
And I, who feared that any more delay
    Might anger him who'd warned me to be quick,
    Turned from those weary souls and went away.
And then I found my leader was already
    Mounted on that repulsive animal.   80
    He told me: 'Now you must be bold and steady.
From now on we'll go down by ways like this:
    Climb up in front; I must be in the middle,
    So that the tail won't be injurious.'
As one who feels the approach of quartan fever,
    With nails already blue, while the mere sight
    Of cooling shade makes him tremble all over –
Such was my feeling when those words were said;
    And then I had that sense of shame which makes
    A servant brave in front of his good lord.   90
I settled on those monstrous shoulders, but
    When I began to speak, my voice would not
    Issue as planned to ask him: 'Hold me tight!'
But he, who'd aided me more than one time
    In other peril, soon as I had mounted
    Wrapped me in both his arms and held me firm;
And said: 'Now Geryon, take off: and make
    Wide circles in descent and travel slowly:
    Think of the novel burden on your back.'
Just as a boat backs slowly from its place   100
    Little by little, so the creature moved;
    And when he knew he had sufficient space,
He turned his tail to where his breast had been,
    And stretched it out, and moved it like an eel,
    And gathered with his paws the soft air in.
I do believe not such tremendous fear
    Struck Phaethon when the reins slipped from his grasp,
    And set the sky, as still appears, on fire;[12]

11. Gianni Buiamonte dei Becchi, a Florentine who died ten years after the date (1300) which Dante gave to his journey.

12. The mythical Phaethon obtained from his father, Helios the Sun, permission to guide the chariot of the sun across the sky. Phaethon proved unequal to this task and lost control of the horses, and they went off course. One result of the conflagration which followed was the Milky Way, which 'still appears' in the sky.

né quando Icaro misero le reni
    sentì spennar per la scaldata cera,   110
    gridando il padre a lui: 'Mala via tieni!' –
che fu la mia, quando vidi ch'i' era
    nell'aere d'ogni parte, e vidi spenta
    ogni veduta fuor che della fera.
Ella sen va notando lenta lenta:
    rota e discende, ma non me n'accorgo
    se non che al viso e di sotto mi venta.
Io sentìa già dalla man destra il gorgo
    far sotto noi un orribile scroscio,
    per che con li occhi 'n giù la testa sporgo.   120
Allor fu' io più timido allo stoscio,
    però ch'i' vidi fuochi e senti' pianti,
    ond'io tremando tutto mi raccoscio.
E vidi poi, ché nol vedea davanti,
    lo scendere e 'l girar per li gran mali
    che s'appressavan da diversi canti.
Come 'l falcon ch'è stato assai sull'ali,
    che sanza veder logoro o uccello
    fa dire al falconiere 'Ohmè, tu cali!' –
discende lasso onde si move snello   130
    per cento rote, e da lunge si pone
    dal suo maestro, disdegnoso e fello –
così ne puose al fondo Gerione
    al piè al piè della stagliata rocca
    e, discarcate le nostre persone,
si dileguò come da corda cocca[a].

a. The notch in the arrow which engages with the bow-string; here used synecdochically for the arrow itself, probably for the sake of the alliteration with 'corda', to emphasise the speed.

Or Icarus when the feathers fell away
    From both his sides, because the wax was melting,   110
    His father crying out: 'Don't go that way!'[13] –
As struck me when I looked around and saw
    Only the monster all about me, and
    No scenery except the ambient air.
Our beast goes swimming slowly, and describing
    Wide circles in descent: I'm only conscious
    Of wind brushing my face and wind arising.[14]
Already I could hear upon our right
    The torrent[15] roaring horribly below,
    And craned my neck as I looked out for it.   120
Then, being terrified that I might drop,
    Seeing such fires and hearing such laments,
    I shuddered, and held on, and huddled up.
I saw what I had not seen previously –
    Our spiralling descent – now that such evils
    At every side were looming up at me.
And as a falcon – one that's lingered on
    The wing too long, and sees no lure[16] or prey,
    And makes the falconer wail: 'You're coming down!' –
Descends exhausted whence it went with speed,   130
    Describes a hundred circles, and alights
    Far from its master, sullen and annoyed –
So, at the very foot of jagged rock,
    Geryon set us down, far down below,
    And, once our weight was lifted from his back,
He shot off like an arrow from a bow.

13. The mythical Icarus was provided by his father with wings made from feathers held together by wax. He was warned not to fly too near the sun, but he did, the wax melted, the wings fell apart, and he fell to his death.
14. The wind brushing Dante's face is caused by Geryon's circling flight, and the wind coming from below is caused by the fact that the beast is descending.
15. Phlegethon.
16. A device to bring a falcon back to its master.

CANTO XVIII

The canto opens with a description of the eighth circle of the Inferno, which consists of ten tiered circular ditches arranged concentrically. The ditches are all cut across by lines of bridges which radiate from the deep well or chasm at the centre of this circle. Different sins are punished in each of the ditches, but all of these sins involve cheating, deceiving, or in some way practising fraud upon people who have no particular reason to trust those who deceive them, except that there is a duty incumbent on everyone to deal honestly.

The first ditch contains pimps and seducers, who move in opposite directions, and are all being scourged by horned demons. Dante speaks with one of the pimps, with whom he was already acquainted and who tries hard to avoid his eyes. This is the Bolognese Venedico Caccianemico who sold his own sister for gain. He is frank about his fault, and gives the impression that this sin is one of which very many Bolognese are guilty, since they are proverbially avaricious.

Now Dante and Virgil climb up one of the bridges which run off at the side of their track. They stand upon its arch to look at the seducers, and they note particularly the mythical Jason, a man of regal bearing and prowess, but a habitual seducer of women. They do not speak with him.

Dante and Virgil cross the bridge and look down into the second ditch, that of the gross flatterers. These sinners are immersed in human excrement (a symbol of the filth in which they trafficked), and so smeared with it that not much can be seen of them. This perversion of the human ability to communicate is seen as not only a serious sin, but a particularly disgusting one.

Luogo è in inferno detto Malebolge[a],   1
    tutto di pietra di color ferrigno,
    come la cerchia che dintorno il volge.
Nel dritto mezzo del campo maligno
    vaneggia un pozzo assai largo e profondo,
    di cui suo loco dicerò l'ordigno.
Quel cinghio che rimane adunque è tondo
    tra 'l pozzo e 'l piè dell'alta ripa dura,
    e ha distinto in dieci valli il fondo.
Quale, dove per guardia delle mura   10
    più e più fossi cingon li castelli,
    la parte dove son rende figura,
tale imagine quivi facean quelli;
    e come a tai fortezze da' lor sogli
    alla ripa di fuor son ponticelli,
così da imo della roccia scogli
    movìen che ricidìen li argini e' fossi
    infino al pozzo che i tronca e racco'gli.
In questo luogo, della schiena scossi
    di Gerion, trovammoci, e 'l poeta   20
    tenne a sinistra, e io dietro mi mossi.
Alla man destra vidi nova pièta,
    novo tormento e novi frustatori,
    di che la prima bolgia era repleta.
Nel fondo erano ignudi i peccatori:
    dal mezzo in qua ci venìen verso 'l volto,
    di là con noi, ma con passi maggiori,
come i Roman per l'essercito molto,
    l'anno del giubileo, su per lo ponte
    hanno a passar la gente modo colto –   30
che dall'un lato tutti hanno la fronte
    verso 'l castello e vanno a Santo Pietro,
    dall'altra sponda vanno verso il monte.
Di qua, di là, su per lo sasso tetro
    vidi demon cornuti con gran ferze,
    che li battìen crudelmente di retro.

a. Lit. 'Evil Pouches': the area is divided into ten concentric pits.

There is in hell a place called Eviltiers,   1
    Which is throughout of iron-coloured stone,
    As the high wall that goes all round it is.
In the dead centre of this wicked space
    There yawns a broad profound abyss or well,
    Whose structure I'll describe in its due place.
The area, between the high surround
    Of hard stone and the well, is circular,
    And cut into ten pits that go all round.
And like the sort of pattern that is made   10
    By the concentric moats around a castle,
    To ensure that it is strongly fortified,
So these ten ditches make the same design;
    And as a castle from its inner gates
    To its perimeter has bridges thrown,
So from the rock wall's foot ridges run down
    Over ditches and banks: the central well
    Cuts them all short and gathers them all in.
This was the very place in which we found
    Ourselves, when Geryon set us down. The poet   20
    Kept to the left, and I went on behind.
Then I saw novel misery on the right,
    Novel torments and novel torturers:
    The first of all the ditches was replete.
The sinners were all naked – on our side
    They came towards us, but the ones beyond
    Along with us, both moving with great speed:
Just as the Romans for the Jubilee[1],
    For all the numbers on the Bridge[2], were able
    To keep the traffic moving steadily,   30
Since on one side[3] they kept their eyes all bent
    Upon the Castle[4], going to St Peter's;
    And, on the other, moved towards the Mount[5].
On both sides, all along the gloomy rock,
    I saw horned demons with enormous whips
    Lashing the sinners cruelly on the back.

1. The first Jubilee of the Roman Catholic Church was instituted by Pope Boniface VIII in 1300.
   It brought many pilgrims into Rome.
2. The Sant'Angelo bridge over the Tiber, leading to St Peter's.
3. One side of the road over the bridge.
4. The Castel Sant'Angelo.
5. Monte Giordano, a small hill on the side of the Tiber opposite to the Castel Sant'Angelo.

Ahi com facean lor levar le berze
   alle prime percosse! Già nessuno
   le seconde aspettava né le terze.
Mentr'io andava, li occhi miei in uno   40
   furo scontrati, e io sì tosto dissi:
   'Già di veder costui non son digiuno;'
per ch'io a figurarlo i piedi affissi –
   e 'l dolce duca meco si ristette,
   e assentìo ch'alquanto in dietro gissi.
E quel frustato celar si credette
   bassando il viso; ma poco li valse,
   ch'io dissi: 'O tu che l'occhio a terra gette,
se le fazion che porti non son false,
   Venedico se' tu Caccianemico…   50
   ma che ti mena a sì pungenti salse?'
Ed elli a me: 'Mal volentier lo dico,
   ma sforzami la tua chiara favella,
   che mi fa sovvenir del mondo antico.
I' fui colui che la Ghisolabella
   condussi a far la voglia del Marchese,
   come che suoni la sconcia novella.
E non pur io qui piango bolognese –
   anzi, n'è questo luogo tanto pieno,
   che tante lingue non son ora apprese   60
a dicer "sipa" tra Sàvena e Reno;
   e se di ciò vuoi fede o testimonio,
   rècati a mente il nostro avaro seno.'
Così parlando il percosse un demonio
   della sua scuriada, e disse: 'Via,
   ruffian, qui non son femmine da conio!'
I' mi raggiunsi con la scorta mia;
   poscia con pochi passi divenimmo
   là 'v'uno scoglio della ripa uscìa.
Assai leggeramente quel salimmo   70
   e, volti a destra su per la sua scheggia,
   da quelle cerchie etterne ci partimmo.

Oh, how the demons made those sinners kick
    Their heels up! Certainly not one was anxious
    To have a third or even second stroke.
While I went on, I was by chance aware   40
    Of one who caught my eye, and I exclaimed:
    'There's somebody I'm sure I've seen before.'
And so I stopped, and tried to make him out;
    My courteous guide stopped also, and he gave
    Me his permission to go back a bit.
That scourged soul thought by lowering his gaze
    To hide himself; but it was all in vain –
    I said: 'O you, who go with downcast eyes,
If your known features are not false or fickle,
    Venedico you'll be – Caccianemico![6]   50
    But what's put you in such a pretty pickle?'
Then he replied: 'I do not want to say,
    But I'm compelled by your clear speech, which brings
    All the old world I lived in back to me.
I was the one who pandered, after all,
    Between Ghisolabella and the Marquis,
    However men may tell the filthy tale.[7]
I'm not the only Bolognese this ditch
    Contains. Indeed, it's crammed so full of them
    Fewer are using *sipa*[8] in their speech   60
Between the Savena and Reno Rivers;[9]
    And if you think this needs to be confirmed,
    Remember we're well-known as avaricious.'
And, as he spoke, a demon with a lash
    Laid on him, and cried out: 'Clear off, you pander!
    There are no women here for you to cash.'
Then I went back and caught up with my guide;
    Not many paces and we came upon
    A ridge of rock that ran out at the side.[10]
We easily climbed up this jagged ground,   70
    And turning to the right along its arch,
    We left that everlasting moving-round.[11]

---

6. A leading Guelph from Bologna (*c.*1228–1302) who sold his own sister, Ghisolabella, to the Marquis of Este. Since the date of Dante's journey is 1300, it seems that he was mistaken about the date of Caccianemico's death.

7. There were, apparently, differing versions of this incident current.

8. The dialect word for *si* (yes) in Bologna.

9. That is, the area under Bolognese control. There are more dead Bolognese in this part of the Inferno than there are Bolognese still alive.

10. This is one of the bridges already mentioned in ll. 14–18 of this canto.

11. The constant movement of the panders and seducers punished in this first ditch of the eighth circle. The panders move facing Dante and Virgil, while the seducers are moving in the opposite direction: both groups of sinners keep to their own right hand.

Quando noi fummo là dov'el vaneggia
    di sotto per dar passo a li sferzati,
    lo duca disse: 'Attienti, e fa' che feggia
lo viso in te di quest'altri mal nati,
    ai quali ancor non vedesti la faccia,
    però che son con noi insieme andati.'
Del vecchio ponte guardavam la traccia
    che venìa verso noi dall'altra banda,   80
    e che la ferza similmente scaccia.
E 'l buon maestro, sanza mia dimanda,
    mi disse: 'Guarda quel grande che vène,
    e per dolor non par lagrima spanda:
quanto aspetto reale ancor ritene!
    Quelli è Iasón, che per cuore e per senno
    li Colchi del monton privati féne.
Ello passò per l'isola di Lenno,
    poi che l'ardite femmine spietate
    tutti li maschi loro a morte dienno.   90
Ivi con segni e con parole ornate
    Isifile ingannò, la giovinetta
    che prima avea tutte l'altre ingannate.
Lasciolla quivi, gravida, soletta –
    tal colpa a tal martiro lui condanna –
    e anche di Medea si fa vendetta.
Con lui sen va chi da tal parte inganna:
    e questo basti della prima valle
    sapere e di color che 'n sé assanna.'
Già eravam là 've lo stretto calle   100
    con l'argine secondo s'incrocicchia,
    e fa di quello ad un altr'arco spalle.
Quindi sentimmo gente che si nicchia
    nell'altra bolgia e che col muso scuffa,
    e sé medesma con le palme picchia.
Le ripe eran grommate d'una muffa,
    per l'alito di giù che vi s'appasta,
    che con li occhi e col naso facea zuffa.

When we came where that ridge has under it
    A hollow passage for those being lashed,
    My leader said: 'Now stop, and let the sight
Of still more ill-born beings catch your eye,
    None of whose faces you have seen as yet,
    Since we have all been walking the same way.'
From the old bridge we looked down at the group
    Coming towards us on the other side,   80
    And like the others driven by the whip.
And my kind guide, without my asking him,
    Said: 'See that mighty one who is approaching,
    And does not seem to weep, for all his pain.
How regal is his bearing still! For this
    Is Jason[12], who by grit and guile deprived
    The men of Colchis of the Golden Fleece.
He landed at the Isle of Lemnos, when
    The bold, unpitying women who lived there
    Had given up to death all of the men.   90
There, with love-signs and flattering phrases, he
    Deceived Hypsipyle, the girl who had
    Deceived the other women previously.[13]
Then he abandoned her, pregnant, alone:
    Such guilt condemns him to such punishment:
    Medea is avenged at the same time.[14]
With him go all deceivers of that sort:
    That's all you need to know about this valley,
    And about everyone whom its fangs bite.'
We were already where the narrow ridge   100
    Crosses the second bank,[15] and where that makes
    A shoulder which supports another bridge.
From here we're conscious of a muffled whine,
    Where people[16] snort and snuffle through their muzzles,
    And slap themselves, inside the next tier down.
Foul vapours smeared the sides as they arose
    Out of the ditch, encrusting it with mould
    Repugnant to the eyes and to the nose.

12. The mythical leader of the Argonauts. They sailed to Colchis in quest of the golden ram's fleece
    which was guarded by a dragon. Jason is, despite his prowess, damned as a serial seducer of women.
13. She had merely pretended to kill her father, and so deceived the other women of Lemnos.
14. The daughter of the King of Colchis, who helped Jason to obtain the golden fleece and whom he
    promised to marry. He later abandoned her.
15. Which divides the first from the second ditch of this eighth circle.
16. Those sinners who gained their ends by gross flattery.

Lo fondo è cupo sì che non ci basta
  luogo a veder sanza montare al dosso   110
  dell'arco, ove lo scoglio più sovrasta.
Quivi venimmo, e quindi giù nel fosso
  vidi gente attuffata in uno sterco
  che dalli uman privadi parea mosso.
E mentre ch'io là giù con l'occhio cerco,
  vidi un col capo sì di merda lordo
  che non parea s'era laico o cherco.
Quei mi sgridò: 'Perché se' tu sì 'ngordo
  di riguardar più me che li altri brutti?'
  E io a lui: 'Perché, se ben ricordo,   120
già t'ho veduto coi capelli asciutti,
  e se' Alessio Interminei da Lucca –
  però t'adocchio più che li altri tutti.'
Ed elli allor, battendosi la zucca:
  'Qua giù m'hanno sommerso le lusinghe
  ond'io non ebbi mai la lingua stucca.'
Appresso ciò lo duca 'Fa' che pinghe,'
  mi disse, 'il viso un poco più avante,
  sì che la faccia ben con l'occhio attinghe
di quella sozza e scapigliata fante   130
  che là si graffia con l'unghie merdose,
  e or s'accoscia, e ora è in piedi stante.
Taidè è, la puttana che rispose
  al drudo suo quando disse "Ho io grazie
  grandi appo te?" – "Anzi maravigliose!"
E quinci sian le nostre viste sazie.'

This ditch's bottom is so deep and dark
    It is not visible unless one climbs   110
    The hump to where the bridge is at its peak.
Once at that point I could look down and see
    The people weltering there in excrement,
    Channelled from earth's latrines apparently.
Soon, as I cast my eyes around it all,
    I saw one with his head so smeared with shit
    That, clerical or lay, I could not tell.
He snarled at me: 'Why's your insatiable
    Stare fixed on me, when all of us are filthy?'
    I answered him: 'Because, as I recall,   120
I used to know you, when your hair was dry,
    Alessio Interminelli, the Lucchese!'[17]
    That's why I look at you especially.'
Then, thumping his own forehead, he replied:
    'I'm drenched down here for all those flatteries
    Of which onetime my tongue was never tired.'
Then, after that, my guide said: 'Try to thrust
    Your head a little further to the front,
    Until you find you're face to face at last
With that dishevelled, filthy prostitute   130
    Who's scratching at herself with shitty nails,
    And sometimes crouches, sometimes stands upright.
That is Thaïs[18], the harlot who replied
    (Her paramour had asked her: "Do I please
    You very much?"): "I'm vastly overjoyed!"
Now let that be enough of sights like these.'

17. All that is known of him, apart from Dante's account, is that he was a White Guelph still alive in 1295.
18. A character in a play by the Roman playwright Terence.

CANTO XIX

The pilgrims can now see the third ditch, where simoniacs – those who traffic in sacred things – are punished by being placed upside down in holes in the rock. Above these holes their legs are visible, and wriggle and jerk to express their torment, while fire licks about their feet.

Dante is interested in one of these pairs of legs which seems to belong to someone who is suffering even more than the others. So Virgil carries Dante down into the ditch, where he is able to talk with this sinner. He is Pope Nicholas III (reigned 1277–80), and he explains that other simoniac popes lie piled up under him, just as he will be pushed further down at the arrival of the next sinner, who we gather will be Pope Boniface VIII (reigned 1294–1303), himself to be pushed down in his turn by Pope Clement V (reigned 1305–14).

Dante expresses to Nicholas III his great detestation of the sin of simony, and reminds him how Christ did not ask for money from St Peter before giving him the keys of the kingdom of heaven, and the Apostles did not ask for money from Matthias before they elected him to take the place of the traitor Judas Iscariot. Dante also seizes the opportunity to deprecate the Donation of Constantine, which was thought to confer temporal power upon the popes. While Dante is speaking, the feet of Nicholas III keep on kicking, though whether to express anger or pangs of conscience Dante does not know. Dante notices that he has clearly pleased Virgil by what he has said.

Virgil picks Dante up once again, and carries him onto the ridge from where they can see into the fourth ditch, and here Virgil sets him down.

O Simon mago, o miseri seguaci   1
    che le cose di Dio, che di bontate
    deon essere spose, e voi rapaci
per oro e per argento avolterate,
    or convien che per voi suoni la tromba,
    però che nella terza bolgia state.
Già eravamo, alla seguente tomba,
    montati dello scoglio in quella parte
    ch'a punto sovra mezzo il fosso piomba.
O somma sapienza, quanta è l'arte   10
    che mostri in cielo, in terra e nel mal mondo,
    e quanto giusto tua virtù comparte!
Io vidi per le coste e per lo fondo
    piena la pietra livida di fori,
    d'un largo tutti e ciascun era tondo.
Non mi parean men ampi né maggiori
    che que' che son nel mio bel San Giovanni,
    fatti per luogo de' battezzatori –
l'un delli quali, ancor non è molt'anni,
    rupp'io per un che dentro v'annegava: 20
    e questo sia suggel ch'ogn'uomo sganni.
Fuor della bocca a ciascun soperchiava
    d'un peccator li piedi e delle gambe
    infino al grosso, e l'altro dentro stava.
Le piante erano a tutti accese intrambe,
    per che sì forte guizzavan le giunte
    che spezzate averìen ritorte e strambe.
Qual suole il fiammeggiar delle cose unte
    muoversi pur su per la strema buccia,
    tal era lì dai calcagni alle punte.   30
'Chi è colui, maestro, che si cruccia
    guizzando più che li altri suoi consorti,'
    diss'io, 'e cui più roggia fiamma succia?'
Ed elli a me: 'Se tu vuo' ch'i' ti porti
    là giù per quella ripa che più giace,
    da lui saprai di sé e de' suoi torti.'

O Simon Magus![1] And all you, his brood!   1
    You take the things of God, which ought to be
    Wedded to good and, such is your great greed,
Prostitute them for gold, because of which
    The trumpet must be sounded for you now:
    You're in your rightful place in this third ditch!
We had already climbed upon the scarp
    To reach the tomb beyond, just at that point
    Which overhangs the centre of the dip.
O Highest Wisdom, see your skill displayed   10
    In heaven, on earth, and in this wicked world!
    How justly do you punish and reward!
I saw, along the bottom and the sides,
    The iron-coloured stone pitted with holes,
    All of them round, and all of them one size,
No narrower and no wider, to my mind,
    Than those in my beloved San Giovanni,
    In which the priests, when they're baptising, stand;[2]
And one of which, not many years ago,
    I broke, to stop somebody suffocating: 20
    To this I set my seal, for all to know.[3]
Out of the mouth of each and every one
    A sinner's feet projected, and his legs
    Up to the thighs: the rest remained within.
The soles of all these feet were set on fire,
    Which made their joints so tremble, jerk, and twitch
    They would have broken bonds of rope or wire.
As flames on well-greased objects only go
    Flickering along them superficially,
    So the flames flickered here, from heel to toe.   30
'Who is that shade, O master, who is kicking,
    And clearly suffering, more than all his fellows,'
    I asked, 'and whom a redder flame is licking?'
He said: 'If you will let me bear you down
    Along that shorter bank lying below,
    He'll tell you of himself and of his sin.'

1. The word 'simony' derives from his name (Acts 8: 9–20).
2. The church of San Giovanni in Florence, a few yards from the Duomo, is now better known as the Baptistery. Nothing remains of the arrangements for baptism, but a fair idea of them can be gained from the baptistery in Pisa, where there is a very large font with several vertical tubes inside it for the priests to stand and remain dry and not be jostled by the crowds: it was the custom then to perform baptisms only twice a year.
3. No more is known of this than can be deduced from Dante's text. There seems to have been some dispute over the rightness of Dante's action, and the language in line 21 is legal, as though Dante is here making an official statement of the truth.

E io: 'Tanto m'è bel quanto a te piace:
    tu se' segnore, e sai ch'i' non mi parto
    dal tuo volere, e sai quel che si tace.'
Allor venimmo in su l'argine quarto: 40
    volgemmo e discendemmo a mano stanca[a]
    là giù nel fondo foracchiato e arto.
Lo buon maestro ancor della sua anca
    non mi dipuose, sì mi giunse al rotto
    di quel che si piangeva con la zanca.
'O qual che se' che 'l di su tien di sotto,
    anima trista come pal commessa,'
    comincia' io a dir, 'se puoi, fa' motto.'
Io stava come 'l frate che confessa
    lo perfido assessin che, poi ch'è fitto,   50
    richiama lui, per che la morte cessa.
Ed el gridò: 'Se' tu già costì ritto,
    se' tu già costì ritto, Bonifazio?
    Di parecchi anni mi mentì lo scritto.
Se' tu sì tosto di quell'aver sazio
    per lo qual non temesti tòrre a 'nganno
    la bella donna, e poi di farne strazio?'
Tal mi fec'io, quai son color che stanno,
    per non intender ciò ch'è lor risposto,
    quasi scornati, e risponder non sanno.   60
Allor Virgilio disse: 'Dilli tosto:
    "Non son colui, non son colui che credi" ' –
    e io rispuosi come a me fu imposto.
Per che lo spirto tutti storse i piedi;
    poi, sospirando e con voce di pianto,
    mi disse: 'Dunque che a me richiedi?
Se di saper ch'i' sia ti cal cotanto
    che tu abbi però la ripa corsa,
    sappi ch'i' fui vestito del gran manto,
e veramente fui figliuol dell'orsa,   70
    cupido sì per avanzar li orsatti
    che su l'avere, e qui me misi in borsa.

a. Archaic for 'sinistra', i.e. 'left'.

I answered him: 'Your wish is my command:
    You are my lord, you know your will is mine,
    And what I do not say you understand.'
We came upon the fourth bulwark; at that   40
    We turned and, keeping to the left, descended
    Into the narrow, perforated pit.
My kindly master did not set me down
    Until we came upon our goal, the hole
    Of him who used his feet to make his moan.[4]
'O you inserted here, heels over head,
    Sad soul stuck like a pole into the ground,'
    I said, 'if you are able, spare a word.'
There I was bending, like the confessor
    Above the assassin who, once he is planted,   50
    Calls the priest back, to keep death from the door.[5]
He cried: 'So you're already standing there,
    Already standing there, eh, Boniface?[6]
    The writing[7] must have lied by a year or more.
Are you already well and truly glutted
    With wealth you did not scruple to obtain
    Deceiving Her[8] whom you then prostituted?'
At that I stood like someone who stands dumb,
    Not understanding the reply that's made:
    Thinking he's mocked, he finds no words will come.   60
Then Virgil said: 'Answer immediately:
    "I'm not the one, the one you think I am."'
    So I replied as was commanded me.
At that the spirit writhed his feet; then he,
    Sighing and with a voice full of despair,
    Replied: 'What is it then you want from me?
If you've taken the trouble to climb down
    Simply to find out who I am, then listen:
    I had the mighty mantle for my own;[9]
A true son of the Bear,[10] in my great greed   70
    To advance the cubs, I pocketed great wealth
    Up in the world, as here I'm pocketed.

---

4. See ll. 31–2 above.

5. Hired assassins were placed upside down in a hole which was then filled with earth once the criminal had made his confession. The temptation to think up more and more sins to confess must have been overwhelming.

6. The sinner's mistake in thinking that Pope Boniface VIII has already come to join him is a neat way of indicating the ultimate destination of one who was still alive in 1300.

7. In the 'book of the future' which the damned are able to read.

8. Holy Mother Church.

9. He was Pope.

10. Pope Nicholas III was a member of the powerful Orsini family. Since *orso* means 'bear', they were known as 'sons of the Bear'. Nicholas is a 'true' son because bears were proverbially greedy creatures.

Di sotto al capo mio son li altri tratti
    che precedetter me simoneggiando,
    per le fessure della pietra piatti.
Là giù cascherò io altressì quando
    verrà colui ch'i' credea che tu fossi
    allor ch'i' feci 'l subito dimando.
Ma più è 'l tempo già che i piè mi cossi
    e ch'io son stato così sottosopra   80
    ch'el non starà piantato coi piè rossi:
ché dopo lui verrà di più laid'opra
    di ver ponente un pastor sanza legge,
    tal che convien che lui e me ricopra.
Novo Iasón sarà, di cui si legge
    ne' Maccabei – e come a quel fu molle
    suo re, così fia lui chi Francia regge.'
I' non so s'i' mi fui qui troppo folle,
    ch'i' pur rispuosi lui a questo metro:
    'Deh, or mi di': quanto tesoro volle   90
Nostro Segnore in prima da san Pietro
    ch'ei ponesse le chiavi in sua balia?
    Certo non chiese se non "Viemmi retro".
Né Pier né li altri tolsero a Mattia
    oro od argento quando fu sortito
    al luogo che perdé l'anima ria.
Però ti sta, ché tu se' ben punito –
    e guarda ben la mal tolta moneta
    ch'esser ti fece contra Carlo ardito.
E se non fosse ch'ancor lo mi vieta   100
    la reverenza delle somme chiavi
    che tu tenesti nella vita lieta,
io userei parole ancor più gravi;
    ché la vostra avarizia il mondo attrista,
    calcando i buoni e sollevando i pravi.
Di voi pastor s'accorse il Vangelista,
    quando colei che siede sopra l'acque
    puttaneggiar coi regi a lui fu vista;

Already underneath my head are thrown
    All those who went before me simonising:
    They're piled up in a heap beneath the stone.
And I like all of them will fall down too
    When he arrives, the one I thought you were[11]
    When I precipitately questioned you.
And now I have already longer stayed
    Cooking my feet and stuck here upside down   80
    Than he'll stay planted with his feet bright red:
Since some years after him will come another,
    A worse, a lawless shepherd from the west,[12]
    One fit to cover both of us together.
He'll be a Jason, like the one we read
    About in *Maccabees*, whose King was kind:
    The King of France will follow that King's lead.'[13]
I was perhaps at this point overbold,
    But all I said to him was in this strain:
    'Now tell me, how much treasure did Our Lord   90
Demand that Peter pay Him before He
    Delivered up the keys[14] into his care?
    Surely all that He said was: "Follow me."[15]
Neither did the Apostles take a toll
    From St Matthias when he was elected
    To take the place of the accursèd soul.[16]
Stay there then, for that punishment's your due;
    And take good care of the ill-gotten gain
    Which made you bold against Charles of Anjou.[17]
And did not those exalted keys restrain   100
    Me still – St Peter's keys I still revere,
    Your charge while you were living in the sun –
The language that I used would be more sharp;
    Because your avarice afflicts the world,
    Stamps on the good, and lifts the wicked up.
You are the pastors *Revelation*[18] brings
    To mind, when she who sits upon the waters
    Is seen by John[19] to fornicate with kings;

11. Pope Boniface VIII.
12. Pope Clement V. He was born in Gascony, and after he became pope he established the Papacy
    at Avignon, in the notorious 'Babylonian Captivity' (1309–77), and never came east to Rome.
13. In 2 Maccabees 4: 7–26 we are told how Jason became high priest by bribing King Antiochus.
    Similarly, Clement V was said to have bought the Papacy by bribing King Philip the Fair of France.
14. 'The keys of the kingdom of heaven' (Matthew 16: 19).
15. See Matthew 4: 19.
16. Judas Iscariot. See Acts 1: 13–26.
17. Nicholas III was said to have been bribed to support the conspiracy (against the rule of Charles
    of Anjou) which led to the massacre of 1282, known as the Sicilian Vespers.
18. Rev. 17. Dante's interpretation of this is that the woman is the Church and her bridegroom the Pope.
19. St John the Evangelist.

quella che con le sette teste nacque,
   e dalle diece corna ebbe argomento,   110
   fin che virtute al suo marito piacque.
Fatto v'avete Dio d'oro e d'argento:
   e che altro è da voi all'idolatre,
   se non ch'elli uno, e voi ne orate cento?
Ahi, Costantin, di quanto mal fu matre,
   non la tua conversion, ma quella dote
   che da te prese il primo ricco patre!'
E mentr'io li cantava cotai note,
   o ira o coscienza che 'l mordesse,
   forte spingava con ambo le piote.   120
I' credo ben ch'al mio duca piacesse,
   con sì contenta labbia sempre attese
   lo suon delle parole vere espresse.
Però con ambo le braccia mi prese,
   e poi che tutto su mi s'ebbe al petto,
   rimontò per la via onde discese.
Né si stancò d'avermi a sé distretto,
   sì men portò sovra 'l colmo dell'arco
   che dal quarto al quinto argine è tragetto.
Quivi soavemente spuose il carco,   130
   soave per lo scoglio sconcio ed erto
   che sarebbe alle capre duro varco.
Indi un altro vallon mi fu scoperto.

She who had seven heads[20] when she was born,
  And from ten horns[21] drew strength and sustenance   110
  So long as virtue gladdened her bridegroom.
Between you and idolaters, what odds?
  You deify your silver and your gold:
  They worship one, and you a hundred gods.
O Constantine, what evil did you mother!
  No, not by your conversion, but the dowry
  Which you donated to the first rich father!'[22]
Now while I was still harping on that note,
  Whether he felt the sting of wrath or conscience,
  He went on kicking hard with both his feet.   120
I do believe I really pleased my guide,
  Because he listened so contentedly
  To every one of those true words I said.
And then he took me in his arms again
  And, when he had me up against his breast,
  He went back by the way we had come down.
Nor did he tire, or let me slip his clutch,
  Until we reached the summit of the arch
  Which leads down from the fourth to the fifth ditch.
And here he gently set his burden down,   130
  Gently because the steep ridge would have been
  A rough road for a goat to travel on.
From there another valley could be seen.[23]

20. The Seven Sacraments.
21. The Ten Commandments.
22. The Roman Emperor Constantine the Great was converted to Christianity in 312. Legend had it that, when Constantine removed the capital of the Empire from Rome to Byzantium, he gave the whole temporal power of the West to the Church. This so-called 'Donation of Constantine' was exposed as a myth by the Italian humanist Lorenzo Valla (1405–57). Dante regards it as genuine, but deplores it.
23. The fourth ditch.

CANTO XX

In this fourth ditch of the eighth circle we find magicians of various kinds, and especially fortune-tellers. They walk slowly and sadly in what is almost a parody of a religious procession. Since they tried to look too far ahead into the future, and tried to go beyond the limits assigned to human knowledge, they are punished by having their heads twisted right round so that, in order to see where they are going, they have to walk backwards. Their appearance is at once pathetic and ludicrous. Virgil warns Dante against having any sympathy for these sinners, explaining how that would be to question divine justice.

It is noteworthy that not one of these shades says anything: their silence now contrasts with their confident assertions while they lived. Virgil, on the other hand, has much to say, and he gives Dante all the information he needs. The inhabitants of this ditch range from legendary figures like Tiresias to historical and near-contemporary ones like Michael Scot, and notably include women, and even unnamed people in humble circumstances who practised magic.

The condemnation of magic here is forthright, but that does not preclude some subtleties in the attitude towards it. Some of the shades are blamed for practising magic (apparently with success), while others are blamed for *pretending* to be able to practise it: the reader is left in some doubt as to the efficacy of magic, although in no doubt at all as to its sinfulness. Moreover, Dante's disgust at this sin does not stop him including – especially in Virgil's descriptions of scenery in Italy – a suggestion of the fascination which magic has for all of us.

With a reminder that, in the world above them, the moon is setting and day breaking, Virgil encourages Dante to go forward on the next stage of his journey.

Di nova pena mi conven far versi   1
   e dar matera al ventesimo canto
   della prima canzon, ch'è de' sommersi.
Io era già disposto tutto quanto
   a riguardar nello scoperto fondo
   che si bagnava d'angoscioso pianto,
e vidi gente per lo vallon tondo
   venir, tacendo e lagrimando, al passo
   che fanno le letane in questo mondo.
Come 'l viso mi scese in lor più basso,   10
   mirabilmente apparve esser travolto
   ciascun tra 'l mento e 'l principio del casso,
ché dalle reni era tornato il volto,
   ed in dietro venir li convenia,
   perché 'l veder dinanzi era lor tolto.
Forse per forza già di parlasìa
   si travolse così alcun del tutto –
   ma io nol vidi, né credo che sia.
Se Dio ti lasci, lettor, prender frutto
   di tua lezione, or pensa per te stesso   20
   com'io potea tener lo viso asciutto
quando la nostra imagine di presso
   vidi sì torta che 'l pianto delli occhi
   le natiche bagnava per lo fesso.
Certo io piangea, poggiato a un de' rocchi
   del duro scoglio, sì che la mia scorta
   mi disse: 'Ancor se' tu delli altri sciocchi?
Qui vive la pietà quand'è ben morta:
   chi è più scellerato che colui
   che al giudicio divin passion porta?   30
Drizza la testa, drizza, e vedi a cui
   s'aperse alli occhi de' Teban la terra,
   per ch'ei gridavan tutti: "Dove rui,
Anfiarao? perché lasci la guerra?"
   E non restò di ruinare a valle
   fino a Minòs che ciascheduno afferra.

I must fill out my verse with further pain,   1
    The subject matter of this twentieth canto
    Of my first book, which is of those cast down.
I was now in a place from which I could
    Look down into the depths that opened up,
    Filled with anguished weeping like a flood;
And I saw silent weeping people pace
    Slowly along the circle of the valley
    As we at holy festivals process.
Then, as my eyes moved from their faces down,   10
    I saw (amazing thing!) each one of them
    Contorted in-between the chest and chin;
I saw their faces had been turned right round,
    And of necessity they travelled backwards,
    Since looking to the front was not allowed.[1]
Perhaps in palsy's worst paralysis
    There have been people twisted in this way;
    But I don't think so: I have not seen this.
And now – God grant you profit from your reading! –
    You may well, Reader, readily imagine   20
    If I was able to refrain from weeping,
The instant that, so close at hand, I'd seen
    Our image so distorted, and the eyes
    Bathing the buttocks and the cleft between.
Of course I wept, leaning upon a scar
    Of the rugged ridge, until my guide demanded:
    'Are you as foolish as the others are?
Here pity lives when it is wholly dead:
    What is more wicked than to deprecate
    God's final judgement once it is declared?   30
Raise, raise your head, until you see the one
    For whom earth opened[2] in the Thebans' eyes;
    To whom they shouted: "Where are you going down
To, Amphiaraus? Why leave the fight?"[3]
    And he just went on falling till he came
    To Minos by whom all of us are caught.[4]

---

1. Those who wished to see into the future cannot now even look straight ahead. There is a sharp
contrast between their high intellectual pretensions and their ridiculous deformity.

2. Literally.

3. Amphiaraus was one of the seven kings who besieged Thebes (see XIV: 68–9 above, and note).
He accurately foresaw his own death in that campaign.

4. See V: 4–12 above.

Mira c'ha fatto petto delle spalle:
    perché volle veder troppo davante,
    di retro guarda e fa retroso calle.
Vedi Tiresia, che mutò sembiante   40
    quando di maschio femmina divenne
    cangiandosi le membra tutte quante –
e prima, poi, ribatter li convenne
    li duo serpenti avvolti, con la verga,
    che riavesse le maschili penne.
Aronta è quei ch'al ventre li s'atterga,
    che ne' monti di Luni, dove ronca
    lo Carrarese che di sotto alberga,
ebbe tra' bianchi marmi la spelonca
    per sua dimora onde a guardar le stelle   50
    e 'l mar non li era la veduta tronca.
E quella che ricuopre le mammelle,
    che tu non vedi, con le treccie sciolte,
    e ha di là ogni pilosa pelle,
Manto fu, che cercò per terre molte:
    poscia si puose là dove nacqu'io,
    onde un poco mi piace che m'ascolte.
Poscia che 'l padre suo di vita uscio
    e venne serva la città di Baco,
    questa gran tempo per lo mondo gìo.   60
Suso in Italia bella giace un laco,
    a piè dell'alpe che serra Lamagna
    sovra Tiralli, c'ha nome Benaco.
Per mille fonti, credo, e più si bagna,
    tra Garda e Val Camonica e Pennino[a]
    dell'acqua che nel detto laco stagna.
Luogo è nel mezzo là dove 'l trentino
    pastore e quel di Brescia e 'l veronese
    segnar porìa, se fesse quel cammino.
Siede Peschiera, bello e forte arnese   70
    da fronteggiar bresciani e bergamaschi,
    ove la riva intorno più discese.

a. The text is uncertain here. Another reading is 'Appennino', which would then be the subject of the verb 'si bagna', giving the meaning 'The Appennines, between Garda and Val Camonica, are bathed…'

Notice his shoulders where his chest should be:
>   Because he wished to see too far ahead,
>   He looks behind and he walks backwardly.
Tiresias next; he changed his looks when he   40
>   Turned from the man he was into a woman,
>   Which altered all his members utterly;
And after that he had to strike again
>   The copulating serpents with his wand
>   Before his manliness came back to him.[5]
Aruns[6] backs onto that one's paunch; he found –
>   In hills of Luni where the Carrarese,
>   Who live beneath them, cultivate the land –
A lonely cave within white marble stone,
>   And made his home there, where the sea and stars   50
>   Were always, without hindrance, to be seen.
And she who uses her loose locks to hide
>   Her breasts, which are not visible to you,
>   She who has hairy skin on the other side,
Was Manto[7], who went searching far and wide;
>   She settled down at last where I was born;[8]
>   And on this topic something must be said.[9]
When her father shook off this mortal coil,
>   And Bacchus' sacred city[10] was enslaved,
>   She wandered through the world for a long while.   60
There lies a lake in lovely Italy,
>   North of the Tyrol, which is called Benaco[11],
>   Under the mountains bounding Germany.
A thousand streams, I think, or even more
>   Bathe Garda, Val Camonica, and Pennino,
>   And all flow from the lake that is up there.
In that lake's centre is a place[12] where three
>   Bishops – of Trent, of Brescia, of Verona –
>   Might bless us, if they ever went that way.
A beautiful strong fortress to confront   70
>   The Brescians and the Bergamese – Peschiera –
>   Stands where the shore is at its lowest point.

---

5. The legend is that, after separating two copulating serpents, Tiresias was turned into a woman. Seven years later he struck the same two serpents again and was changed back into a man.
6. A Tuscan soothsayer, who foretold the war between Pompey and Caesar and the latter's triumph.
7. Daughter of Tiresias.
8. Mantua.
9. The account of the founding of Mantua which follows is at odds with what Virgil says in his *Aeneid* x: 198–200. The apparent digression here enables Dante to scout the notion of deciding on the foundation of a city, or the naming of it, by casting lots or looking for auguries.
10. Thebes.
11. The modern Lake Garda.
12. Probably the island now known as Lechi, on which there was a church subject to the authority of three bishops.

Ivi convien che tutto quanto caschi
    ciò che 'n grembo a Benaco star non pò,
    e fassi fiume giù per verdi paschi.
Tosto che l'acqua a correr mette co[b],
    non più Benaco, ma Mencio si chiama
    fino a Governol, dove cade in Po.
Non molto ha corso ch'el trova una lama,
    nella qual si distende e la 'mpaluda,   80
    e suol di state talor esser grama.
Quindi passando la vergine cruda
    vide terra, nel mezzo del pantano,
    sanza coltura e d'abitanti nuda.
Lì, per fuggire ogni consorzio umano,
    ristette con suoi servi a far sue arti,
    e visse, e vi lasciò suo corpo vano.
Li uomini poi che 'ntorno erano sparti
    s'accolsero a quel luogo, ch'era forte
    per lo pantan ch'avea da tutte parti.   90
Fer la città sovra quell'ossa morte
    e, per colei che 'l luogo prima elesse,
    Mantua l'appellar sanz'altra sorte.
Già fuor le genti sue dentro più spesse,
    prima che la mattia da Casalodi
    da Pinamonte inganno ricevesse.
Però t'assenno che se tu mai odi
    originar la mia terra altrimenti,
    la verità nulla menzogna frodi.'
E io: 'Maestro, i tuoi ragionamenti   100
    mi son sì certi e prendon sì mia fede
    che li altri mi sarìen carboni spenti.
Ma dimmi, della gente che procede,
    se tu ne vedi alcun degno di nota,
    ché solo a ciò la mia mente rifiede.'
Allor mi disse: 'Quel che dalla gota
    porge la barba in su le spalle brune
    fu, quando Grecia fu di maschi vota

b. i.e. 'mette capo' ('begins').

There all the water that cannot be held
    Within Benaco's bosom overflows:
    This river runs through many a green field.
The moment that this water starts to flow,
    Men know it as the Mincio, not Benaco,
    Till at Governolo it joins the Po.
It comes to flat land after a short way,
    On which it spreads itself into a marsh –   80
    And sometimes in the summer it runs dry.
When she went by that way the uncouth maid
    Discovered land, in the middle of the marsh,
    Untilled, and wholly uninhabited.
There, to avoid all human intercourse,
    She and her slaves stayed, to pursue her arts[13] –
    Lived there, then left her body spiritless.[14]
The people who were scattered round about
    Gathered there then, since it was fensible
    By reason of the marsh surrounding it.   90
They built the city over her dead bones,
    And called it Mantua, because she chose it,
    And sought no augury but her remains.
Once the inhabitants were more numerous,
    Before the foolishness of Casalodi
    Was caught by Pinamonte's sly device.[15]
So I suggest that, if you ever see
    A different record of my city's birth,
    You let no fable drive the truth away.'
'Master,' I answered, 'all you've said upon   100
    This matter's so persuasive any version
    Were dust and ashes in comparison.
But say, among these people moving on,
    If you see anybody worth our notice,
    Since all my thoughts turn back to that alone.'
Then he replied: 'That man who lets his beard
    Spread from his cheeks and down his swarthy shoulders
    Was, at a time when Greece was so devoid

13. Magic arts.
14. That is, when she died and soul and body were separated.
15. Alberto da Casalodi, a Guelph Count of Mantua, was persuaded by a Ghibelline lord, Pinamonte de'
    Buonaccorsi, to expel many of the city's nobles. Once they were gone Pinamonte was able, in 1272,
    to seize the city for himself.

sì ch'a pena rimaser per le cune,
    augure, e diede 'l punto con Calcanta   110
    in Aulide a tagliar la prima fune.
Eurìpilo ebbe nome, e così 'l canta
    l'alta mia tragedìa in alcun loco:
    ben lo sai tu che la sai tutta quanta.
Quell'altro che ne' fianchi è così poco,
    Michele Scotto fu, che veramente
    delle magiche frode seppe il gioco.
Vedi Guido Bonatti – vedi Asdente,
    ch'avere inteso al cuoio ed allo spago
    ora vorrebbe, ma tardi si pente.   120
Vedi le triste che lasciaron l'ago,
    la spuola e 'l fuso, e fecersi 'ndivine –
    fecer malie con erbe e con imago.
Ma vienne omai, ché già tiene 'l confine
    d'amendue li emisperi e tocca l'onda
    sotto Sobilia Caino e le spine –
e già iernotte fu la luna tonda:
    ben ten de' ricordar, ché non ti nocque
    alcuna volta per la selva fonda.'
Sì mi parlava, ed andavamo introcque.   130

Of males that there were scarcely sons in cradles,[16]
    The augur who, in company with Calchas[17],   110
    At Aulis fixed the time to cut the cables –
Eurypylus[18]. In my high tragedy[19]
    You'll find him mentioned in a certain passage.
    You'll know the place: you've read it thoroughly.
And that one over there was Michael Scot[20],
    That one whose hips are slim; he really, truly
    Knew every magic trick and every sleight.
See Guido Bonatti[21]; and Asdente[22] that
    Is wishing he had stuck to thread and leather,
    But whose repentance has arrived too late.   120
See the sad women who gave up the needle,
    Shuttle, and spindle to become diviners;
    They worked with herbs,[23] or sometimes a wax model.[24]
But let us go now; for already Cain's
    Touching the boundary of both hemispheres
    Below Seville, and watering his thorns;[25]
Last night the moon was full: you really should
    Remember this: the moon, you must recall,
    Was not unhelpful in the first dark wood.'
Those were his words, and we walked on meanwhile.   130

16. Most of the men were embarking for Troy.
17. A famous augur, who advised a human sacrifice to gain a favourable wind for the Grecian fleet.
18. An augur sent by the Greeks to consult the oracle of Apollo at Delphi about their departure for Troy. It was one function of soothsayers to decide on the best time to begin any great undertaking.
19. Virgil calls his *Aeneid* a 'tragedy' because it is written in high, epic style.
20. A Scottish doctor and philosopher at the court of Frederick II of Sicily.
21. Another astrologer at the court of Frederick II.
22. A shoemaker of Parma in the second half of the 13th century, also known for predicting the future.
23. For magic potions.
24. Effigies, into which pins could be stuck or which could be melted down, used to cast spells on people.
25. Cain with a thorn-bush corresponds to our Man in the Moon. The moon is now setting: it is about 6:00 a.m.

CANTO XXI

Dante and Virgil look down into the fifth ditch of the eighth circle, which is amazingly dark. It is filled with boiling pitch – a reminder to Dante of the Venetian arsenals with men working through the winter to repair their ships. At first only the surface of the pitch is visible. Later Dante learns that barrators – those traffickers in public offices and other abusers of positions of public trust for profit – are boiling in this pitch, and that there are devils at hand to push them under.

Dante is terrified to see a black demon running towards them. He is carrying over his shoulder a human body, a new arrival among the barrators. Throwing this person onto the ground, for the other devils to deal with, he announces that he is rushing back to Lucca where there are so many more barrators requiring his attention.

Virgil suggests that the frightened Dante should hide behind a rock, and goes to parley with the devils. Virgil is confident that he can deal with the situation but, even when it seems that he has come to an agreement with the devils, Dante is still afraid.

Muckrake, who is acting as a representative of the devils, restrains his followers from attacking Dante, as they are eager to do, and sends ten of them to guide Virgil and Dante on their journey. He says, truly, that the next bridge that they are looking for has been destroyed, and also, untruly, that there is another bridge further on, to which his devils will lead them.

Dante is still terrified by the devils, but Virgil, who lacks his usual caution, feels quite safe. The devils salute their leader in an unusual manner, and he sounds an unusual bugle as signal for them to depart.

The most striking feature of this canto is its harsh comedy. The demons here are reminiscent of those shown in so many medieval depictions of the Last Judgement, both terrifying and ridiculous.

Così, di ponte in ponte – altro parlando   1
  che la mia comedìa cantar non cura –
  venimmo, e tenavamo il colmo quando
restammo per veder l'altra fessura
  di Malebolge e li altri pianti vani –
  e vidila mirabilmente oscura.
Quale nell'arzanà de' Viniziani
  bolle l'inverno la tenace pece
  a rimpalmare i legni lor non sani,
ché navicar non ponno – in quella vece   10
  chi fa suo legno novo e chi ristoppa
  le coste a quel che più viaggi fece,
chi ribatte da proda e chi da poppa,
  altri fa remi e altri volge sarte,
  chi terzeruolo e artimon rintoppa –
tal, non per foco, ma per divin'arte,
  bollia là giuso una pegola spessa,
  che 'nviscava la ripa d'ogni parte.
I' vedea lei, ma non vedea in essa
  mai che le bolle che 'l bollor levava,   20
  e gonfiar tutta, e riseder compressa.
Mentr'io là giù fisamente mirava,
  lo duca mio, dicendo: 'Guarda, guarda!'
  mi trasse a sé del loco dov'io stava.
Allor mi volsi come l'om cui tarda
  di veder quel che li convien fuggire
  e cui paura subita sgagliarda,
che, per veder, non indugia 'l partire –
  e vidi dietro a noi un diavol nero
  correndo su per lo scoglio venire.   30
Ahi quant'elli era nell'aspetto fero!
  e quanto mi parea nell'atto acerbo,
  con l'ali aperte e sovra i piè leggero!
L'omero suo, ch'era aguto e superbo,
  carcava un peccator con ambo l'anche,
  e quei tenea de' piè ghermito il nerbo.

And so we travelled on from bridge to bridge,   1
    Speaking of things with which my comedy
    Is not concerned, and when we'd climbed the ridge,
We saw the next crack open in the rock[1]
    Of Eviltiers, with all its futile weeping –
    It seemed to me exceptionally black.
As, when Venetian arsenals are working
    In winter, sticky pitch is on the boil,
    For caulking any vessels that are leaking,
Since nobody can sail; and some repair   10
    Their ships and make them good as new; some others
    Strengthen a frame before it's gone too far;
Some hammer nails in prow and stern; meanwhile
    Some fashion oars, and some fresh sheets and shrouds;
    Some patch the jib, and others the mainsail –
So here, though not by fire, but by God's art,
    A stretch of sticky pitch was boiling over,
    And clinging to the sides all round the pit.[2]
I saw the mass, but could not see inside it,
    Only the bubbles coming to the surface,   20
    As it all swelled, then once again subsided.
While I was staring down at this, my guide
    Said to me suddenly: 'Look out! Look out!'
    And then he grabbed me up against his side.
I turned around, like somebody who is
    Eager to see what he is fleeing from,
    Whom sudden fear has weakened at the knees,
And yet does not slow down, but still looks back;
    At which I saw behind us a black devil
    Racing our way along the rocky crag.   30
And what a devil! What a savage sight!
    He looked like sheer ferocity in action,
    With wings spread wide, and light upon his feet!
Upon one shoulder, that was hunched up high,
    He had a sinner's haunches, while in front
    It was his ankle-bones he held him by.

1. This is the fifth ditch of the eighth circle (Eviltiers), occupied by those who have trafficked in public offices or been in other ways guilty of the misuse of public positions.

2. The simile's most obvious point of comparison is simply the boiling pitch, but the description of the Venetian shipyards is developed far beyond this. The apparent digression is justified, because it sets the tone for the busy and tumultuous canto it introduces.

Del nostro ponte disse: 'O Malebranche[a],
    ecco un delli anzian di santa Zita!
    Mettetel sotto, ch'i' torno per anche
a quella terra che n'è ben fornita: 40
    ogn'uom v'è barattier, fuor che Bonturo –
    del no per li denar vi si fa ita[b].'
Là giù il buttò, e per lo scoglio duro
    si volse – e mai non fu mastino sciolto
    con tanta fretta a seguitar lo furo.
Quel s'attuffò, e tornò su convolto –
    ma i demon che del ponte avean coperchio
    gridar: 'Qui non ha luogo il Santo Volto:
qui si nuota altrimenti che nel Serchio!
    Però, se tu non vuo' di nostri graffi,   50
    non far sopra la pegola soverchio.'
Poi l'addentar con più di cento raffi,
    disser: 'Coverto convien che qui balli,
    sì che, se puoi, nascosamente accaffi.'
Non altrimenti i cuoci a' lor vassalli
    fanno attuffare in mezzo la caldaia
    la carne con li uncin, perché non galli.
Lo buon maestro: 'Acciò che non si paia
    che tu ci sia,' mi disse, 'giù t'acquatta
    dopo uno scheggio, ch'alcun schermo t'aia;   60
e per nulla offension che mi sia fatta,
    non temer tu, ch'i' ho le cose conte,
    ché altra volta fui a tal baratta.'
Poscia passò di là dal co del ponte,
    e com'el giunse in su la ripa sesta,
    mestier li fu d'aver sicura fronte.
Con quel furore e con quella tempesta
    ch'escono i cani a dosso al poverello
    che di subito chiede ove s'arresta,
usciron quei di sotto al ponticello,   70
    e volser contra lui tutt'i runcigli –
    ma el gridò: 'Nessun di voi sia fello!

a. The generic, and highly descriptive, name (lit. 'Evil Claws') for the devils in this ditch.
b. A Latin word (meaning 'thus'), signifying assent.

He called out from our bridge: 'Look here, Clawboys!
    I've brought along an elder of Saint Zita!3
    Just pop him in;4 I'm rushing back because
The city where I got him's got so many –   40
    Barrators all, except for old Bonturo;5
    "Nay" there turns into "Yea" for ready money.'6
He flung him down upon the stony cliff,
    And turned to go: no watchdog off the leash
    Was ever in such haste to catch a thief.
The sinner plunged, then came up black as pitch;
    At which, 'The Holy Face here's out of place!'7
    Hollered the demons hidden by the bridge.
'It's not like swimming in the Serchio8 here!
    So, unless you have a mind to taste our hooks,   50
    Don't stick your head above the boiling tar.'
They got their teeth into him hungrily,
    A hundred hooks, and said: 'Stay under cover;
    Steal still, if you can steal round stealthily.'
Just so do cooks, when meat is in the pot,
    Order their scullions to press it under
    With their long forks, because it must not float.
'So that your presence may remain concealed,'
    My kindly master said, 'you must crouch down
    Behind a rock, to serve you as a shield.   60
And then whatever outrage I endure,
    Don't be afraid: I have it all in hand:
    I've been in such a squabble once before.'9
With that he walked on to the bridge's end
    But, when he came upon the sixth embankment,
    Found it more effort to look unconcerned.
With all that fury and that storm of storms
    With which the dogs rush out on some poor beggar
    Who's halted at the door to beg for alms,
Out from beneath the bridge the devils flew   70
    And turned their hooks against him; but he shouted:
    'I'll have no trouble now from any of you!

---

3. A leading citizen of Lucca. Zita was born near that city, where she died in 1278. She was popularly acclaimed a saint.

4. Into the boiling pitch.

5. This is said ironically, to indicate that Bonturo Dati (fl. early 14th century in Lucca) is worse than any.

6. The reference is to the selling of votes.

7. The Holy Face is a famous crucifix of black wood still venerated in the Cathedral of San Martino in Lucca. The devils' taunting chant is inspired by the pitch-blackened face of this new arrival in the Inferno.

8. A river near Lucca.

9. Virgil is referring to his previous descent into the Inferno, mentioned at IX: 22–30 above.

Innanzi che l'uncin vostro mi pigli,
    traggasi avante l'un di voi che m'oda,
    e poi d'arruncigliarmi si consigli.'
Tutti gridaron: 'Vada Malacoda^c!';
    per ch'un si mosse – e li altri stetter fermi –
    e venne a lui dicendo: 'Che li approda?'
'Credi tu, Malacoda, qui vedermi
    esser venuto,' disse 'l mio maestro,   80
    'sicuro già da tutti vostri schermi,
sanza voler divino e fato destro?
    Lascian'andar, ché nel cielo è voluto
    ch'i' mostri altrui questo cammin silvestro.'
Allor li fu l'orgoglio sì caduto
    che si lasciò cascar l'uncino a' piedi,
    e disse alli altri: 'Omai non sia feruto.'
E 'l duca mio a me: 'O tu che siedi
    tra li scheggion del ponte quatto quatto,
    sicuramente omai a me ti riedi.'   90
Per ch'io mi mossi, ed a lui venni ratto,
    e i diavoli si fecer tutti avanti,
    sì ch'io temetti ch'ei tenesser patto –
così vid'io già temer li fanti
    ch'uscivan patteggiati di Caprona,
    veggendo sé tra nemici cotanti.
I' m'accostai con tutta la persona
    lungo 'l mio duca, e non torceva li occhi
    dalla sembianza lor, ch'era non bona.
Ei chinavan li raffi e: 'Vuo' che 'l tocchi,'   100
    diceva l'un con l'altro, 'in sul groppone?'
    E rispondìen: 'Sì, fa' che lile accocchi!'
Ma quel demonio che tenea sermone
    col duca mio si volse tutto presto
    e disse: 'Posa, posa, Scarmiglione^d!'
Poi disse a noi: 'Più oltre andar per questo
    iscoglio non si può, però che giace
    tutto spezzato al fondo l'arco sesto.

c. Name (lit. 'Evil Tail') of the leader of the devils in this ditch.
d. Formed from 'scarmigliare', 'to ruffle (hair)'.

Before you start to use your hooks on me,
 Let one of you step forward. Hear me out:
 Then see if it is wise to grapple me.'
At this they hollered: 'Muckrake ought to go!'
 And so one moved – with all the others waiting –
 Towards him, asking: 'What good will this do?'
'Do you imagine, Muckrake, I have got
 As far as this already,' asked my master,   80
 'Unharmed by you, who failed to keep me out,
Without the favour and the will of God?
 Let us pass on: it is decreed in heaven
 That I must show another this rough road.'
Muckrake was now completely at a loss,
 And felt his own hook slipping through his fingers,
 And said to the others: 'Leave him after this.'
Then Virgil said to me: 'You, crouching there
 Behind those rocky boulders on the bridge,
 You may come back: there's nothing now to fear.'   90
So I came out, and ran towards my guide;
 And all the devils started edging forward,
 Which made me wonder if they'd keep their word:
So I remember Pisan infantry
 Under safe conduct coming from Caprona
 In fear, surrounded by the enemy.[10]
I kept on drawing closer to my guide,
 And did not move my eyes away from them,
 Whose attitude seemed anything but kind.
They lowered their hooks, and 'Shall I touch him up,'   100
 One asked the other devils, 'on the back?'
 And all the others answered, 'Make him hop!'
But Muckrake, who was having a discussion
 With my good guide, turned round at that abruptly,
 And said to him: 'Bollweevil, don't be rushing!'
'You cannot go much further on this ridge,'
 He said to us, 'because down there it's broken:
 Nothing but rubble's left of the sixth bridge.

---

10. Dante took part in the campaign of the Tuscan Guelphs in 1289 which resulted in the capture of
 the Pisan fortress of Caprona.

E se l'andare avante pur vi piace,
   andatevene su per questa grotta –   110
   presso è un altro scoglio che via face.
Ier, più oltre cinqu'ore che quest'otta,
   mille dugento con sessanta sei
   anni compié che qui la via fu rotta.
Io mando verso là di questi miei
   a riguardar s'alcun se ne sciorina:
   gite con lor, che non saranno rei.'
'Tra'ti avante Alichino, e Calcabrina,'
   cominciò elli a dire, 'e tu, Cagnazzo –
   e Barbariccia guidi la decina.   120
Libicocco vegn'oltre e Draghignazzo,
   Ciriatto sannuto e Graffiacane
   e Farfarello e Rubicante pazzo.ᵉ
Cercate intorno le boglienti pane:
   costor sian salvi infino all'altro scheggio
   che tutto intero va sopra le tane.'
'Ohmè, maestro, che è quel ch'i' veggio?'
   diss'io. 'Deh, sanza scorta andianci soli,
   se tu sa' ir, ch'i' per me non la cheggio.
Se tu se' sì accorto come suoli,   130
   non vedi tu ch'e' digrignan li denti,
   e con le ciglia ne minaccian duoli?'
Ed elli a me: 'Non vo' che tu paventi:
   lasciali digrignar pur a lor senno,
   ch'e' fanno ciò per li lessi dolenti.'
Per l'argine sinistro volta dienno –
   ma prima avea ciascun la lingua stretta
   coi denti verso lor duca per cenno,
ed elli avea del cul fatto trombetta.

---

e. The name 'Alichino' derives from the French Hallequin, one of the devils engaged in the legendary
devilish hunt of sinners, see XIII: 124–6, and also Boccaccio, *Decameron*, V: 8. The name 'Calcabrina'
suggests 'Passes over the hoar-frost', perhaps with reference to his speed. 'Cagnazzo' means 'Nasty
Dog'. Barbariccia means 'Curly Beard'. 'Libicocco' is perhaps a combination of 'libeccio' (south-west
wind) and 'scirocco' (sirocco, south-east wind). 'Draghignazzo' is again, possibly, a combination of
'drago' ('dragon') and 'ghigno' ('sneer'), with the suffix '-azzo' denoting nastiness. 'Ciriatto' (who is
shown with tusks) means 'Boar'. 'Graffiacane' means 'Scratch-Dog'. The etimology of 'Farfarello' is
not clear, and the name can be interpreted in many ways: it was, perhaps, a real nickname in Dante's
time. 'Rubicante' means 'Red' or 'Rabid'.

So if you really want to go ahead,
    Then make your way along this same embankment: 110
    Another bridge nearby can be your road.[11]
Yesterday, five hours later than this hour,
    One thousand and two hundred and sixty-six
    Years had passed since the bridge was broken here.[12]
I'm sending some men out there to discover
    If anybody's trying to get some air:
    You go with them; they won't be any bother.'
'One pace forward, Flibbertigibbet and
    Pollutus,' then he ordered, 'and Hellhound;
    Take nine men, Bandersnatch, and take command.   120
Step forward, Scumbag, and Snapdragon there,
    And toothy Hogwash, and beside him Scrotter,
    And Dandiprat, and raving mad Hacksore.
Scout everywhere around the boiling pitch.
    And keep this couple safe until that spur
    That goes across the ditches like a bridge.'
'Master,' I said, 'alas, what's this I see?
    Can't we go on alone, without an escort?
    We don't need any, if you know the way.
And you, who up to now have been so shrewd,   130
    Haven't you noticed how they grind their teeth,
    All of them looking daggers, all black-browed?'
'I would not have you fearful,' he replied.
    'Let them go grinding to their hearts' content:
    They're thinking of those wretches who are stewed.'
They wheeled along the ridge to the left hand;
    But first they stuck their tongues out as a signal
    Directed to the leader of their band,
And he had made his arse blow like a bugle.

11. It is true that the sixth bridge has been destroyed, but not that there is another bridge nearby.
12. As a result of the earthquake at the time of the Crucifixion.

CANTO XXII

This canto opens with a vivid description of medieval warfare, such as Dante had himself witnessed, followed by his comment that he had never before heard on the field of battle such a signal as issued from Bandersnatch at the end of the previous canto. By recalling this signal he sets a humorous tone for the events which follow.

Dante and Virgil continue their journey, escorted by the ten demons. As Dante says, who else would one expect to be escorted by in the Inferno? The barrators are leaping into the air like dolphins, but not, as dolphins do, to warn sailors of a coming storm, but in order to get some brief respite from their torment. Any sinner who appears above the surface of the boiling pitch is likely to be caught by the devils' grapnels. Soon one is caught: he is brought out of the pitch on the end of a hook, like an otter.

This sinner, whom Dante does not name but who appears to be a certain Ciampolo, explains who he is and why he is being punished, and mentions two of his companions. There is a fierce argument, and some even fiercer physical maltreatment, while the demons consider what to do with him. However, they, who delight in deceiving and tormenting, are themselves deceived and tormented by Ciampolo, who offers to call other sinners up out of the ditch by whistling and so give the devils more people to torment. It is a trick, of course, and Ciampolo manages to get away. The devils turn on each other to vent their anger and frustration. Two of them, Pollutus and Flibbertigibbet, are so intent on fighting that they tumble into the boiling pitch. This stops the fight, but they still cannot get out onto the embankment, because their wings are sticky with pitch. While the other devils are preoccupied, apparently with trying to help their two boiling companions, Dante and Virgil go on their way.

Io vidi già cavalier muover campo,   I
    e cominciare stormo e far lor mostra,
    e tal volta partir per loro scampo –
corridor vidi per la terra vostra,
    o Aretini, e vidi gir gualdane,
    fedir torneamenti e correr giostra
quando con trombe, e quando con campane,
    con tamburi e con cenni di castella,
    e con cose nostrali e con istrane –
né già con sì diversa cennamella   10
    cavalier vidi muover né pedoni,
    né nave a segno di terra o di stella.
Noi andavam con li diece demoni –
    ahi fiera compagnia! – ma nella chiesa
    coi santi, ed in taverna co' ghiottoni.
Pur alla pegola era la mia intesa,
    per veder della bolgia ogni contegno
    e della gente ch'entro v'era incesa.
Come i dalfini, quando fanno segno
    a' marinar con l'arco della schiena   20
    che s'argomentin di campar lor legno,
talor così, ad alleggiar la pena,
    mostrav'alcun de' peccatori il dosso,
    e nascondea in men che non balena.
E come all'orlo dell'acqua d'un fosso
    stanno i ranocchi pur col muso fori,
    sì che celano i piedi e l'altro grosso,
sì stavan d'ogne parte i peccatori,
    ma come s'appressava Barbariccia,
    così si ritraén sotto i bollori.   30
I' vidi, e anco il cor me n'accapriccia,
    uno aspettar così – com'elli 'ncontra
    ch'una rana rimane ed altra spiccia –
e Graffiacan, che li era più di contra,
    li arrunciglò le 'mpegolate chiome
    e trassel su, che mi parve una lontra.

I had seen cavalry strike camp, move out,   1
    Lead an assault, or muster on parade;
    I'd even seen them beating a retreat;
Over your territory I'd seen the scouts,
    O Aretines, and raiding parties ranging;[1]
    Seen clash of tournament, seen rush of joust;
With trumpeting sometimes, and sometimes bells,[2]
    With thud of drums, and signals from the castles,
    Some of them ours, and some from somewhere else;
But never yet had I seen foot or horse   10
    Move in response to such a bagpipe-blast[3] –
    Nor ship steering by landmarks or by stars.
So led by the ten demons we went on:
    What dreadful company! But, as they say,
    'With saints in church, with gluttons at the inn.'
All my attention was upon the pitch:
    I wanted to make out each single detail,
    And all the people burning in the ditch.
Just as a dolphin, with its arching back,
    Signals to sailors that they must take care   20
    To save their vessel from impending wreck,[4]
Just so at times, to mitigate his pain,
    One of the sinners would disclose his back,
    Then quick as lightning hide it once again.
And as, just at a ditch's edge, frogs squat,
    And only poke their muzzles out of water,
    Keeping their feet and bodies out of sight,
So here on every hand the sinners crouch;
    But at the instant Bandersnatch approaches,
    They just as quickly hide in boiling pitch.   30
I saw – the memory still makes me writhe –
    One sinner slow to move, as it can happen
    One frog delays, another's quick to dive;
The nearest devil, who happened to be Scrotter,
    Got his hook into his pitch-blackened locks
    And drew him out: he looked just like an otter.

1. Dante was present at the Battle of Campaldino (1289) at which the Ghibellines of Arezzo were defeated by the Florentine Guelphs.
2. Each of the Italian states had at this time a *carroccio*, or war-wagon, drawn by oxen, and furnished with a bell: it was a rallying-point in battle.
3. This is the signal mentioned at XXI: 139.
4. It was an old tradition that dolphins warned sailors of coming storms. The comparison here of dolphins to sinners is visually exact, but in other respects deliberately at odds: the dolphins help the sailors, while the sinners are thinking only of helping themselves – one of Dante's many subtle ways of stressing the hellishness of hell.

I' sapea già di tutti quanti il nome,
    sì li notai quando fuorono eletti,
    e poi ch'e' si chiamaro, attesi come.
'O Rubicante, fa' che tu li metti   40
    li unghioni a dosso, sì che tu lo scuoi!'
    gridavan tutti insieme i maladetti.
E io: 'Maestro mio, fa', se tu puoi,
    che tu sappi chi è lo sciagurato
    venuto a man delli avversari suoi.'
Lo duca mio li s'accostò a lato,
    domandollo ond'ei fosse, e quei rispuose:
    'I' fui del regno di Navarra nato.
Mia madre a servo d'un segnor mi pose
    che m'avea generato d'un ribaldo,   50
    distruggitor di sé e di sue cose.
Poi fui famiglia del buon re Tebaldo:
    quivi mi misi a far barratteria;
    di ch'io rendo ragione in questo caldo.'
E Ciriatto, a cui di bocca uscìa
    d'ogni parte una sanna come a porco,
    li fe' sentir come l'una sdrucia.
Tra male gatte era venuto il sorco –
    ma Barbariccia il chiuse con le braccia
    e disse: 'State in là, mentr'io lo 'nforco.'   60
E al maestro mio volse la faccia:
    'Domanda,' disse, 'ancor, se più disii
    saper da lui, prima ch'altri 'l disfaccia[a].'
Lo duca dunque: 'Or di', delli altri rii
    conosci tu alcun che sia latino
    sotto la pece?' E quelli: 'I' mi partii,
poco è, da un che fu di là vicino –
    così foss'io ancor con lui coperto,
    ch'i' non temerei unghia né uncino!'
E Libicocco: 'Troppo avem sofferto,'   70
    disse, e preseli 'l braccio col runciglio,
    sì che, stracciando, ne portò un lacerto.

---

a. At that time 'disfare' had the sense of 'kill'. The expression is therefore hyperbolical, since the damned cannot be killed.

(I knew their names already: I'd been rather
    Careful to listen when I heard them chosen,
    And then I'd noted what they called each other.)
'Now Hacksore, it is up to you to sever   40
    The skin from off his back: don't waste your talons!'
    The accursèd demons shouted all together.
And I said: 'Master, if you're able, please
    Find out the name of that unfortunate
    Who's just been captured by his enemies.'
My leader asked him, having drawn quite near,
    About his birthplace, and the wretch replied:
    'My homeland was the kingdom of Navarre.[5]
My mother placed me in service to a lord,
    Since she had borne me to a waster who   50
    Destroyed himself and everything he had.
I found myself in good King Thibaut's[6] court;
    And there I gave myself to barratry,
    For which I pay the reckoning in this heat.'
Then Hogwash, from whose mouth, each side, stuck out
    A wild boar's tusk, allowed him to discover
    How just the one of them could lacerate.
Now the fiends want to play at cat and mouse.
    But Bandersnatch embraces him, and cries:
    'I'll see to him! You keep away from us!'   60
Then, turning to my guide, he said: 'Ask on,
    If there is something more you want to know;
    Quickly, before somebody does him in.'
At that my guide said: 'Tell me: do you know
    Of any sinners here who are Italian
    Under the pitch?' The shade replied: 'Just now
I've come from one who lived not far away:[7]
    I wish I were still covered up with him!
    Then hooks and claws would strike no fear in me.'
Then Scumbag said: 'This has gone far enough!'   70
    And caught him on his arm so with his grapnel
    He tore the flesh and pulled a muscle off.

5. Nothing is known of him apart from what Dante says, except that the ancient commentators give his name as Ciampolo.

6. King Thibaut II of Navarre (reigned 1253–70).

7. From Sardinia.

Draghignazzo anco i volle dar di piglio
    giuso alle gambe – onde 'l decurio loro
    si volse intorno intorno con mal piglio.
Quand'elli un poco rappacciati foro,
    a lui, ch'ancor mirava sua ferita,
    domandò 'l duca mio sanza dimoro:
'Chi fu colui da cui mala partita
    di' che facesti per venire a proda?'   80
    Ed ei rispuose: 'Fu frate Gomita,
quel di Gallura, vasel d'ogne froda –
    ch'ebbe i nemici di suo donno in mano,
    e fe' sì lor che ciascun se ne loda.
Danar si tolse, e lasciolli di piano,
    sì com'e' dice – e nelli altri offici anche
    barattier fu non picciol, ma sovrano.
Usa con esso donno Michel Zanche
    di Logodoro – e a dir di Sardigna
    le lingue lor non si sentono stanche.   90
Ohmè, vedete l'altro che digrigna:
    i' direi anche, ma i' temo ch'ello
    non s'apparecchi a grattarmi la tigna.'
E 'l gran proposto, vòlto a Farfarello
    che stralunava li occhi per fedire,
    disse: 'Fatti 'n costà, malvagio uccello.'
'Se voi volete vedere o udire,'
    ricominciò lo spaurato appresso,
    'Toschi o Lombardi, io ne farò venire –
ma stieno i Malebranche un poco in cesso,   100
    sì ch'ei non teman delle lor vendette –
    e io, seggendo in questo luogo stesso,
per un ch'io son, ne farò venir sette
    quand'io suffolerò, com'è nostro uso
    di fare allor che fori alcun si mette.'
Cagnazzo a cotal motto levò 'l muso,
    crollando il capo, e disse: 'Odi malizia
    ch'elli ha pensata per gittarsi giuso!'

Snapdragon also seemed about to strike
 And tear his legs; at which their captain turned
 Right round, and gave them all an ugly look.
When they were calmer, and the sinner too
 Was silently still staring at his wound,
 My leader asked him without more ado:
'Who was that man from whom in evil hour,
 As you yourself have said, you separated?'   80
 The sinner then replied: 'Oh, that was Friar
Gomita from Gallura, full of fraud,[8]
 Who had his lord's foes under his control,
 And dealt with them in ways that they thought good.
He took their money, and he freed them all,
 As he admits; and was in other matters
 No petty jobber, but the nonpareil.
Michele Zanche from Logudoro's there[9]
 With him; they always talk about Sardinia;
 On that one subject their tongues never tire.   90
But see that demon grind his teeth and grin!
 I would say more, but I'm afraid that he
 Is just about to scratch my scabby skin.'
Their great commander turned to Dandiprat,
 Who rolled his eyes and seemed about to strike,
 And ordered: 'Get away, you filthy bat!'
'If you would really like to see or hear,'
 The sinner, somewhat reassured, went on,
 'Tuscans or Lombards, I can get them here.
But let the Clawboys stand apart somewhat,   100
 So my companions need not fear their vengeance;
 And I, still sitting on this selfsame spot,
For the one I am, will make seven appear,
 Simply by whistling, as our custom is
 To do whenever one of us gets clear.'
Hearing this, Hellhound lifted up his snout,
 And shook his head, and told them: 'That's a trick:
 This is his way to get back in the pit!'

8. Deputy of Nino Visconti of Pisa, judge of the district of Gallura in Sardinia (a possession of Pisa at that time). When Fra Gomita connived at the escape of some prisoners who were under his control, Nino had him hanged.

9. Little is known about his life. He was killed treacherously by his son-in-law, Branca Doria (see XXXIII).

Ond'ei, ch'avea lacciuoli a gran divizia,
　　rispuose: 'Malizioso son io troppo,　　　　　　　110
　　quand'io procuro a' miei maggior tristizia.'
Alichin non si tenne e, di rintoppo
　　alli altri, disse a lui: 'Se tu ti cali,
　　io non ti verrò dietro di gualoppo,
ma batterò sovra la pece l'ali –
　　lascisi 'l collo, e sia la ripa scudo,
　　a veder se tu sol più di noi vali.'
O tu che leggi, udirai nuovo ludo:
　　ciascun dall'altra costa li occhi volse –
　　quel prima ch'a ciò fare era più crudo.　　　　　120
Lo Navarrese ben suo tempo colse:
　　fermò le piante a terra, ed in un punto
　　saltò e dal proposto lor si sciolse.
Di che ciascun di colpa fu compunto,
　　ma quei più che cagion fu del difetto;
　　però si mosse e gridò: 'Tu se' giunto!'
Ma poco i valse, ché l'ali al sospetto
　　non potero avanzar: quelli andò sotto,
　　e quei drizzò volando suso il petto –
non altrimenti l'anitra di botto,　　　　　　　　130
　　quando 'l falcon s'appressa, giù s'attuffa,
　　ed ei ritorna su crucciato e rotto.
Irato Calcabrina della buffa,
　　volando dietro li tenne, invaghito
　　che quei campasse per aver la zuffa;
e come 'l barattier fu disparito,
　　così volse li artigli al suo compagno,
　　e fu con lui sopra 'l fosso ghermito.
Ma l'altro fu bene sparvier grifagno
　　ad artigliar ben lui, ed amendue　　　　　　　140
　　cadder nel mezzo del bogliente stagno.
Lo caldo sghermitor subito fue –
　　ma però di levarsi era neente,
　　sì avieno invischiate l'ali sue.

Then he, who had no shortage of devices,
>Admitted: 'I'm a tricky chap indeed,   110
>Fixing to give my neighbours such surprises.'
Pollutus can't restrain himself at this;
>He says, to spite the others: 'If you dive,
>It won't be at a gallop I give chase:
I'll fly on faster wings above the pitch.
>To see if you are smarter than we are,
>We'll hide behind this ditch's lower edge.'
Now, Reader, here's a most unusual sport!
>All of them turned their eyes the other way,
>He first, the one against it at the start.[10]   120
The sinner acted when he saw their blunder:
>He planted both his feet upon the ground,
>And leapt, and broke away from their commander.
At this they were all stricken with remorse,
>Pollutus most, the cause of the disaster;
>And yet he moved, and shrieked: 'You're in my claws!'
Which was no help, for wings were not as fast
>As terror was: the Navarrese went under;
>And up the fiend flew, with uplifted breast.
Just so the duck's reaction's not belated,   130
>Who, when the hawk's upon her, plunges under,
>While he flies up again, tired and frustrated.
Flibbertigibbet, furious at the bluff,
>Flew at Pollutus, glad to see the sinner
>Escape, since he was keen to cut up rough;
And once the barrator was out of touch,
>He turned his talons onto his companion,
>And got to grips with him above the ditch.
And then Pollutus was not far behind
>In clawing like a falcon, till both tumbled   140
>Into the middle of the boiling pond.
They were, so great the heat, soon disentangled;
>And yet their wings stayed so gummed up with pitch
>Every attempt they made to rise was bungled.

---

10. This is Hellhound. See ll. 106–8.

Barbariccia, con li altri suoi dolente,
    quattro ne fe' volar dall'altra costa
    con tutt'i raffi, ed assai prestamente
di qua, di là discesero alla posta:
    porser li uncini verso li 'mpaniati,
    ch'eran già cotti dentro dalla crosta –   150
e noi lasciammo lor così 'mpacciati.

Then Bandersnatch, like all the rest annoyed,
    Sent four of them to line the other shore,
    All with their hooks; and these were soon deployed
On this side and on that, and standing to;
    And then they held their hooks out hopefully;
    But both the fiends by now were cooked right through.   150
And so we left them in that quandary.[11]

11. This incident, in which the duplicitous devils are themselves duped and made to fall out with each other, reveals the Inferno as a place (and a state of mind or soul) where there is nothing good and no one to trust, a place 'where there is no light at all' (IV: 151). The incident suggests also, in its grotesque comedy, that going against the moral order is not only a repulsive, but a ridiculous thing to do.

CANTO XXIII

After the tumult of the previous canto, this one begins on a quiet note. Dante and Virgil have escaped from the demons of the fifth ditch, and now they walk on while Dante thinks over the violent scenes they have just witnessed. Soon however, Dante has more troubling thoughts. What if the devils are coming after them?

Virgil understands Dante's concern, he snatches him up, and they slide down together into the sixth ditch of Eviltiers. There they see the hypocrites, who are punished by having to walk endlessly, weighed down by cloaks which gleam with gold outside, yet are lined with lead. Dante and Virgil walk in the same direction as these sinners.

Two of the hypocrites, the Bolognese Frisky Friars Catalano and Loderingo, are curious about Dante, since they realise he must be alive. He does not say who he is, but he does say he is a citizen of Florence. In reply the others say that they were chosen jointly to rule Florence, in order to patch up the political differences there, and that they only made matters worse. They were thought to be impartial, but they were not, and so they are punished for their hypocrisy.

Suddenly Dante notices a figure lying crucified across the road – Caiaphas, who urged the Jews to deliver Christ to the Romans for crucifixion, saying that it was right for one man to die for the good of the whole people. His father-in-law, Annas, who went along with this, is also crucified in the same manner.

Virgil asks Catalano if there is a way by which they may travel out of this ditch without calling on the dubious help of the black angels who guard the barrators. Catalano tells him they can climb up the broken rock, which was originally a bridge, and so find their way.

Virgil strides out, angered by the realisation that Muckrake deceived him into believing that there was an unbroken bridge there, and also by Catalano's mocking parting words. Dante follows his beloved guide.

Taciti, soli, sanza compagnia   1
    n'andavam l'un dinanzi e l'altro dopo,
    come i frati minor vanno per via.
Volt'era in su la favola d'Isopo
    lo mio pensier per la presente rissa,
    dov'el parlò della rana e del topo –
ché più non si pareggia 'mo' e 'issa'[a]
    che l'un con l'altro fa, se ben s'accoppia
    principio e fine con la mente fissa.
E come l'un pensier dell'altro scoppia,   10
    così nacque di quello un altro poi,
    che la prima paura mi fe' doppia.
Io pensava così: 'Questi per noi
    sono scherniti con danno e con beffa
    sì fatta ch'assai credo che lor nòi.
Se l'ira sovra 'l mal voler fa gueffa,
    ei ne verranno dietro più crudeli
    che 'l cane a quella lievre ch'elli acceffa.'
Già mi sentìa tutti arricciar li peli
    della paura, e stava in dietro intento,   20
    quand'io dissi: 'Maestro, se non celi
te e me tostamente, i' ho pavento
    de' Malebranche – noi li avem già dietro:
    io li 'magino sì che già li sento.'
E quei: 'S'i' fossi di piombato vetro,
    l'imagine di fuor tua non trarrei
    più tosto a me che quella d'entro impetro.
Pur mo venieno i tuo' pensier tra' miei,
    con simile atto e con simile faccia,
    sì che d'intrambi un sol consiglio fei.   30
S'elli è che sì la destra costa giaccia
    che noi possiam nell'altra bolgia scendere,
    noi fuggirem l'imaginata caccia.'
Già non compié di tal consiglio rendere
    ch'io li vidi venir con l'ali tese
    non molto lungi, per volerne prendere.

a. 'Mo' and 'issa' both mean 'now' in old Italian, 'mo' from the Latin 'modo', and 'issa' from the Latin 'ipsa (hora)'.

Alone, and silently, we went on further,   1
    One of us in the front and one behind,
    Like Friars Minor¹ when they walk together.
My thoughts all ran on that Aesopian fable
    Which gives the story of the frog and mouse²
    (Suggested to me by the recent quarrel);
For 'no' and 'nay' are not more like each other
    Than these two stories are, if you consider
    The start and close of each of them together.
And, as one thought gives rise to a further thought,   10
    Thinking about that fable made me think
    Of something that increased my former fright.
The thought was this: 'These fiends, because of us,
    Have been both injured and held up to scorn,
    Which must, I think, have made them furious.
Once anger's joined with that ill will of theirs,
    They will come after us more cruelly
    Than hound hunts after hare with gaping jaws.'
I felt my hair was standing up on end
    In terror, as I stood there looking back,   20
    And saying: 'Master, if you cannot find
Somewhere to hide us quickly, then I fear them,
    The Clawboys! They are coming up behind us:
    Already I imagine I can hear them.'
He said to me: 'Were I a silvered mirror
    I could not take your outer image in
    More swiftly than I've taken in your inner.³
Your thoughts just now were so entwined with mine,
    With the same attitude, the selfsame features,
    That from them all I soon worked out one plan.   30
If that slope on the right is not too steep,
    We can descend into the lower ditch,
    And so escape the hunt you think is up.'
Well, he had hardly finished saying this
    When I could see them coming, wings outspread,
    And not far off, and keen on catching us.

1. The Franciscans are known as Friars Minor, to indicate their humility.
2. A frog promised to carry a mouse over a river. It tied the mouse to itself, and then, once in the water, dived under in an attempt to drown it. A hawk swooped down and seized the mouse, and the frog went with it. It is the fight between Flibbertigibbet and Pollutus (XXII: 133–44) which reminds Dante of this fable.
3. Dante's 'inner' image is his thought. This is one of the many occasions when it is shown that Virgil can read Dante's thoughts.

Lo duca mio di subito mi prese,
 come la madre ch'al romore è desta
 e vede presso a sé le fiamme accese –
che prende il figlio e fugge e non s'arresta,   40
 avendo più di lui che di sé cura,
 tanto che solo una camicia vesta –
e giù dal collo della ripa dura
 supin si diede alla pendente roccia,
 che l'un de' lati all'altra bolgia tura.
Non corse mai sì tosto acqua per doccia
 a volger ruota di molin terragno,
 quand'ella più verso le pale approccia,
come 'l maestro mio per quel vivagno,
 portandosene me sovra 'l suo petto,   50
 come suo figlio, non come compagno.
A pena fuoro i piè suoi giunti al letto
 del fondo giù ch'e' furono in sul colle
 sovresso noi – ma non li era sospetto,
ché l'alta provedenza che lor volle
 porre ministri della fossa quinta,
 poder di partirs'indi a tutti tolle.
Là giù trovammo una gente dipinta
 che giva intorno assai con lenti passi,
 piangendo e nel sembiante stanca e vinta.   60
Elli avean cappe con cappucci bassi
 dinanzi alli occhi, fatte della taglia
 che in Clugnì per li monaci fassi.
Di fuor dorate son, sì ch'elli abbaglia,
 ma dentro tutte piombo, e gravi tanto
 che Federigo le mettea di paglia.
Oh in etterno faticoso manto!
 Noi ci volgemmo ancor pur a man manca
 con loro insieme, intenti al tristo pianto,
ma per lo peso quella gente stanca   70
 venìa sì pian che noi eravam novi
 di compagnia ad ogni mover d'anca.

My guide wasted no time at all in snatching
    Me – as a mother wakened by the roar
    Of burning, and observing flames approaching,
Snatches her son and runs and does not pause: 40
    She has such care of him (none for herself)
    She does not stop to put on any clothes;
And, down from the hard ridge, upon his back
    He slid and slithered, down the steep embankment
    Which closes on one side the lower dyke.
No rushing water in a strait mill race,
    With all its energy to turn the wheel,
    And moving faster coming near the blades,
Could move as fast as he did, sliding down,
    And always bearing me against his breast,   50
    And not as a companion, but a son.
His feet had hardly touched upon the bed
    Below, when fiends were on the ridge above us;
    But now we had no cause to feel afraid,
Because high providence, that had assigned
    These filthy demons to the foul fifth ditch,
    Deprived them of all power to go beyond.
Down there we came on people who were painted,[4]
    Moving about the place with lagging steps,
    Weeping, with all the signs of being defeated.   60
They had on cloaks which had their cowls pulled down
    So low they hid their eyes, cut in the fashion
    Favoured at Cluny by the monks therein.[5]
They were gilded outside, and dazzling bright,
    But inside all of lead, and all so heavy
    That Frederick's, weighed with them, would seem but light.[6]
A tiring mantle for eternity!
    We turned once more, as always, to the left,
    And went with them, engrossed in misery.
But, such the weight they wore, those weary folk   70
    Came on so slowly, that we came upon
    Fresh company with every step we took.

4. It is their robes which are 'painted (with gold)', as we see in ll. 61–6.
5. The ample and sumptuous habits worn by the monks in the Benedictine monastery at Cluny were well known.
6. The Emperor Frederick II (1194–1250) was believed to put traitors into leaden robes which were then melted over a fire.

Per ch'io al duca mio: 'Fa' che tu trovi
    alcun ch'al fatto o al nome si conosca,
    e li occhi, sì andando, intorno movi.'
E un che 'ntese la parola tosca,
    di retro a noi gridò: 'Tenete i piedi,
    voi che correte sì per l'aura fosca!
Forse ch'avrai da me quel che tu chiedi.'
    Onde 'l duca si volse e disse: 'Aspetta,   80
    e poi secondo il suo passo procedi.'
Ristetti, e vidi due mostrar gran fretta
    dell'animo, col viso, d'esser meco,
    ma tardavali 'l carco e la via stretta.
Quando fuor giunti, assai con l'occhio bieco
    mi rimiraron sanza far parola;
    poi si volsero in sé, e dicean seco:
'Costui par vivo all'atto della gola –
    e s'e' son morti, per qual privilegio
    vanno scoperti della grave stola?'   90
Poi disser me: 'O Tosco, ch'al collegio
    dell'ipocriti tristi se' venuto,
    dir chi tu se' non avere in dispregio.'
E io a loro: 'I' fui nato e cresciuto
    sovra 'l bel fiume d'Arno alla gran villa,
    e son col corpo ch'i' ho sempre avuto.
Ma voi chi siete a cui tanto distilla
    quant'i' veggio dolor giù per le guance?
    E che pena è in voi che sì sfavilla?'
E l'un rispuose a me: 'Le cappe rance   100
    son di piombo sì grosse che li pesi
    fan così cigolar le lor bilance.
Frati Godenti fummo, e bolognesi –
    io Catalano e questi Loderingo
    nomati, e da tua terra insieme presi,
come suole esser tolto un uom solingo,
    per conservar sua pace – e fummo tali,
    ch'ancor si pare intorno dal Gardingo.'

I therefore begged my leader: 'Try to find
    Someone whose name or history is known,
    And as we walk, please cast your eyes around.'
And one behind us, who'd become aware
    That I was speaking Tuscan, shouted: 'Stop!
    You who are rushing[7] through this gloomy air!
And maybe I can give you what you need.'
    At this my guide turned round, and told me: 'Wait,   80
    And then continue walking, at his speed.'
I stopped, and saw two show great urgency
    Of mind, by their expressions, to come up;
    But their weight slowed them, and the narrow way.
When they came up, they did not say a word
    For quite some time, but looked at me askance;
    Then turned to one another, and they said:
This man seems living – see him move his throat.
    If they're alive, why are they privileged,
    When we wear heavy stoles, to go without?'   90
'Tuscan, admitted to the sacred college
    Of the sad hypocrites,'[8] they said to me,
    'Say who you are: do not conceal that knowledge.'
This was my answer: 'I was born and bred
    In the great city[9] on the River Arno;
    I'm with the body I have always had.
But who are you, in such great misery
    That I can see it running down your cheeks?
    What punishment can shine so brilliantly?'
'All of these gilded mantles,' answered one,   100
    'Are made of such thick lead that their great weight
    Makes us, like balances they're laid on, groan.
We're from Bologna, and both Frisky Friars[10] –
    I Catalano, and he Loderingo –
    And both appointed – though your city was
Accustomed to appoint a single man –
    To keep the peace; and what we did accomplish
    Is still around Gardingo to be seen.'[11]

7. Dante and Virgil are not 'rushing'; but to the sinners, who are hindered by heavy robes, they seem to be.
8. The sinners naturally assume that Dante is being punished, as they are, for the sin of hypocrisy.
    The word 'college' suggests a religious community.
9. Florence.
10. The religious order of the Cavalieri di Maria Vergine Gloriosa (Knights of the Glorious Virgin Mary),
    was founded in Bologna in 1261, to promote peace and protect the weak. Its members were familiarly
    known as Frati Gaudenti (Frisky Friars), because of their free and easy way of life.
11. The Guelph Catalano (d. 1285) and the Ghibelline Loderingo (d. 1293) were appointed jointly to
    the office of *podestà* of Florence. They were not impartial, and their bias led to the destruction of the
    property of the Uberti family in the Gardingo area of the city. (It was not exceptional to appoint
    someone from outside the city to this office, but normally only one person was appointed.)

Io cominciai: 'O frati, i vostri mali...'
   ma più non dissi, ch'all'occhio mi corse   110
   un, crucifisso in terra con tre pali.
Quando mi vide, tutto si distorse,
   soffiando nella barba con sospiri –
   e 'l frate Catalan, ch'a ciò s'accorse,
mi disse: 'Quel confitto che tu miri,
   consigliò i Farisei che convenìa
   porre un uom per lo popolo a' martiri.
Attraversato è, nudo, nella via,
   come tu vedi, ed è mestier ch'el senta,
   qualunque passa, come pesa pria.   120
E a tal modo il socero si stenta
   in questa fossa, e li altri dal concilio
   che fu per li Giudei mala sementa.'
Allor vid'io maravigliar Virgilio
   sovra colui ch'era disteso in croce
   tanto vilmente nell'etterno essilio.
Poscia drizzò al frate cotal voce:
   'Non vi dispiaccia, se vi lece, dirci
   s'alla man destra giace alcuna foce
onde noi amendue possiamo uscirci,   130
   sanza costringer delli angeli neri
   che vegnan d'esto fondo a dipartirci.'
Rispuose adunque: 'Più che tu non speri
   s'appressa un sasso che dalla gran cerchia
   si move e varca tutt'i vallon feri;
salvo che 'n questo è rotto e nol coperchia:
   montar potrete su per la ruina
   che giace in costa e nel fondo soperchia.'
Lo duca stette un poco a testa china,
   poi disse: 'Mal contava la bisogna   140
   colui che i peccator di qua uncina.'
E 'l frate: 'Io udi' già dire a Bologna
   del diavol vizi assai, tra' quali udi'
   ch'elli è bugiardo, e padre di menzogna.'

I started off: 'O Friars, your evil state...'
    But said no more, because one crucified   110
    By three stakes on the ground had come in sight.
He writhed and twisted, catching sight of me,
    And mingled breaths with sighs inside his beard;
    Seeing this, Catalano said to me:
'That man impaled there, upon whom you look,
    Advised the Pharisees that it was better
    One man should suffer for the people's sake.[12]
He's stretched out naked right across the road,
    As you can see, and therefore he must feel
    All who walk over him as a great load.   120
His father-in-law[13] is suffering likewise
    In this same ditch, with the others of that council
    Which brought calamity upon the Jews.'[14]
I stared at Virgil who was standing, filled
    With sheer amazement, by him, crucified
    So vilely, and eternally exiled.[15]
Then he spoke to the friar, saying: 'Let
    It not displease you, if you may, to tell us
    If any passage opens on the right
Through which we two may travel and get clear,   130
    Without being forced to order the black angels
    To plumb the depths and get us out of here.'
'Nearer than you may think,' he answered then.
    'A rocky ridge starts from the outer wall[16]
    And crosses all the dykes as it runs down,
Except this one, for it is broken here;
    But it's still possible to climb the rubble
    Lining the side and heaped up on the floor.'
My leader bowed his head – he felt unsure –
    Then said: 'I heard a very different story   140
    From him who hooks the sinners over there.'[17]
'Well, in Bologna everybody says,'
    The friar replied, 'the devil's bad, and even
    That he's a liar, the father of all lies.'

12. The Jewish high priest, Caiaphas, who urged that Christ should be given up to the Romans for execution (John 11: 49–50).
13. The high priest Annas (John 18: 12–4).
14. The destruction of Jerusalem in AD 70 and the dispersion of the Jewish people.
15. Virgil had not seen Caiaphas on his previous descent into the Inferno, because that was before the Crucifixion.
16. The outer wall of Eviltiers (XVIII: 1–3).
17. Muckrake.

Appresso il duca a gran passi sen gì,
    turbato un poco d'ira nel sembiante –
    ond'io dalli 'ncarcati mi parti'
dietro alle poste delle care piante.

At that my guide stalked off with giant strides,
   And he was obviously a touch irate;[18]
   I left the sinners with their heavy loads,
And followed in the prints of those dear feet.

18. Virgil's uncharacteristic anger is caused by Muckrake's deception and Catalano's mockery in ll. 142–4.

CANTO XXIV

This canto begins with an unusually long simile, whose purpose is partly to emphasise how brief is Virgil's annoyance and, more importantly, to provide a homely scene from the world above to throw into relief the strange events which follow.

Virgil and Dante manage with difficulty to climb up the rubble until they can look down into the seventh ditch, reserved for the shades of thieves. Dante is intrigued by the sound of a voice below, whose words he cannot make out. Looking into the ditch, Dante sees that it is filled with repulsive serpents, of many different kinds. Terrified, naked people are running about among these monsters, without any hope of evading them. Their hands are bound behind them with serpents, which pierce their loins and are then tied in a knot in front.

Suddenly one sinner who is near them is transfixed by a serpent, and then immediately falls into a heap of ash. The ash gathers itself together, and the sinner regains his usual shape. In response to Virgil's question this sinner says he is a recent arrival in the Inferno, Vanni Fucci, a notorious murderer, thug, and – something which Dante is surprised to hear – sacrilegious thief. The sacrilege he committed, for which another man was executed, is the reason that he is here among the thieves, and not higher up among the violent.

Out of sheer spite Vanni Fucci makes a prophecy to Dante. Its main theme is the coming defeat of the Florentine White Guelphs, of whom Dante is one. Vanni Fucci's assertion that all the Whites will suffer is a hint of Dante's coming exile from his native city.

In quella parte del giovanetto anno   1
    che 'l sole i crin sotto l'Acquario tempra
    e già le notti al mezzo dì sen vanno –
quando la brina in su la terra assempra
    l'imagine di sua sorella bianca,
    ma poco dura alla sua penna tempra –
lo villanello a cui la roba manca
    si leva e guarda, e vede la campagna
    biancheggiar tutta – ond'ei si batte l'anca,
ritorna in casa, e qua e là si lagna,   10
    come 'l tapin che non sa che si faccia –
    poi riede, e la speranza ringavagna,
veggendo il mondo aver cangiata faccia
    in poco d'ora, e prende suo vincastro,
    e fuor le pecorelle a pascer caccia.
Così mi fece sbigottir lo mastro
    quand'io li vidi sì turbar la fronte,
    e così tosto al mal giunse lo 'mpiastro –
ché, come noi venimmo al guasto ponte,
    lo duca a me si volse con quel piglio   20
    dolce ch'io vidi prima a piè del monte.
Le braccia aperse, dopo alcun consiglio
    eletto seco riguardando prima
    ben la ruina, e diedemi di piglio.
E come quei ch'adopera ed estima,
    che sempre par che 'nnanzi si proveggia,
    così, levando me su ver la cima
d'un ronchione, avvisava un'altra scheggia
    dicendo: 'Sovra quella poi t'aggrappa –
    ma tenta pria s'è tal ch'ella ti reggia.'   30
Non era via da vestito di cappa,
    ché noi a pena, ei lieve e io sospinto,
    potavam su montar di chiappa in chiappa;
e se non fosse che da quel precinto
    più che dall'altro era la costa corta,
    non so di lui, ma io sarei ben vinto.

When the sun, while the year is still but young,   I
    Is in Aquarius, warming his bright hair,
    And nights grow shorter, as the days grow long –
And Jack Frost copies out upon the ground
    A perfect semblance of his sister snow,
    Not long to last with that warm sun around –
See farmers, short of food and forage, rise,
    And go to look, and find the countryside
    All white, and turn around, and slap their thighs,[1]
And go back in, and grumble, and despair,   10
    And moon about, with nothing to be done;
    But suddenly come back, in hope once more,
Seeing the world assume a different face
    In such short space of time, and seize their crooks
    And drive their flocks of sheep abroad to graze.
Just so my master filled me with despair
    When I saw how his brow was clouded over;
    But then the ointment came to soothe the sore,
For, when we reached the broken bridge, my guide
    Turned round to face me with that calm demeanour   20
    I noticed first under the mountainside.[2]
He spread his arms – once he had carefully
    Studied the bridge's ruin and decided
    His course of action – and took hold of me.
And, like one who, while working, reckons up
    What's needed next, and always thinks ahead,
    So he, placing me first upon the top
Of one great rock, would trouble to find out
    Another, saying: 'You must grab that next;
    But first make sure that it will take your weight.'   30
No way for someone in a leaden cloak![3]
    For we, though I was helped and he was weightless,[4]
    Could hardly make our way from rock to rock;
And if the bank had not been less in height
    On that rim than the upper one, I cannot
    Speak for my guide, but I'd have faced defeat.

1. In frustration.
2. 'The delightful mountain' of I, at the foot of which Dante first met Virgil.
3. Dante is still thinking of the hypocrites whom he has just left behind.
4. There is a contradiction, with no attempt to resolve it, between the immateriality of the shades and their capacity for physical suffering, or, as here, Virgil's physical help for Dante.

Ma perché Malebolge inver la porta
   del bassissimo pozzo tutta pende,
   lo sito di ciascuna valle porta
che l'una costa surge e l'altra scende: 40
   noi pur venimmo al fine in su la punta
   onde l'ultima pietra si scoscende.
La lena m'era del polmon sì munta,
   quand'io fui su, ch'i' non potea più oltre,
   anzi m'assisi nella prima giunta.
'Omai convien che tu così ti spoltre,'
   disse 'l maestro, 'ché, seggendo in piuma,
   in fama non si vien, né sotto coltre –
sanza la qual chi sua vita consuma,
   cotal vestigio in terra di sé lascia   50
   qual fummo in aere ed in acqua la schiuma.
E però leva su: vinci l'ambascia
   con l'animo che vince ogni battaglia,
   se col suo grave corpo non s'accascia.
Più lunga scala convien che si saglia –
   non basta da costoro esser partito:
   se tu m'intendi, or fa' sì che ti vaglia.'
Leva'mi allor, mostrandomi fornito
   meglio di lena ch'i' non mi sentìa,
   e dissi: 'Va, ch'i' son forte e ardito.'   60
Su per lo scoglio prendemmo la via,
   ch'era ronchioso, stretto e malagevole,
   ed erto più assai che quel di pria.
Parlando andava per non parer fievole,
   onde una voce uscì dall'altro fosso,
   a parole formar disconvenevole.
Non so che disse, ancor che sovra 'l dosso
   fossi dell'arco già che varca quivi,
   ma chi parlava ad ire parea mosso[a].
Io era vòlto in giù, ma li occhi vivi   70
   non poteano ire al fondo per lo scuro;
   per ch'io: 'Maestro, fa' che tu arrivi

---

a. 'Ad ire parea mosso' – lit. 'seemed to be on the move'. There is a reading 'ad ira' which would give the sense 'moved to anger'; but 'ad ire' seems preferable, since it fits with l. 66 and its indication of difficulty in speaking, probably because the speaker is panting.

But since the whole of Eviltiers[5] inclines
    Towards the well's mouth lying at its foot,
    Each valley's situation always means
One rim is higher than the other one.   40
    Well then, at length we did arrive up where
    We found the final lump of broken stone.
My lungs were utterly devoid of air
    When I got to that place – my strength was gone;
    I sat down straight away once we got there.
'From now on in this way,' my master said,
    'You'll cast off laziness: no one gets fame,
    Taking it easy in a feather bed;
And he who lives without achieving fame
    Leaves no more trace of what he was on earth   50
    Than smoke in air or, in the water, foam.
And so, stand up! You're panting – you must get
    Your breath back: the strong mind wins every battle,
    Unless it sinks under the body's weight.
A longer ladder waits:[6] it's not enough
    That you have left the hypocrites behind.
    You've heard me. Now show whether you are tough.'
So I stood up, pretending I had more
    Breath than I had been feeling that I had,
    And said: 'Lead on! I'm strong. I have no fear.'   60
We made our way up, and along the ridge,
    Which was rugged, and narrow, hard to manage,
    And much more steep than was the previous bridge.
I walked and talked, not wanting to seem faint;
    And then a voice came from the lower ditch,
    Which seemed unable to articulate.
I caught no word, although I stood above
    The ditch itself, at midpoint of the bridge;
    But he who spoke seemed to be on the move.
I stood there looking down, but living eyes   70
    Could not pierce to the depth through all that dark;
    So I said: 'Master, try to get us please,

5. See XVIII: 1–18.
6. The ascent from the lowest point of the Inferno, the centre of the globe, to the surface of the earth.

dall'altro cinghio e dismontiam lo muro,
 ché, com'i' odo quinci e non intendo,
 così giù veggio e neente affiguro.'
'Altra risposta,' disse, 'non ti rendo
 se non lo far, ché la dimanda onesta
 si de' seguir con l'opera tacendo.'
Noi discendemmo il ponte dalla testa
 dove s'aggiugne con l'ottava ripa,   80
 e poi mi fu la bolgia manifesta –
e vidivi entro terribile stipa
 di serpenti, e di sì diversa mena
 che la memoria il sangue ancor mi scipa.
Più non si vanti Libia con sua rena,
 ché se chelidri, iaculi e faree
 produce, e cencri con anfisibena,
né tante pestilenzie né sì ree
 mostrò già mai con tutta l'Etiopia ,
 né con ciò che di sopra al Mar Rosso èe.   90
Tra questa cruda e tristissima copia
 correan genti nude e spaventate,
 sanza sperar pertugio o elitropia:
con serpi le man dietro avean legate –
 quelle ficcavan per le ren la coda
 e il capo, ed eran dinanzi aggroppate.
Ed ecco a un, ch'era da nostra proda,
 s'avventò un serpente che 'l trafisse
 là dove 'l collo alle spalle s'annoda.
Né *o* sì tosto mai né *i* si scrisse   100
 com'el s'accese ed arse, e cener tutto
 convenne che cascando divenisse;
e poi che fu a terra sì distrutto,
 la polver si raccolse per sé stessa,
 e 'n quel medesmo ritornò di butto:
così per li gran savi si confessa
 che la fenice more e poi rinasce,
 quando al cinquecentesimo anno appressa –

To the other rim, and then descend the wall;
  I stand here hearing, and not understanding,
  And look down there, and see nothing at all.'
'I will not give,' he said, 'any reply
  Except to do it – for a fair request
  Ought to be met with action, silently.'
We went on, till we came to where the bridge
  Runs down to join up with the eighth embankment,   80
  And then I could see clearly in the ditch.[7]
And saw that it was frighteningly filled
  With coiling serpents – great monstrosities:
  The mere remembrance makes my blood run cold.
Let Libya boast no more, although her sand
  Produces jaculi and amphisboenae,
  Chelydri, cenchri, and phareae.[8] And
The whole of Ethiopia and those regions
  That lie along the shores of the Red Sea
  Never produced such pestilential legions.   90
I could see terrified and naked folk
  Running among these cruel wicked swarms,
  Hopeless of hiding place or heliotrope[9];
They had their hands tied up with snakes behind,
  Which threaded through their loins, with head and tail
  Knotted together on the other side.
Then suddenly one sinner where we stand
  Is savaged by a serpent and transfixed
  Just where the neck and shoulders are conjoined.
And never was *O* or *I* written so soon[10]   100
  As he caught fire and burnt up, utterly
  Dissolving into ash as he fell down;
And as he lay there in a heap of ash,
  The powder drew itself up altogether
  To reassume his figure in a flash.
Just so the greatest sages all aver
  The phoenix perishes and is reborn
  When she approaches her five-hundredth year:

7. This is the seventh ditch of Eviltiers, reserved for thieves.
8. These fabulous reptiles are taken from Lucan's *Pharsalia*. Jaculi fly through the air like javelins; amphisboenae have a head at each end; chelydri, amphibious creatures, leave a trail of smoke behind them; cenchri always move in a straight line; phareae, as they move, cut a furrow in the ground with their tails.
9. The bloodstone, said to heal snake-bites, and also to make its wearer invisible.
10. Each of these letters can be written with a single stroke of the pen, and therefore very quickly.

erba né biada in sua vita non pasce,
    ma sol d'incenso lacrime e d'amomo,   110
    e nardo e mirra son l'ultime fasce.
E qual è quel che cade, e non sa como,
    per forza di demon ch'a terra il tira,
    o d'altra oppilazion che lega l'omo –
quando si leva, che 'ntorno si mira
    tutto smarrito della grande angoscia
    ch'elli ha sofferta, e guardando sospira –
tal era il peccator levato poscia.
    Oh potenza di Dio, quant'è severa,
    che cotai colpi per vendetta croscia!   120
Lo duca il domandò poi chi ello era,
    per ch'ei rispuose: 'Io piovvi di Toscana,
    poco tempo è, in questa gola fera.
Vita bestial mi piacque, e non umana,
    sì come a mul ch'i' fui – son Vanni Fucci
    bestia, e Pistoia mi fu degna tana.'
E io al duca: 'Dilli che non mucci,
    e domanda che colpa qua giù 'l pinse,
    ch'io 'l vidi uomo di sangue e di crucci.'
E 'l peccator, che 'ntese, non s'infinse,   130
    ma drizzò verso me l'animo e 'l volto,
    e di trista vergogna si dipinse;
poi disse: 'Più mi duol che tu m'hai colto
    nella miseria dove tu mi vedi
    che quando fui dell'altra vita tolto.
Io non posso negar quel che tu chiedi:
    in giù son messo tanto perch'io fui
    ladro alla sagrestia de' belli arredi,
e falsamente già fu apposto altrui.
    Ma perché di tal vista tu non godi,   140
    se mai sarai di fuor da' luoghi bui,
apri li orecchi al mio annunzio, e odi:
    Pistoia in pria de' Neri si dimagra –
    poi Fiorenza rinova gente e modi –

She feeds, lifelong, on neither grass nor grain,
>But only tears of frankincense and balsam;   110
>Her winding sheet is myrrh and cinnamon.[11]
Like someone who falls down, not knowing why –
>Whether a demon has him in a seizure,
>Or other blockage binds him physically –
Then stands and looks around as he comes round,
>Bewildered utterly by all the anguish
>He's undergone, and sighs as he looks round –
That's how this sinner was when he arose.
>And oh, the power of God, how stern it is,
>Dealing in vengeance such almighty blows!   120
My master asked the sinner who he was;
>He answered: 'I poured down from Tuscany,
>And not long since, into these cruel jaws.
I lived a beast's life, not a human one,
>Mule[12] that I was: Vanni Fucci the Beast[13];
>Pistoia suited me: it was my den.'
I begged my guide: 'Tell him not to slip off,
>And ask about the fault that brought him here:
>I knew him as a man of blood and wrath.'[14]
The sinner understood, and did not feign,   130
>But turned his face to me, and his attention,
>And coloured up, so dreadful was his shame;
Then said: 'I am more grieved that you have found me
>In such a wretched state as you can see,
>Than I was grieved to leave my life behind me.
I can't deny whatever you ask of me:
>I'm stowed here so low down because I stole
>The holy vessels from the sacristy,
For which the judgement fell upon another.[15]
>But to ensure you have no cause to gloat   140
>If you should leave these lands of darkness ever,
Prick up your ears, and hear my prophecy:
>Pistoia first will weed out all her Blacks,
>Then Florence change her men and polity.[16]

11. The thief is compared to the phoenix because of its unusual method of regeneration. In other respects a sharp contrast is implied: the phoenix was normally spoken of with respect, and was indeed often taken as a symbol of Christ's Resurrection.

12. Bastard.

13. 'Beast' may have been a nickname. He was a citizen of Pistoia, a Black Guelph who played a brutal part in the civil strife in that city.

14. Dante is surprised to find Vanni Fucci among the thieves, rather than higher up among the violent.

15. The truth about this sacrilege came to light only after Vanni Fucci's death, which occurred in early 1300. 1300 is the date of Dante's vision: he does not know the facts until Vanni Fucci tells him.

16. In 1301 the White Guelphs were victorious in Pistoia over the Black Guelphs. Not long afterwards the Blacks were victorious in Florence over the Whites, and Dante was among those proscribed.

tragge Marte vapor di Val di Magra
   ch'è di torbidi nuvoli involuto,
   e con tempesta impetuosa e agra
sovra Campo Picen fia combattuto –
   ond'ei repente spezzerà la nebbia,
   sì ch'ogni Bianco ne sarà feruto.   150
E detto l'ho perché doler ti debbia!'

Enveloped in a black and stormy cloud,
   Mars will bring lightning out of Val di Magra;
   And in a bitter tempest, and a loud,
Over Piceno's field will rage the fight;
   Sudden the lightning will break through the storm,
   And wound, successively, each single White.[17]   150
And I have told you this to make you squirm!'

17. In this highly coloured and obscure language, suitable to prophecy, Vanni Fucci alludes to the victory
   of the Blacks of Florence and Lucca combined, under Moroello Malaspina (the 'lightning out of Val di
   Magra'), at Piceno in 1302.

CANTO XXV

Having completed his malevolent prophecy to Dante, Vanni Fucci makes an obscene gesture to God. Dante is glad to see two serpents wind themselves around the sinner and prevent his saying anything more: what pleases Dante is the demonstration that God cannot be mocked.

There is a brief condemnation of Pistoia. Then Vanni Fucci flees, and a centaur arrives, with all his animal parts covered with reptiles. This is Cacus, condemned for theft with fraud, as Virgil explains.

More thieves arrive, Florentines, and we see the second and third metamorphoses in this part of the Inferno, both very complicated ones. (The first metamorphosis was that of Vanni Fucci in the previous canto.)

A monster grapples with one of the shades, and the two become a mysterious being, which moves away slowly. Another reptile attacks a sinner, at his navel to begin with, and gradually the man becomes a reptile and the reptile a man.

Dante rejoices in his own artistry, saying that his descriptions of metamorphoses are superior to those of Lucan and Ovid. In this canto Vanni Fucci has been blamed for pride, as Capaneus was previously. Theirs is rebellious pride in the face of God, a determination not to accept the nature of things. Dante's pride in his own workmanship – a theme which will recur in the *Comedy* – is a different matter entirely.

It would be a mistake to think of these descriptions as merely an excuse for Dante to display his verbal skill. Behind them is the conviction that a thief attacks the owner himself in depriving him of his property, which may be viewed as part of himself: theft is an offence against the person. Those who do not observe the distinction between *meum et tuum* have lost the sense of human personality. The transformed sinners have become their sin.

Al fine delle sue parole il ladro   1
    le mani alzò con amendue le fiche,
    gridando: 'Togli, Dio, ch'a te le squadro!'
Da indi in qua mi fuor le serpi amiche,
    perch'una li s'avvolse allora al collo,
    come dicesse: 'Non vo' che più diche' –
e un'altra alle braccia, e rilegollo,
    ribadendo sé stessa sì dinanzi
    che non potea con esse dare un crollo.
Ahi Pistoia, Pistoia, ché non stanzi   10
    d'incenerarti sì che più non duri,
    poi che in mal far lo seme tuo avanzi?
Per tutt'i cerchi dello 'nferno scuri
    non vidi spirto in Dio tanto superbo –
    non quel che cadde a Tebe giù da' muri.
El si fuggì che non parlò più verbo,
    e io vidi un centauro pien di rabbia
    venir chiamando: 'Ov'è, ov'è l'acerbo?'
Maremma non cred'io che tante n'abbia,
    quante bisce elli avea su per la groppa   20
    infin ove comincia nostra labbia.
Sovra le spalle, dietro dalla coppa,
    con l'ali aperte li giacea un draco:
    e quello affuoca qualunque s'intoppa.
Lo mio maestro disse: 'Questi è Caco,
    che sotto il sasso di monte Aventino
    di sangue fece spesse volte laco.
Non va co' suoi fratei per un cammino,
    per lo furto che frodolente fece
    del grande armento ch'elli ebbe a vicino,   30
onde cessar le sue opere biece
    sotto la mazza d'Ercule, che forse
    li ne diè cento, e non sentì le diece.'
Mentre che sì parlava, ed[a] el trascorse
    e tre spiriti venner sotto noi,
    de' qua né io né 'l duca mio s'accorse,

a. In the sense of 'ecco che', the same use as in l. 50, to stress the simultaneity of the actions mentioned.

That said, the robber[1], with no more ado,   1
    Lifted his hands, and made the fig with both,[2]
    Shouting: 'Take that, God! They are both for you!'
The serpents were my friends from that time on,
    For one of them coiled round the sinner's neck,
    As if to say: 'Now all your talking's done';
Another took him into its constriction,
    And tied itself so tightly up in front
    He could not move his arms even a fraction.
Men of Pistoia, the decision's yours!   10
    Burn down your city! Leave not one stone standing!
    Your evil goes beyond your ancestors'.[3]
In all the circles of obscurest hell
    I saw no shade so blasphemously proud,
    Not him who tumbled from the Theban wall.[4]
He fled, and did not say another word;
    And then I saw a centaur full of anger
    That came and shouted: 'Where's this rebel shade?'
Even Maremma[5] has not such a swarm
    Of snakes, I think, as it had on its haunches,   20
    Right up to where it takes on human form.[6]
On its shoulders, behind the nape, it bore
    A dragon with enormous wings outspread:
    All whom it breathes upon it sets on fire.
'Now this is Cacus here,' my master said,
    'That in a cave beneath Mount Aventine[7]
    Times without number made a lake of blood.
He does not take the road his brothers take,
    Because he stole from out of the great herd
    That was nearby, and did it with a trick;[8]   30
For that his crooked ways were ended, when
    Hercules clubbed him, giving him perhaps
    A hundred blows, of which he felt not ten.'
My master spoke, the centaur ran away,
    And three shades came beneath our vantage point,
    Whom my leader and I both failed to see,

1. Vanni Fucci.
2. An insulting and obscene gesture, made by placing the thumb between the first two fingers.
3. Legend had it that Pistoia was founded by soldiers from the army of the Roman conspirator Catiline.
4. Capaneus, punished in the third ring of the seventh circle. See XIV: 43–72.
5. An unhealthy marshy area on the Tuscan coast.
6. Centaurs are usually represented as having a human upper body.
7. One of the seven hills of Rome.
8. Cacus is not with the other centaurs, guardians of the violent in the first ring of the seventh circle, but here among the thieves, because he stole cattle from Hercules and tried to disguise their whereabouts by dragging them backwards into his cave by their tails, so that the hoofprints seemed to lead out of the cave.

se non quando gridar: 'Chi siete voi?'
    Per che nostra novella si ristette,
    ed intendemmo pur ad essi poi.
Io non li conoscea, ma ei seguette,   40
    come suol seguitar per alcun caso
    che l'un nomar un altro convenette,
dicendo: 'Cianfa dove fia rimaso?'
    Per ch'io, acciò che 'l duca stesse attento,
    mi puosi il dito su dal mento al naso.
Se tu se' or, lettore, a creder lento
    ciò ch'io dirò, non sarà maraviglia,
    ché io che 'l vidi a pena il mi consento.
Com'io tenea levate in lor le ciglia,
    e un serpente con sei piè si lancia   50
    dinanzi all'uno, e tutto a lui s'appiglia.
Co' piè di mezzo li avvinse la pancia,
    e con li anterior le braccia prese,
    poi li addentò e l'una e l'altra guancia –
li diretani alle cosce distese,
    e miseli la coda tra 'mbedue,
    e dietro per le ren su la ritese.
Ellera abbarbicata mai non fue
    ad alber sì, come l'orribil fera
    per l'altrui membra avviticchiò le sue.   60
Poi s'appiccar come di calda cera
    fossero stati e mischiar lor colore,
    né l'un né l'altro già parea quel ch'era,
come procede innanzi dall'ardore
    per lo papiro suso un color bruno
    che non è nero ancora, e 'l bianco more.
Li altri due 'l riguardavano, e ciascuno
    gridava: 'Ohmè, Agnel, come ti muti!
    Vedi che già non se' né due né uno.'
Già eran li due capi un divenuti,   70
    quando n'apparver due figure miste
    in una faccia, ov'eran due perduti.

Until they cried out: 'Who are you?' When we
    Immediately broke off our conversation,
    And paid attention only to those three.
I did not know them; but it then occurred,   40
    As frequently by chance it does occur,
    One of them named another, and he said:
'Now where is Cianfa[9]? Is he coming?' Then,
    So that my guide might pay good heed, I rested
    My finger on my mouth from nose to chin.
If, Reader, you're unwilling to believe
    What I shall tell you, that is not surprising,
    Since I, who've seen it, can't believe I have.
While I still have my eyes fastened on them,
    A reptile with six feet[10] comes springing out   50
    In front of one of them, and fastens him.
It gripped his belly with its middle feet,
    With its forefeet laid hold of both his arms,
    And then it sank its teeth in either cheek;
It stretched each hind foot out to either thigh,
    Then put its tail between the sinner's legs,
    Whence, passing by his loins, it rose on high.
Rooted ivy never became attached
    So strongly to its tree as that foul monster
    Was found adhering to the limbs it clutched.   60
They stuck together, just as if they were
    Of molten wax; their colours ran and mingled –
    And neither looked like what it was before –
Just as, when paper burns, the advancing heat
    Is steadily preceded by a darkness
    That is not black, and yet no longer white.
The other two shades cried, as they looked on:
    'Alas, Agnolo[11], you are really altered!
    Look at yourself! You're neither two nor one!'
By now the two heads had become one head,   70
    And we could see two intermingled aspects
    In one face, where the two had disappeared.

9. A Florentine of the Donati family.
10. This is Cianfa, who has been turned into a reptile.
11. A Florentine.

Fersi le braccia due di quattro liste –
    le cosce con le gambe e 'l ventre e 'l casso
    divenner membra che non fuor mai viste.
Ogni primaio aspetto ivi era casso:
    due e nessun l'imagine perversa
    parea – e tal sen gìo con lento passo.
Come 'l ramarro sotto la gran fersa
    dei dì canicular, cangiando sepe,   80
    folgore par se la via attraversa,
sì pareva, venendo verso l'epe
    delli altri due, un serpentello acceso,
    livido e nero come gran di pepe;
e quella parte onde prima è preso
    nostro alimento, all'un di lor trafisse,
    poi cadde giuso innanzi lui disteso.
Lo trafitto 'l mirò, ma nulla disse –
    anzi, co' piè fermati, sbadigliava
    pur come sonno o febbre l'assalisse.   90
Elli 'l serpente, e quei lui riguardava –
    l'un per la piaga, e l'altro per la bocca
    fummavan forte, e 'l fummo si scontrava.
Taccia Lucano ormai là dove tocca
    del misero Sabello e di Nassidio,
    e attenda a udir quel ch'or si scocca.
Taccia di Cadmo e d'Aretusa Ovidio,
    ché se quello in serpente e quella in fonte
    converte poetando, io non lo 'nvidio:
ché due nature mai a fronte a fronte   100
    non trasmutò sì ch'amendue le forme
    a cambiar lor matera fosser pronte.
Insieme si rispuosero a tai norme,
    che 'l serpente la coda in forca fesse,
    e il feruto ristrinse insieme l'orme.
Le gambe con le cosce seco stesse
    s'appiccar sì che 'n poco la giuntura
    non facea segno alcun che si paresse.

Two arms were fashioned where four lengths had been –
    The thighs, the legs, the bellies, and the breasts
    Became such members as were never seen.
Nothing of what had been was left to see:
    The twisted image looked like both, yet neither.
    Such as it was, it slowly moved away.
And like a lizard underneath the lash
    Of the dog days, moving from hedge to hedge   80
    Over the roadway like a lightning flash,
A blazing little brute came on the scene,
    Straight for the bellies of the other two,
    As black and livid as a peppercorn;
And at that part through which at first he'd drawn
    His nourishment,[12] it transfixed one of them;
    Then, at full length in front of him, fell down.
The one transfixed stared, but he did not speak –
    He merely stood his ground, and he was yawning,
    As overcome by fever or by sleep.   90
He and the brute were looking at each other –
    From the shade's wound, and from the monster's jaws
    Smoke snorted, and the two fumes came together.
Let Lucan hold his tongue now, with his tale
    Of poor Sabellus and Nasidius,[13]
    Until he hears what wonders I reveal.
Let Ovid hold his tongue: though he recount
    Such tales of Cadmus and of Arethusa,
    I do not envy him his snake and fount:[14]
He never brought two creatures face to face   100
    And changed them so that both of them were ready
    To swap themselves around, as in this case.
This is how they responded to each other:
    The reptile split its tail into a fork;
    The wounded sinner placed his feet together.
The legs, including the whole thigh, were soon
    So closely stuck together that their juncture
    Could not by any mark or sign be seen.

12. The navel.
13. Lucan tells in his *Pharsalia* how these two soldiers were bitten by snakes, and Sabellus was reduced
    to ashes, while Nasidius swelled up until he became a shapeless mass.
14. In his *Metamorphoses* Ovid describes in vivid detail Cadmus being changed into a snake and Arethusa
    into a spring.

Togliea la coda fessa la figura
   che si perdeva là, e la sua pelle   110
   si facea molle, e quella di là dura.
Io vidi intrar le braccia per l'ascelle,
   e i due piè della fiera, ch'eran corti,
   tanto allungar quanto accorciavan quelle.
Poscia li piè di rietro, insieme attorti,
   diventaron lo membro che l'uom cela,
   e 'l misero del suo n'avea due porti.
Mentre che 'l fummo l'uno e l'altro vela
   di color novo, e genera il pel suso
   per l'una parte e dall'altra il dipela,   120
l'un si levò e l'altro cadde giuso,
   non torcendo però le lucerne empie,
   sotto le quai ciascun cambiava muso.
Quel ch'era dritto, il trasse ver le tempie,
   e di troppa matera ch'in là venne
   uscir li orecchi delle gote scempie:
ciò che non corse in dietro e si ritenne
   di quel soverchio, fe' naso alla faccia,
   e le labbra ingrossò quanto convenne.
Quel che giacea, il muso innanzi caccia,   130
   e li orecchi ritira per la testa
   come face le corna la lumaccia;
e la lingua, ch'avea unita e presta
   prima a parlar, si fende, e la forcuta
   nell'altro si richiude – e 'l fummo resta.
L'anima ch'era fiera divenuta
   suffolando si fugge per la valle,
   e l'altro dietro a lui parlando sputa.
Poscia li volse le novelle spalle,
   e disse all'altro: 'I' vo' che Buoso corra,   140
   com'ho fatt'io, carpon per questo calle.'
Così vid'io la settima zavorra
   mutare e trasmutare – e qui mi scusi
   la novità se fior la penna abborra.

The cleft tail took the shape that disappeared
    Into itself; and the reptilian skin   110
    Grew soft and smooth; the sinner's skin grew hard.
I saw each arm shrink into its armpit,
    And saw the monster's little forepaws lengthen
    In just proportion as those arms went short.
The hindpaws after, twisted into one,
    Became that member[15] which a man conceals,
    While the wretch stretched two paws out from his own.[16]
They are still veiled in smoke, they both change colour,
    And hair has started sprouting out on one,
    While all the hair starts falling from the other.   120
One rises at the downfall of the other,
    But neither turns aside his baleful eyeballs,
    Under whose glare their snouts are now changed over.
The one erect pulled his snout up and out,
    And from the excess matter that he had
    Grew ears upon a head that was without:
Then all the matter not pulled up and out –
    Matter left over – gave the face a nose,
    And both the lips were duly swelled with it.
The fallen one thrusts out his snout instead,   130
    And, as a snail withdraws into its shell,
    He draws his ears right back into his head;
The tongue, that was united once and quick
    To speak, divides; the forked tongue of the other
    Becomes united – and there's no more smoke.
The human soul that had become a brute[17]
    Went hissing off in flight along the valley;
    The other followed on, to speak and spit.[18]
Then, turning his new shoulders, said to the one
    Who still remained:[19] 'I must see Buoso scurry   140
    On all fours down this road, as I have done.'
So I saw the garbage in the seventh pit
    Changed and transformed: sheer novelty's the reason,
    If my account has somewhat garbled it.

15. The genitals.
16. His genitals.
17. Buoso, a Florentine.
18. The Florentine Francesco dei Cavalcanti, the 'blazing little brute' of line 82, now restored to human shape. He is identified by Dante only at line 151.
19. Puccio Sciancato, named in line 148.

E avvegna che li occhi miei confusi
    fossero alquanto, e l'animo smagato,
    non poter quei fuggirsi tanto chiusi
ch'i' non scorgessi ben Puccio Sciancato –
    ed era quel che sol, de' tre compagni
    che venner prima, non era mutato: 150
l'altr'era quel che tu, Gaville, piagni.

And, though my mind was dreadfully disturbed,
    And my eyesight was dazzled and bewildered,
    Those who remained could not fly unobserved:
Puccio the Cripple[20] I could recognise –
    Of those we came on first, the only one
    Who had not changed in any way his guise;   150
The other one made you, Gaville, mourn.[21]

20. Of a Florentine Ghibelline family. Dante recognises him easily because he is lame, as his nickname
    indicates.
21. Francesco dei Cavalcanti was killed by inhabitants of the Tuscan village of Gaville, and his death
    was avenged on them by his relatives.

CANTO XXVI

The canto opens with an ironic encomium of Florence, famous not only throughout our world but also the underworld. Then Dante forecasts, and even reveals his longing for, the punishment that other Tuscan states will inflict on his native city for its arrogance.

Dante and Virgil climb back up the rocks by which they had descended, and leave the ditch of the thieves behind. They look down into the eighth ditch, where they can see many fires twinkling in the darkness. Every fire conceals a sinner, for this is where those who counselled fraud are punished.

One flame is moving towards them. It is divided into two horns at the top. Inside it, Virgil tells Dante, are the shades of Diomed and Ulysses, Greek commanders at the siege of Troy. They are being punished for several ruses, but particularly for that of the wooden horse, by means of which the Greeks managed to get inside Troy's walls. Dante is anxious to speak with these shades, but Virgil says that he himself must do the talking: the Greeks were proverbially a proud people, and Virgil is able to claim some respect from Diomed and Ulysses for including them in his *Aeneid*.

A voice issues from the higher of the flame's two horns, that belonging to Ulysses. He gives an account of a voyage he undertook after his return home from Troy, a voyage inspired by the desire for knowledge, which ends disastrously when his ship is sunk in sight of a lone mountain rising out of the sea. This mountain, we learn much later, is Mount Purgatory.

This canto (the source of Tennyson's *Ulysses*) exemplifies the conflict between men's desire for knowledge, which is in itself praiseworthy, and the futility of this desire when it is not backed up by the grace of God. Ulysses is probably the most sympathetic of the shades we meet in the Inferno: it is interesting that his main rival for this distinction, Brunetto Latini, displays a similar intellectual curiosity.

Godi, Fiorenza, poi che se' sì grande,   1
    che per mare e per terra batti l'ali,
    e per lo 'nferno tuo nome si spande!
Tra li ladron trovai cinque cotali
    tuoi cittadini onde mi ven vergogna –
    e tu in grande orranza non ne sali.
Ma se presso al mattin del ver si sogna,
    tu sentirai di qua da picciol tempo
    di quel che Prato, non ch'altri, t'agogna.
E se già fosse, non saria per tempo: 10
    così foss'ei, da che pur esser dee –
    ché più mi graverà, com' più m'attempo!
Noi ci partimmo, e su per le scalee
    che n'avean fatte i borni a scender pria,
    rimontò 'l duca mio e trasse mee;
e proseguendo la solinga via,
    tra le schegge e tra' rocchi dello scoglio
    lo piè sanza la man non si spedìa.
Allor mi dolsi, e ora mi ridoglio
    quando drizzo la mente[a] a ciò ch'io vidi,   20
    e più lo 'ngegno affreno ch'i' non soglio,
perché non corra che virtù nol guidi,
    sì che, se stella bona o miglior cosa
    m'ha dato 'l ben, ch'io stessi nol m'invidi.
Quante il villan ch'al poggio si riposa,
    nel tempo che colui che 'l mondo schiara
    la faccia sua a noi tien meno ascosa,
come la mosca cede a la zanzara,
    vede lucciole giù per la vallea –
    forse colà dov'e' vendemmia ed ara –   30
di tante fiamme tutta risplendea
    l'ottava bolgia, sì com'io m'accorsi
    tosto che fui là 've 'l fondo parea.
E qual colui che si vengiò con li orsi
    vide 'l carro d'Elia al dipartire –
    quando i cavalli al cielo erti levorsi,

a. memory.

Florence, rejoice, now that you have such fame,   1
    And over land and sea you spread your wings!
    The whole Inferno's ringing with your name!
Among the thieves I found five citizens
    Of yours, all nobles, causing me some shame,
    While you yourself take little honour thence.
And yet, if dreams we dream at dawn come true,[1]
    You shall before long feel the weight of what
    Prato desires for you, and others too.[2]
It would, if it had come, not be too soon;   10
    Since come it must, I wish that it had happened:
    It will but hurt me more as time goes on.
We left that place, and slowly, step by step,
    Using the rocks by which we had descended,
    My guide climbed up once more and drew me up;
And so we made our solitary way
    Among the crags and splinters of the ridge:
    Feet without hands would have made no headway.
I grieved to see, and now I grieve again
    When I call back to mind the things I saw,   20
    And hold my genius on a tighter rein,
For fear it run where virtue does not guide,
    So that, if a kind star or something better[3]
    Has made me gifts, I do not make them void.
Just as some peasant – when he takes his rest
    Upon a little hillside in that season
    When he that lights the world[4] hides his face least,
That hour when mites go and mosquitoes come[5] –
    Sees countless fireflies crowded in the valley,
    His scene of husbandry and harvest home –   30
So the eighth ditch was scatteringly bright
    With countless fires, as I became aware
    The instant its depression came in sight.
And just as he who was avenged by bears[6]
    Saw, as it left, the chariot of Elijah,[7]
    Its horses rearing heavenwards as it rose,

1. A common belief in ancient and medieval times.
2. Prato was at this time subject to Florence, whose power was feared by other Tuscan cities also.
3. God's grace.
4. The sun. The season is summer.
5. The evening.
6. Some children teased the prophet Elisha for his baldness, he cursed them, and two bears came and killed them.
7. Elisha saw his master, the prophet Elijah, ascend into heaven in a chariot of fire.

che nol potea sì con li occhi seguire
    ch'el vedesse altro che la fiamma sola,
    sì come nuvoletta, in su salire –
tal si move ciascuna per la gola   40
    del fosso, ché nessuna mostra il furto,
    e ogni fiamma un peccatore invola.
Io stava sovra 'l ponte a veder surto,
    sì che, s'io non avessi un ronchion preso,
    caduto sarei giù sanz'esser urto.
E 'l duca, che mi vide tanto atteso,
    disse: 'Dentro dai fuochi son li spirti –
    ciascun si fascia di quel ch'elli è inceso.'
'Maestro mio,' rispuos'io, 'per udirti
    son io più certo, ma già m'era avviso   50
    che così fosse, e già voleva dirti:
chi è in quel fuoco che vien sì diviso
    di sopra, che par surger della pira
    dov'Eteòcle col fratel fu miso?'
Rispuose a me: 'Là dentro si martira
    Ulisse e Diomede, e così insieme
    alla vendetta vanno come all'ira;
e dentro dalla lor fiamma si geme
    l'agguato del caval che fe' la porta
    onde uscì de' Romani il gentil seme.   60
Piangevisi entro l'arte per che, morta,
    Deidamìa ancor si duol d'Achille,
    e del Palladio pena vi si porta.'
'S'ei posson dentro da quelle faville
    parlar,' diss'io, 'maestro, assai ten priego
    e ripriego – che il priego vaglia mille –
che non mi facci dell'attender niego
    fin che la fiamma cornuta qua vegna:
    vedi che del disio ver lei mi piego!'
Ed elli a me: 'La tua preghiera è degna   70
    di molta loda, e io però l'accetto –
    ma fa' che la tua lingua si sostegna.

And could not keep it under observation
    Except by following the blaze alone,
    Like a small burning cloud in its ascension –
So each flame makes its way along the inner   40
    Parts of the ditch, and none reveals the theft,
    Though each of them contains a stolen sinner.
I stood tiptoe upon the bridge to look,
    And would have toppled down without being pushed,
    Had I not taken hold of a great rock.
My leader, seeing how I was concerned,
    Then told me: 'There are souls inside those flames,
    Each one involved in that by which it's burnt.'
'My master,' I replied, 'now I can hear
    You saying that, I'm certain, but I thought   50
    That it was so; I wanted to inquire:
Who's coming in that flame which we see sever
    Itself on top, as coming from the pyre
    On which Eteocles burnt with his brother?'[8]
He made this answer: 'There, within that flame,
    Diomed and Ulysses go together,
    As once in guilt, now in avenging pain;
And, burning in that flame, they both regret
    Their trickery and the horse that made the breach
    Through which the noble Roman seed came out.[9]   60
Now they regret that guile which makes the dead
    Deidamia mourn Achilles still; now also
    The price for the Palladium is paid.'[10]
'If they, inside the flashing of those flames,
    Can speak,' I said, 'my master, I request,
    Repeating the request a thousand times,
That you do not forbid my waiting here
    Until that flame that has two horns arrives:
    You see me lean towards it in desire!'
He answered: 'Your request is laudable,   70
    And so I grant it willingly – however,
    Take care to hold your tongue a little while.

8. Eteocles and his brother Polynices, sons of King Oedipus of Thebes, killed each other in battle. When their bodies were burnt on the same pyre, the flames divided into two, which was taken as a sign of their continuing enmity.
9. Diomed and Ulysses, Greek commanders at the siege of Troy, devised the stratagem of the wooden horse, by means of which Greek soldiers managed to enter the city. As Troy was falling, Aeneas and his companions escaped and eventually reached Italy, where their descendants founded the city of Rome.
10. Diomed and Ulysses persuaded Achilles to go with them to Troy: his lover Deidamia died of her grief. They also stole from Troy the Palladium, a statue of Pallas Athena on which the safety of Troy was believed to depend.

Lascia parlare a me, ch'i' ho concetto
    ciò che tu vuoi – ch'ei sarebbero schivi,
    perché fuor greci, forse del tuo detto.'
Poi che la fiamma fu venuta quivi
    dove parve al mio duca tempo e loco,
    in questa forma lui parlare audivi:
'O voi che siete due dentro ad un foco,
    s'io meritai di voi mentre ch'io vissi,   80
    s'io meritai di voi assai o poco
quando nel mondo li alti versi scrissi,
    non vi movete, ma l'un di voi dica
    dove per lui perduto a morir gissi.'
Lo maggior corno della fiamma antica
    cominciò a crollarsi mormorando
    pur come quella cui vento affatica;
indi la cima qua e là menando,
    come fosse la lingua che parlasse,
    gittò voce di fuori, e disse: 'Quando   90
mi diparti' da Circe, che sottrasse
    me più d'un anno là presso a Gaeta,
    prima che sì Enea la nomasse,
né dolcezza di figlio, né la pièta[b]
    del vecchio padre, né 'l debito amore
    lo qual dovea Penelopè far lieta,
vincer potero dentro a me l'ardore
    ch'i' ebbi a divenir del mondo esperto,
    e delli vizi umani e del valore;
ma misi me per l'alto mare aperto   100
    sol con un legno e con quella compagna
    picciola dalla qual non fui diserto.
L'un lito e l'altro vidi infin la Spagna,
    fin nel Morrocco, e l'isola de' Sardi,
    e l'altre che quel mare intorno bagna.
Io e' compagni eravam vecchi e tardi
    quando venimmo a quella foce stretta
    dov'Ercule segnò li suoi riguardi,

b. Here equivalent to the Latin *pietas*, frequently used by Virgil in the sense of 'respect' and 'reverence'.

I'll do the talking, for I understand
    What you would like to ask – and they, being Greeks,
    Might think your speech was something to be scorned.'[11]
So, when the flame had come to where my guide
    Judged that both time and place were opportune,
    I heard him speak, and this is what he said:
'O you, who share one flame and yet are two,
    If I earned honour from you while I lived,   80
    If great or small the honour I earned from you,
When in the world I wrote my tragedy[12],
    Do not move off, but one of you recount
    Where, when he went astray, he came to die.'
That ancient fire's great horn[13] began to bend
    And straighten, shake itself about, and murmur,
    Like a flame that's troubled by the wind;
And, as it waved its tip from side to side,
    As though it were the tongue itself that spoke,
    It managed to emit a voice, which said: 90
'When I left Circe's charms, strong to detain
    Me near Gaeta more than one whole year
    (Before Aeneas called it by that name),[14]
Neither paternal fondness,[15] nor the duty
    I owed to my old father,[16] nor the love
    I owed Penelope, to make her happy,[17]
Could overcome the great desire I had
    To widen my experience of the world,
    Of human wickedness and human good;
And so I set out on the open sea   100
    With one ship only and that tiny band
    Of men who never had deserted me.
I saw the shores that stretch on either hand
    To Spain and to Morocco; and Sardinia
    And other countries with that Sea[18] all round.
My companions and I were old and weak
    When we came to those straits where Hercules
    Set up on either side a great landmark[19] –

11. The Greeks were proverbially an arrogant race.
12. The *Aeneid*.
13. Ulysses' flame rises higher than Diomed's.
14. Circe bewitched Ulysses on his way home from Troy and kept him with her for a year. A little later Aeneas, on his voyage from Troy to Italy, founded a city on Circe's island and named it after his nurse.
15. Ulysses had a son, Telemachus.
16. When Ulysses returned from Troy, his father Laertes was still alive.
17. Ulysses' wife Penelope remained faithful to him throughout the years he was away at Troy.
18. The Mediterranean.
19. The Straits of Gibraltar. There is a mountain on each side, and together they were known as the Pillars of Hercules. There was a common belief that the Pillars were there to indicate that men should not sail beyond them.

acciò che l'uom più oltre non si metta –
    dalla man destra mi lasciai Sibilia,   110
    dall'altra già m'avea lasciata Setta.
"O frati," dissi, "che per cento milia
    perigli siete giunti all'occidente,
    a questa tanto picciola vigilia
de' nostri sensi ch'è del rimanente,
    non vogliate negar l'esperienza,
    di retro al sol, del mondo sanza gente.
Considerate la vostra semenza:
    fatti non foste a viver come bruti,
    ma per seguir virtute e canoscenza."   120
Li miei compagni fec'io sì aguti,
    con questa orazion picciola, al cammino,
    che a pena poscia li avrei ritenuti;
e volta nostra poppa nel mattino,
    dei remi facemmo ali al folle volo,
    sempre acquistando dal lato mancino.
Tutte le stelle già dell'altro polo
    vedea la notte, e 'l nostro tanto basso
    che non surgea fuor del marin suolo.
Cinque volte racceso e tante casso   130
    lo lume era di sotto dalla luna,
    poi che 'ntrati eravam nell'alto passo,
quando n'apparve una montagna, bruna
    per la distanza, e parvemi alta tanto
    quanto veduta non avea alcuna.
Noi ci allegrammo, e tosto tornò in pianto,
    ché della nova terra un turbo nacque,
    e percosse del legno il primo canto.
Tre volte il fe' girar con tutte l'acque:
    alla quarta levar la poppa in suso   140
    e la prora ire in giù, com'altrui piacque,
infin che 'l mar fu sopra noi richiuso.'

His warning that nobody should go further:[21]
    Upon the right I left Seville behind,   110
    Having upon the left abandoned Ceuta.
"O brothers who have reached the west," I cried,
    "With a hundred thousand dangers overcome,
    You will not let yourselves now be denied –
Now your brief lives have little time to run –
    Experience at first hand of the unpeopled
    World we shall find by following the sun.
Consider well your origin, your birth:
    You were not made to live like animals,
    But to pursue and gain wisdom and worth."   120
Now I had made my company so keen,
    With this oration, to be on their way,
    I would have found them difficult to restrain;
So, having turned our stern towards the east,
    We used our oars like wings in our mad flight,
    Making continual headway west-south-west.
And now at night we could see every star
    Of the south hemisphere: ours were so low
    They did not rise above the ocean floor.[22]
The light beneath the moon had been five times   130
    Rekindled, and as many times extinguished,[23]
    Since we began on this hard enterprise,
When up in front there rose a mountain[24], dark
    In the distance, and it seemed to me to be
    Higher than any northern mountain peak.
Then we were glad, but soon began to weep;
    For out of that new world a whirlwind rose
    And struck against the forepart of the ship.
It turned us round three times with all the water:
    And at the fourth it lifted up the stern   140
    So that the prow sank down, as pleased Another[25],
Until the sea closed over us again.

21. The Pillars of Hercules were taken as marking the boundary of the known world, and often of
    the knowable world.
22. The voyagers have crossed the equator.
23. Five lunar months had passed.
24. This, although naturally Ulysses does not know it, is Mount Purgatory.
25. God.

CANTO XXVII

The shade of Ulysses stops talking and moves away. Its place is taken by another soul hidden in a flame, which seems to be trying to speak. This, as we learn later, is Guido da Montefeltro, another counsellor of fraud. He asks whether Romagna is at peace or war. Dante replies that there is at present no open warfare, but that war is always in the hearts of the rulers there: he emphasises this by referring to the various rulers not by name, but by their coats of arms, which all bear creatures of prey. Dante then asks the shade to reveal his identity.

Guido replies that he would not say who he was if he thought that there was any chance of this information reaching the world of the living: he assumes that Dante and Virgil are shades who have recently arrived in the Inferno.

After a lifetime of fighting and deceit, Guido explains, he decided to retire, and he entered the Order of St Francis as a way of atoning for his sins. Pope Boniface VIII, however, called him out of retirement to get his advice on how to subdue his enemies and destroy Palestrina. Guido was at first unwilling but, encouraged by the Pope's assertion that his sins were forgiven in advance, he suggested that large promises should be made and then broken. By following this advice, the Pope succeeded in his object, but Guido himself, when he died, was damned: the Pope's advance absolution proves to be invalid.

Dante and Virgil go further along the rocky ridge until they come to where they can see into the next ditch of the eighth circle, where the sowers of discord are punished.

In keeping with the theme of fraud or deception, this canto is full of dramatic irony. Guido thinks that his secret is safe with Dante, who will in fact give a public account of it; Guido, the great deceiver, is himself deceived by Pope Boniface; the outward forms of religion (for which Dante always shows a great respect) prove in this instance to be valueless, since the right intention is ultimately what matters.

Già era dritta in su la fiamma e queta   1
    per non dir più, e già da noi sen gìa
    con la licenza del dolce poeta,
quand'un'altra, che dietro a lei venìa,
    ne fece volger li occhi alla sua cima
    per un confuso suon che fuor n'uscìa.
Come 'l bue cicilian, che mugghiò prima
    col pianto di colui – e ciò fu dritto –
    che l'avea temperato con sua lima,
mugghiava con la voce dell'afflitto,   10
    sì che, con tutto che fosse di rame,
    pur el parea dal dolor trafitto,
così, per non aver via né forame
    dal principio nel foco, in suo linguaggio
    si convertian le parole grame.
Ma poscia ch'ebber colto lor viaggio
    su per la punta, dandole quel guizzo
    che dato avea la lingua in lor passaggio,
udimmo dire: 'O tu a cu' io drizzo
    la voce e che parlavi mo lombardo,   20
    dicendo "Istra[a] ten va; più non t'adizzo",
perch'io sia giunto forse alquanto tardo,
    non t'incresca restare a parlar meco:
    vedi che non incresce a me, e ardo!
Se tu pur mo in questo mondo cieco
    caduto se' di quella dolce terra
    latina ond'io mia colpa tutta reco,
dimmi se i Romagnuoli han pace o guerra,
    ch'io fui de' monti là intra Urbino
    e 'l giogo di che Tever si diserra.'   30
Io era in giuso ancora attento e chino,
    quando il mio duca mi tentò di costa,
    dicendo: 'Parla tu, questi è latino.'
E io, ch'avea già pronta la risposta,
    sanza indugio a parlare incominciai:
    'O anima che se' là giù nascosta,

a. A Tuscan and northern Italian word meaning 'now'. See 'issa' of XXIII: 7 and note.

That flame, now standing upright, had gone quiet   1
    With nothing more to say, and was departing
    With the permission of the kindly poet,
When one more flame, that came right after it,
    Forced us to turn our eyes up to its crest
    Because of those strange noises coming out.
As the Sicilian bull – bellowing first
    With his wild cries who filed it into shape
    (An outcome that was only right and just) –
Would bellow with men's voices under torture,   10
    So that, although it was a brazen image,
    It seemed as though the bull itself must suffer[1] –
Just so, because there was no way for them
    To issue at the start, the grieving words
    Were changed into the language of the flame.
But once they had discovered how to go
    To the flame's tip, and given it that flicker
    Given them by the tongue as they went through,
We heard them: 'You, who just this moment were
    Talking like one from Lombardy, and saying,   20
    "You may go now; I'm urging you no more",[2]
Although I am a little late arriving,
    Don't be displeased, but stay and talk with me:
    You see I'm not displeased, and I am burning!
Say – if you've fallen only recently
    Into this blind world from that Latin land[3],
    So lovely, whence I bring my guilt with me –
Whether Romagna lives in war or peace:
    I'm from those hills between Urbino and
    That ridge from which the Tiber is unleashed.'   30
While I was still intently gazing down,
    My leader nudged me lightly on the side,
    And said: 'He is a Latin: you begin.'
I had the answer on my lips unbidden,
    And so began to speak with no delay:
    'O soul down there, so well and truly hidden,

---

1. A Sicilian tyrant had a brass bull made, in which he roasted his victims, whose shrieks came out as though the bull was bellowing. The tyrant used it first on the man who made it for him.

2. The shade is addressing Virgil (born near Mantua in Lombardy) and referring to Virgil's dismissal of Ulysses in ll. 2–3.

3. Italy. The shade presumes that Virgil has only recently been damned.

Romagna tua non è, e non fu mai,
    sanza guerra ne' cuor de' suoi tiranni,
    ma 'n palese nessuna or vi lasciai.
Ravenna sta come stata è molt'anni: 40
    l'aguglia da Polenta la si cova,
    sì che Cervia ricuopre co' suoi vanni.
La terra che fe' già la lunga prova,
    e di Franceschi sanguinoso mucchio,
    sotto le branche verdi si ritrova.
E 'l mastin vecchio e 'l nuovo da Verrucchio,
    che fecer di Montagna il mal governo,
    là dove soglion fan de' denti succhio.
Le città di Lamone e di Santerno
    conduce il lioncel dal nido bianco,   50
    che muta parte dalla state al verno.
E quella cu' il Savio bagna il fianco,
    così com'ella sie' tra 'l piano e 'l monte
    tra tirannia si vive e stato franco.
Ora chi se' ti priego che ne conte:
    non esser duro più ch'altri sia stato,
    se 'l nome tuo nel mondo tegna fronte.'
Poscia che 'l foco alquanto ebbe rugghiato
    al modo suo, l'aguta punta mosse
    di qua, di là, e poi diè cotal fiato: 60
'S'i' credesse che mia risposta fosse
    a persona che mai tornasse al mondo,
    questa fiamma starìa sanza più scosse –
ma però che già mai di questo fondo
    non tornò vivo alcun, s'i' odo il vero,
    sanza tema d'infamia ti rispondo.
Io fui uom d'arme, e poi fui cordigliero,
    credendomi, sì cinto, fare ammenda –
    e certo il creder mio venìa intero,
se non fosse il gran prete, a cui mal prenda!   70
    che mi rimise nelle prime colpe –
    e come e quare, voglio che m'intenda.

Your Romagna is not, nor was it ever,
    Quite free of war within its tyrants' hearts,
    But when I left there was no open rupture.
Ravenna stands as it has stood for years: 40
    The Eagle of Polenta[4] broods above it,
    And covers Cervia[5] with its wings and claws.
That city, under siege more than a year,
    That raised a bloody mountain of dead Frenchmen,[6]
    Finds itself under the Green Paws[7] once more.
Both bulldogs of Verrucchio, old and new,[8]
    Who used Montagna with such cruelty,[9]
    Still use their teeth as they're accustomed to.
The Lion Cub in White Lair[10] has his claws on
    The cities on Lamone and Santerno:[11]   50
    He changes sides according to the season.[12]
That city which the Savio ripples by,[13]
    Just as it lies between low land and mountain
    Lives between tyranny and being free.
And now, I beg you, tell us who you are;
    Be no more taciturn than I have been;
    So may your fame throughout the world endure.'
After the flame had been roaring somewhat
    In its own way, it moved its pointed end
    From side to side, and finally breathed out: 60
'If I believed the words I'm saying were
    To somebody returning to the world,
    This flame of mine would not move any more;
But since no one has ever made his way
    Alive from this abyss, or so I'm told,
    I'll answer with no fear of infamy.
I was a soldier, then a Cordelier,
    Hoping, thus girdled, to make full amends;[14]
    And so my conscience would have been quite clear,
Had not the High Priest[15] – may he rot in hell! –   70
    Plunged me right back into my former guilt:
    And how and why is what I wish to tell.

4. The coat of arms of the da Polenta family bore an eagle.
5. A town on the Adriatic, south of Ravenna.
6. The shade to whom Dante is speaking shone in the defence of Forlì against French troops (1281–3).
7. The coat of arms of the Ordelaffi family bore a green lion.
8. The father and son Malatesta and Malatestino da Verrucchio.
9. Montagna, a Ghibelline lord of Rimini, was imprisoned by Malatesta and killed by Malatestino.
10. The coat of arms of Maghinardo Pagani da Susinana bore a blue lion on a white field.
11. Faenza on the River Lamone, and Imola on the River Santerno.
12. Inclining sometimes to the Ghibellines, and sometimes to the Guelphs.
13. Cesena.
14. The speaker is Guido da Montefeltro (c.1220–98), leader of the Ghibellines in Romagna.
15. Pope Boniface VIII.

Mentre ch'io forma fui d'ossa e di polpe
    che la madre mi diè, l'opere mie
    non furon leonine, ma di volpe.
Li accorgimenti e le coperte vie
    io seppi tutte, e sì menai lor arte,
    ch'al fine della terra il suono uscìe.
Quando mi vidi giunto in quella parte
    di mia etade ove ciascun dovrebbe   80
    calar le vele e raccoglier le sarte,
ciò che pria mi piacea, allor m'increbbe,
    e pentuto e confesso mi rendei –
    ahi miser lasso! E giovato sarebbe.
Lo principe de' novi Farisei,
    avendo guerra presso a Laterano –
    e non con Saracin né con Giudei,
ché ciascun suo nimico era Cristiano,
    e nessun era stato a vincer Acri,
    né mercatante in terra di Soldano –   90
né sommo officio né ordini sacri
    guardò in sé, né in me quel capestro
    che solea fare i suoi cinti più macri.
Ma come Costantin chiese Silvestro
    d'entro Siratti a guerir della lebbre,
    così mi chiese questi per maestro
a guerir della sua superba febbre:
    domandommi consiglio, e io tacetti
    perché le sue parole parver ebbre.
E' poi ridisse: "Tuo cuor non sospetti –   100
    finor t'assolvo, e tu m'insegna fare
    sì come Penestrino in terra getti.
Lo ciel poss'io serrare e diserrare,
    come tu sai, però son due le chiavi
    che 'l mio antecessor non ebbe care."
Allor mi pinser li argomenti gravi
    là 've 'l tacer mi fu avviso il peggio,
    e dissi: "Padre, da che tu mi lavi

While I was living, with the flesh and blood
 My mother gave me, then not lion-like
 But vulpine rather were the things I did.
Every underhand trick and stratagem
 Was at my beck and call; I had such skill
 That the wide world resounded with my fame.
When finally I saw myself attain
 That stage of life when everybody ought to   80
 Lower his sails and take the rigging in,
What had onetime so pleased me, now so irked
 Me I repented and confessed and entered;[16]
 And – oh, I am a wretch! – it should have worked.
The ruler of the modern Pharisees[17] –
 Engaged in warfare near the Lateran,[18]
 And not with Saracens, and not with Jews,
For all his enemies were Christians, and
 Not one of them had been besieging Acre[19]
 Or merchandising in the Sultan's land[20] –   90
Abused his office and those vows of mine –
 His priestly orders, and my knotted cord
 Which onetime made its wearers good and thin.[21]
And, just as Constantine called Pope Sylvester
 Down from Soracte, to cure leprosy,[22]
 So this man chose me out to be his master
And cure him of the fever of his pride:
 He asked for my advice, and I was silent
 Because his words seemed wandering and wild.
But he insisted: "Set your mind at rest;   100
 I absolve you from now on; so just advise me
 How to lay Palestrina in the dust.[23]
I can lock heaven's gates, as you're aware,
 And unlock heaven's gates:[24] I hold both keys
 My predecessor did not hold so dear."[25]
I, influenced by those weighty arguments,
 And thinking silence a worse fault than speech,
 Said: "Father, since you cleanse me in advance

16. Entered the Franciscan Order.
17. Pope Boniface VIII.
18. In Rome itself: the Lateran Palace was the Pope's residence. The Pope's quarrel was with the Colonna family who did not recognise the abdication of his predecessor Celestine V and Boniface's election.
19. Acre, in the Holy Land, had fallen to the Saracens in 1291.
20. Egypt. The Church banned trade with Muslim countries.
21. The rope girdle of the Franciscans was a sign of their poverty and asceticism.
22. According to legend, the Roman Emperor Constantine was cured of his leprosy by Pope Sylvester I.
23. Boniface was at the time besieging the Colonnas in their fortress of Palestrina, near Rome.
24. 'And I will give unto thee the keys of the kingdom of heaven..' (Matthew 16: 19)
25. A sneer at Pope Celestine V who relinquished the Papacy.

di quel peccato ov'io mo cader deggio,
 lunga promessa con l'attender corto   110
 ti farà triunfar nell'alto seggio."
Francesco venne poi, com'io fu' morto,
 per me, ma un de' neri cherubini
 li disse: "Non portar – non mi far torto.
Venir se ne dee giù tra' miei meschini
 perché diede il consiglio frodolente,
 dal quale in qua stato li sono a' crini;
ch'assolver non si può chi non si pente,
 né pentére e volere insieme puossi,
 per la contradizion che nol consente."   120
Oh me dolente! come mi riscossi
 quando mi prese dicendomi: "Forse
 tu non pensavi ch'io loico fossi!"
A Minòs mi portò, e quelli attorse
 otto volte la coda al dosso duro;
 e poi che per gran rabbia la si morse,
disse: "Questi è de' rei del foco furo" –
 per ch'io là dove vedi son perduto
 e, sì vestito, andando mi rancuro.'
Quand'elli ebbe 'l suo dir così compiuto,   130
 la fiamma dolorando si partìo,
 torcendo e dibattendo il corno aguto.
Noi passamm'oltre, e io e 'l duca mio,
 su per lo scoglio infino in su l'altr'arco
 che cuopre il fosso in che si paga il fio
a quei che scommettendo acquistan carco.

Of that sin which I'm going to commit:
    Large promises, but minimally kept,   110
    Will make you triumph in the Holy Seat."[27]
When I was dead, and Francis came to bear
    Me off to heaven, one of the black angels
    Cried out: "Don't take him: that would be unfair.
Servitude under me is this man's doom:
    The counsel that he gave was fraudulent,
    And since that time I've had my eye on him;
Without repentance there's no absolution,
    And no one can repent while willing sin,
    For that would be an obvious contradiction."   120
Oh, wretched me! I realised my position
    When he grabbed hold of me, and said: "Perhaps
    You did not know I was a strict logician!"
He took me off to Minos; Minos twisted
    His tail around his scaly back eight times,[28]
    And then announced in anger as he bit it:
"Another sinner for the thieving fire!"
    So that is why, as you can see, I'm lost,
    And walk in bitterness and strange attire.'[29]
When all his talking was completely done,   130
    The miserable flame departed, mourning,
    Still wriggling and still writhing its sharp horn.
And so we carried on, the two of us,
    Along the ridge to reach an arch which led
    Over the ditch where sinners pay the price
For all the seeds of discord that they sowed.[30]

27. Boniface promised an amnesty to the Colonnas and then, once they had surrendered, destroyed
    Palestrina.
28. See V: 4–12.
29. He is clothed in fire.
30. This is the ninth ditch of the eighth circle.

CANTO XXVIII

The ninth ditch of the eighth circle reveals a sight which, Dante says, no one could describe adequately. Here are innumerable sowers of religious and political discord, and they are dreadfully and disgustingly mutilated.

Mahomet is here; he was regarded in the Middle Ages as a Christian schismatic and, if it does not seem quite so natural today to look at him in that light, we can still see how he represents in this canto the greatest religious, political, and cultural schism in the smaller world which Dante knew. Mahomet's body is cut open from his chin to his belly, while his son-in-law Ali has his face cut open from his chin to the top of his head.

Also present are Pier da Medicina who has, amongst other mutilations, his throat slit, and speaks through the gash; Curio, whose tongue is slit because he advised Caesar to take the action which led to civil war in the Roman Empire; Mosca de' Lamberti, the originator of the feud between the Guelphs and Ghibellines, who has both his hands cut off so that, as he lifts them in the air, the blood falls down to drench his face; and Bertran de Born, who sowed dissension among the children of Henry II of England, and who carries his own severed head in front of him like a lantern.

Dante does not in any way attempt to mitigate our natural reaction of physical disgust. It would, however, be a mistake to see this canto as a mere chamber of horrors: here, as elsewhere in the Inferno, the punishment fits the sin, and those who tore society apart are themselves torn apart. The disgust we feel at such physical horrors is a disgust which Dante makes us feel also at the sin which incurred them.

Chi porìa mai pur con parole sciolte   I
    dicer del sangue e delle piaghe a pieno
    ch'i' ora vidi, per narrar più volte?
Ogne lingua per certo verrìa meno
    per lo nostro sermone e per la mente
    c'hanno a tanto comprender poco seno.
S'el s'aunasse ancor tutta la gente
    che già in su la fortunata terra
    di Puglia fu del suo sangue dolente
per li Troiani e per la lunga guerra   10
    che dell'anella fe' sì alte spoglie –
    come Livio scrive, che non erra –
con quella che sentìo di colpi doglie
    per contastare a Ruberto Guiscardo,
    e l'altra il cui ossame ancor s'accoglie
a Ceperan, là dove fu bugiardoᵃ
    ciascun pugliese, e là da Tagliacozzo,
    dove sanz'arme vinse il vecchio Alardo,
e qual forato suo membro e qual mozzo
    mostrasse, d'aequar sarebbe nulla   20
    il modo della nona bolgia sozzo.
Già veggia, per mezzul perdere o lulla,
    com'io vidi un, così non si pertugia,
    rotto dal mento infin dove si trulla:
tra le gambe pendevan le minugia –
    la corata pareva e 'l tristo sacco
    che merda fa di quel che si trangugia.
Mentre che tutto in lui veder m'attacco,
    guardommi, e con le man s'aperse il petto,
    dicendo: 'Or vedi com'io mi dilacco!   30
Vedi come storpiato è Maometto!
    Dinanzi a me sen va piangendo Alì,
    fesso nel volto dal mento al ciuffetto.
E tutti li altri che tu vedi qui,
    seminator di scandalo e di scisma
    fur vivi, e però son fessi così.

a. Generally 'liar', here means 'traitor' or 'deceitful'.

Who could describe, even in words set free   1
    From rhyme and metre, all the wounds and blood
    I now saw, though he tried to, tirelessly?
There is no doubt that every tongue would fail,
    Together with the words and memory:
    They cannot hope to comprehend it all.
If we could reunite the multitude
    That fought onetime upon your fatal earth,
    Apulia[1], and lamented all their blood
Shed by the Trojans[2] or in that long war   10
    That culminated in a mound of rings[3]
    (As Livy[4] tells us, and he does not err),
With all of those who suffered heavy blows
    In their engagements with Robert Guiscard[5];
    And all those others who are heaps of bones
At Ceperano, there where turn by turn
    Apulians broke their faith,[6] or Tagliacozzo
    Where old Alardo did not fight but won;[7]
And some showed wounded limbs, and some limbs which
    Had been hacked off – that would not give a notion   20
    Of how things were within that foul ninth ditch.
I never saw a barrel gape apart,
    Through loss of hoop or stave, as I saw one
    Ripped from his chin right down to where we fart;
His guts between his legs, his inside out,
    Intestines on display, with that foul pouch
    That changes what we swallow into shit.
While I was all intent upon this sight,
    He looked, tore his breast open with his hands,
    And said: 'See how I pull myself apart!   30
See how Mahomet is discomfited![8]
    Ali[9] is walking off in front and weeping,
    His face split open – chin to top of head.
And all these other shades here whom you see –
    Because, while still alive, they sowed dissension
    And scandal – have been riven in this way.

1. Apulia, now the 'heel' of Italy, is used here to indicate southern Italy in general.
2. Aeneas and his descendants who, refugees from Troy, gradually took possession of all Italy.
3. The reference is to the Second Punic War (219–202 BC) and the Battle of Cannae, after which the Carthaginians were said to have collected three bushels of rings from the fingers of dead Romans.
4. Roman historian (59 BC–AD 17).
5. A Norman invader of the eleventh century.
6. This treachery led to the defeat of King Manfred at Benevento in 1266.
7. In 1268 Alardo, although he did not himself take part in the fighting, devised a winning strategy by which Charles of Anjou defeated Manfred's nephew Conradin.
8. In the Middle Ages Mahomet was often regarded as a Christian schismatic.
9. Mahomet's son-in-law and his eventual successor. He came to represent a schism within Islam itself.

Un diavolo è qua dietro che n'accisma
 sì crudelmente, al taglio della spada
 rimettendo ciascun di questa risma,
quand'avem volta la dolente strada –   40
 però che le ferite son richiuse
 prima ch'altri dinanzi li rivada.
Ma tu chi se' che 'n su lo scoglio muse,
 forse per indugiar d'ire alla pena
 ch'è giudicata in su le tue accuse?'
'Né morte 'l giunse ancor, né colpa 'l mena,'
 rispuose 'l mio maestro, 'a tormentarlo –
 ma per dar lui esperienza piena,
a me, che morto son, convien menarlo
 per lo 'nferno qua giù di giro in giro: 50
 e quest'è ver così com'io ti parlo.'
Più fuor di cento che, quando l'udiro,
 s'arrestaron nel fosso a riguardarmi
 per maraviglia, obliando il martiro.
'Or di' a fra Dolcin dunque che s'armi –
 tu che forse vedra' il sole in breve,
 s'ello non vuol qui tosto seguitarmi –
sì di vivanda che stretta di neve
 non rechi la vittoria al Noarese,
 ch'altrimenti acquistar non saria leve.'   60
Poi che l'un piè per girsene sospese,
 Maometto mi disse esta parola,
 indi a partirsi in terra lo distese.
Un altro, che forata avea la gola
 e tronco il naso infin sotto le ciglia,
 e non avea mai ch'una orecchia sola,
ristato a riguardar per maraviglia
 con li altri, innanzi alli altri aprì la canna,
 ch'era di fuor d'ogni parte vermiglia,
e disse: 'O tu cui colpa non condanna   70
 e cu' io vidi su in terra latina[b],
 se troppa simiglianza non m'inganna,

b. 'Italian', as at XXII: 65, XXVII: 27 and 33, and XXIX: 88.

A hidden fiend back there renews our trouble
    Continually, by putting to the sword
    All of the shades included in this rabble,
Each time we travel round this road of pain,   40
    Because each time we come to face that devil
    Our open wounds have all healed up again.
But who are you, standing up there and gaping?
    Perhaps you're trying to postpone the torment
    Which after your confession you are facing?'[10]
'Death has not reached him yet, nor does guilt bring
    This man,' my master said, 'to be tormented;
    But, that he may experience everything,
I, who am dead, act as his leader here,
    Down through the Inferno, circle after circle: 50
    This is as true as that I'm standing here.'
Souls by the hundred stopped to stare at me,
    And stood and wondered, when they heard this said,
    For once oblivious of their agony.
'You who, shortly perhaps, will see the sun,
    Tell Fra Dolcino to provide himself –
    Unless he wants to join me very soon –
With victuals; or the snow, blocking him in,
    Will bring a victory to the Novarese,
    Which otherwise he would find hard to win.'[11]   60
With one foot in the air, with half a mind
    To go away, Mahomet said these words;
    Then moved off, as he put it to the ground.
Another – with his throat slit open wide,
    His nose cut off right up to his eyebrows,
    And only one ear left upon his head,
And who, in his surprise at us, had stood
    Still like the others – was the first to clear
    His windpipe's fissure, all blood-red outside,
To speak through: 'You, who do not stand condemned,   70
    Are one, unless the likeness is deceptive,
    I've seen before above on Latin ground.

10. Mahomet assumes that Dante is a soul who has confessed to Minos (v: 4–12) and been damned.
11. Dolcino Tornielli was the leader of a heretical sect who, with his followers, was blockaded in the hills
    between Novara and Vercelli, then forced by starvation to surrender, and burnt alive in 1307. The
    'Novarese' is the Bishop of Novara who led the crusade against Dolcino.

rimembriti di Pier da Medicina,
    se mai torni a veder lo dolce piano
    che da Vercelli a Marcabò dichina.
E fa sapere a' due miglior da Fano,
    a messer Guido e anco ad Angiolello,
    che se l'antiveder qui non è vano,
gittati saran fuor di lor vasello
    e mazzerati presso alla Cattolica   80
    per tradimento d'un tiranno fello.
Tra l'isola di Cipri e di Maiolica
    non vide mai sì gran fallo Nettuno,
    non da pirate, non da gente argolica.
Quel traditor che vede pur con l'uno,
    e tien la terra che tale qui meco
    vorrebbe di vedere esser digiuno,
farà venirli a parlamento seco;
    poi farà sì ch'al vento di Focara
    non sarà lor mestier voto né preco.'   90
E io a lui: 'Dimostrami e dichiara,
    se vuo' ch'i' porti su di te novella,
    chi è colui dalla veduta amara.'
Allor puose la mano alla mascella
    d'un suo compagno e la bocca li aperse,
    gridando: 'Questi è desso, e non favella.
Questi, scacciato, il dubitar sommerse
    in Cesare, affermando che 'l fornito
    sempre con danno l'attender sofferse.'
Oh quanto mi pareva sbigottito   100
    con la lingua tagliata nella strozza
    Curio, ch'a dir fu così ardito!
E un ch'avea l'una e l'altra man mozza,
    levando i moncherin per l'aura fosca,
    sì che 'l sangue facea la faccia sozza,
gridò: 'Ricordera'ti anche del Mosca,
    che disse – lasso! – "Capo ha cosa fatta",
    che fu 'l mal seme per la gente tosca.'

I'm Pier da Medicina[12]. If you go
    Back ever to revisit that dear plain
    That from Vercelli slopes to Marcabò,
Remember me.[13] Tell Fano's two best men,
    Guido I mean, and also Angiolello:
    If our apparent foresight here's not vain,
They will be weighted down, drowned in the sea,
    Thrown overboard close by Cattolica,   80
    Through a brute tyrant and his treachery.[14]
Neptune has never witnessed such a crime
    Between the isles of Cyprus and Majorca,
    By pirates now or Greeks in ancient time.
That one-eyed traitor[15] wielding power within
    The city which somebody here with me
    Heartily wishes he had never seen,[16]
Will make them meet with him and talk together,
    Then so arrange it that they'll need no prayers
    To shield them from Focara's wind and weather.'[17]   90
I said: 'Explain that – point him out to me
    (If you want news of you spread up above)
    That man who hates the sight of Rimini.'
He laid his hand on a companion's cheek,
    And prised his jaws apart for him, and shouted:
    'This is the fellow, and he does not speak!
This man, an exile, managed to allay
    All Caesar's doubts: "The man who's good and ready
    Will only suffer harm if he delay." '[18]
Oh how aghast, dismayed that man appeared,   100
    His tongue slit in his gullet – Curio –
    Always so ready to put in a word!
And one who had his hands docked, both of them,
    Lifted his stumps in that dark atmosphere
    So that his face was fouled as blood dripped down,
And cried: 'Remember Mosca too, who said,
    With what result! "A thing once done is done",
    Which for the Tuscans sowed such evil seed.'[19]

12. Nothing is known of him apart from what Dante tells us here.
13. Many of the damned share this anxiety to be remembered in the land of the living.
14. This murder was committed on the orders of Malatestino, lord of Rimini, in 1312.
15. Malatestino da Rimini.
16. Because it was there that he committed the sin for which he is damned.
17. The implication is that they will be drowned before their ship reaches the proverbially dangerous weather off the headland of Focara on Italy's Adriatic coast.
18. The sinner is Curio, the Roman who in 49 BC urged Julius Caesar to cross the Rubicon, an action which precipitated civil war.
19. In 1215 Mosca de' Lamberti urged the killing of Buondelmonte de' Buondelmonti which started the feud in Florence between the Guelphs and Ghibellines.

E io li aggiunsi: 'E morte di tua schiatta.'
    Per ch'elli, accumulando duol con duolo,   110
    sen gìo come persona trista e matta.
Ma io rimasi a riguardar lo stuolo,
    e vidi cosa ch'io avrei paura,
    sanza più prova, di contarla solo –
se non che coscienza m'assicura,
    la buona compagnia che l'uom francheggia
    sotto l'asbergo del sentirsi pura.
Io vidi certo, ed ancor par ch'io 'l veggia,
    un busto sanza capo andar sì come
    andavan li altri della trista greggia –   120
e 'l capo tronco tenea per le chiome,
    pésol con mano a guisa di lanterna –
    e quel mirava noi, e dicea: 'Oh me!'
Di sé facea a se stesso lucerna,
    ed eran due in uno e uno in due:
    com'esser può, quei sa che sì governa.
Quando diritto al piè del ponte fue,
    levò 'l braccio alto con tutta la testa,
    per appressarne le parole sue,
che fuoro: 'Or vedi la pena molesta   130
    tu che, spirando, vai veggendo i morti:
    vedi s'alcuna è grande come questa.
E perché tu di me novella porti,
    sappi ch'i' son Bertram dal Bornio, quelli
    che diedi al Re giovane i ma' conforti.
Io feci il padre e 'l figlio in sé ribelli:
    Achitofèl non fe' più d'Absalone
    e di Davìd coi malvagi punzelli.
Perch'io parti' così giunte persone,
    partito porto il mio cerebro – lasso! –   140
    dal suo principio ch'è in questo troncone.
Così s'osserva in me lo contrapasso.'

I added: 'And sowed death to all your race!'[20]
    And, at these words, which piled grief onto grief,   110
    He went like someone maddened by distress.
But I remained to gaze upon that crowd,
    And I saw what I'd hardly dare to mention
    Without someone supporting what was said,
If conscience did not now encourage me,
    The good companion that emboldens men
    Under their breastplate of integrity.
I really saw, and still I seem to see,
    A trunk without a head, moving along
    With all the others in that company;   120
It held its severed head up by the hair,
    Swinging it in one hand just like a lantern;
    The head saw us and moaned in its despair.
It made itself a lamp of its own head,
    And they were two in one and one in two:
    But how, He only knows, who so decreed.
When it arrived just under where we were,[21]
    It lifted up both arm and head together,
    To bring the words it had to say more near.
Those words were: 'Now you see outrageous pain,   130
    You who, still breathing, visit all the dead:
    Tell me, is any grief as great as mine?
So that you may take up some news of me,
    You must know I'm Bertran de Born, the man
    Who led the Young King into treachery,
Setting the father and the son at odds:[22]
    Achitophel did not do worse to David
    And Absalom, with his contentious words.[23]
Because I severed people joined like this,
    I carry here my brain which has been severed   140
    From where it drew its life – this trunk, alas!
And thus fit retribution is delivered.'

20. The Lamberti family were expelled from Florence in 1258.
21. Dante and Virgil are on a bridge, looking down into the ninth ditch.
22. The famous troubadour Bertran de Born (*c.*1140–*c.*1214) encouraged Prince Henry, the son of Henry II of England, to rebel against his father. Prince Henry was known as the Young King because he was crowned during his father's lifetime.
23. Achitophel persuaded Absalom to rebel against his father King David (2 Samuel: 15–18).

CANTO XXIX

Dante finds it difficult to tear himself away from the sowers of discord, and it becomes apparent that his anguish is for one in particular of those mutilated shades. This is Geri del Bello, a relative of Dante, who is angry that his murder has not been avenged. Dante shows some sympathy with his relative's plight, but Virgil has already insisted that he should turn his attention elsewhere: such sympathy is out of place, and also time is pressing.

The travellers then come to where they can look down into the last ditch of Eviltiers, reserved for falsifiers of all kinds. The description of this ditch, like an enormous hospital where all the sinners are punished with illness, will continue into the next canto. The falsifiers of metal, the alchemists, are punished with a sort of leprosy or scabies; the falsifiers of people, the impersonators, with hydrophobia; the falsifiers of money, the coiners, with dropsy; and the falsifiers of words, who use them for deception, with a burning fever.

We see in this canto two members of the first group, the alchemists, whose lives are revealed as not only sinful, but absurd. This absurdity provokes some comments on the pretentiousness of the Sienese, and particularly on their tendency to indulge in wildly extravagant living.

Dante and Virgil, here as everywhere in the Inferno, have time to speak with only a few of those who represent the sins which are being punished. It is, however, not difficult for the reader to provide his own, perhaps contemporary, instances. This is strikingly the case with the big spenders of Siena, the mention of whom may seem at first to give us merely an insight into a quaint, and repulsive, thirteenth-century fad, but which, after a moment's thought, is very likely to strike home to the reader. And this is, of course, the intention behind the whole of *The Divine Comedy*.

La molta gente e le diverse piaghe   1
   avean le luci mie sì inebriate
   che dello stare a piangere eran vaghe;
ma Virgilio mi disse: 'Che pur guate?
   perché la vista tua pur si soffolge
   là giù tra l'ombre triste smozzicate?
Tu non hai fatto sì all'altre bolge:
   pensa, se tu annoverar le credi,
   che miglia ventidue la valle volge.
E già la luna è sotto i nostri piedi: 10
   lo tempo è poco omai che n'è concesso,
   e altro è da veder che tu non vedi.'
'Se tu avessi,' rispuos'io appresso,
   'atteso alla cagion per ch'io guardava,
   forse m'avresti ancor lo star dimesso.'
Parte sen giva, e io retro li andava,
   lo duca, già faccendo la risposta,
   e soggiugnendo: 'Dentro a quella cava
dov'io tenea or li occhi sì a posta,
   credo ch'un spirto del mio sangue pianga   20
   la colpa che là giù cotanto costa.'
Allor disse 'l maestro: 'Non si franga
   lo tuo pensier da qui innanzi sovr'ello:
   attendi ad altro, ed ei là si rimanga:
ch'io vidi lui a piè del ponticello
   mostrarti, e minacciar forte, col dito,
   e udi' 'l nominar Geri del Bello.
Tu eri allor sì del tutto impedito
   sovra colui che già tenne Altaforte
   che non guardasti in là, sì fu partito.'   30
'O duca mio, la violenta morte
   che non li è vendicata ancor,' diss'io,
   'per alcun che dell'onta sia consorte,
fece lui disdegnoso – ond'el sen gìo
   sanza parlarmi, sì com'io estimo:
   ed in ciò m'ha el fatto a sé più pio.'

Such crowds, such frightful wounds! My eyes filled up –   1
    I found myself with a compelling urge
    Simply to linger there, and stand and weep,
But Virgil said: 'Why do you stand and gaze?
    Why do you pause and let your vision linger
    Among the sad and mutilated shades?
Think, if you mean to number all these souls –
    Something you did not do in other ditches –
    This valley runs for two and twenty miles.
By now the moon is underneath our feet:[1]   10
    Not much of our allotted time is left,
    And there's much more to see than you've seen yet.'
'If you had known,' I answered straight away,
    'The reason why I wished to go on looking,
    I think perhaps you would have let me stay.'
My leader simply went ahead meanwhile;
    But as I followed him I went on talking,
    Explaining what I meant: 'Within that hole
On which I was intent, I think I saw
    A spirit, one of my own blood, regretting   20
    The guilt for which they pay so dearly there.'
At this my master said: 'Henceforth refrain
    From thoughts of him, for more important things;
    And where that sinner is, let him remain;
I saw him pointing at you, from the hollow
    Beneath our bridge, and threaten, with his finger,
    And heard him being called Geri del Bello[2].
And then you had your eyes so fixed upon
    The shade which was the ruler of Hautefort[3]
    You did not look that way till he was gone.'   30
'O my good lord, the violent death he died,
    Which up to now is unavenged,' I answered,
    'By anyone who shares his shame and blood,
Made him disdainful – that is why he parted
    Without a word to me, or so I think;
    And that has made me feel more tender-hearted.'[4]

---

1. The moon is in the southern hemisphere. In the northern hemisphere the time is about noon.
2. He was a cousin of Dante's father.
3. Bertran de Born, seen in the previous canto in the ditch reserved for the sowers of discord.
4. Dante is sensitive to the custom of blood revenge, and even feels the obligation emotionally, but he clearly does not believe in honouring it.

Così parlammo infino al luogo primo
    che dello scoglio l'altra valle mostra,
    se più lume vi fosse, tutto ad imo.
Quando noi fummo sor[a] l'ultima chiostra   40
    di Malebolge, sì che i suoi conversi
    potean parere alla veduta nostra,
lamenti saettaron me diversi,
    che di pietà ferrati avean li strali,
    ond'io li orecchi con le man copersi.
Qual dolor fora, se delli spedali
    di Valdichiana tra 'l luglio e 'l settembre
    e di Maremma e di Sardigna i mali
fossero in una fossa tutti insembre,
    tal era quivi, e tal puzzo n'usciva   50
    qual suol venir delle marcite membre.
Noi discendemmo in su l'ultima riva
    del lungo scoglio, pur da man sinistra;
    e allor fu la mia vista più viva
giù ver lo fondo, la 've la ministra
    dell'alto sire infallibil giustizia
    punisce i falsador che qui registra.
Non credo ch'a veder maggior tristizia
    fosse in Egina il popol tutto infermo –
    quando fu l'aere sì pien di malizia   60
che li animali, infino al picciol vermo,
    cascaron tutti, e poi le genti antiche,
    secondo che i poeti hanno per fermo,
si ristorar di seme di formiche –
    ch'era a veder per quella oscura valle
    languir li spirti per diverse biche.
Qual sovra 'l ventre, e qual sovra le spalle
    l'un dell'altro giacea, e qual carpone
    si trasmutava per lo tristo calle.
Passo passo andavam sanza sermone,   70
    guardando e ascoltando li ammalati,
    che non potean levar le lor persone.

a. 'Sopra'.

We went on talking till we were in sight
    Of the next valley and its lowest parts,
    Or would have been, if there had been more light.
And when we'd finished walking, and we stood   40
    Above the last cloister of Eviltiers,
    And could distinguish all the brotherhood[5],
Such lamentation struck me, sharp and fierce
    As arrowheads, and barbed with sympathy,
    I had to clap my hands upon my ears.
There'd be such pain, if all the hospitals
    Of Val di Chiana, in the summer months,
    Sardinia, and Maremma, and all their ills,[6]
Were thrown into a single ditch together,
    As there was here; and such a stench arose   50
    As we expect from limbs that rot and fester.
We climbed right down onto the final ridge
    That runs across our pathway, keeping left,
    And there I found at last my sight could reach
Down where the handmaid of the highest lord,
    Justice that is unerring, punishes
    The falsifiers she has registered.
I do not think they made a sorrier sight –
    The sickly population of Aegina,
    Whose atmosphere was so infected that   60
All creatures, even to the little worm,
    Had to succumb, until that ancient race,
    Or so the poets strenuously affirm,
Was recreated, now with ants as seed[7] –
    Than those we saw along the sombre valley,
    Spirits languishing and diversified,
Some on their bellies, and some on the back
    Of someone else, and some upon all fours
    Dragging themselves along the gloomy track.
We went on step by step without a sound,   70
    But listening to and watching those sick souls,
    Who could not raise their bodies from the ground:

5. The religious terms 'cloister' and 'brotherhood' are ironical. Virgil and Dante are now looking down
    into the ditch reserved for the falsifiers of metals and money, people, and words.
6. These regions were all notoriously marshy and malarial.
7. According to the myth, ants were changed into human beings in order to repopulate the Greek island
    of Aegina.

Io vidi due sedere a sé poggiati,
 com'a scaldar si poggia tegghia a tegghia,
 dal capo al piè di schianze macolati;
e non vidi già mai menare stregghia
 a ragazzo aspettato dal segnorso,
 né a colui che mal volentier vegghia,
come ciascun menava spesso il morso
 dell'unghie sopra sé per la gran rabbia   80
 del pizzicor, che non ha più soccorso;
e sì traevan giù l'unghie la scabbia,
 come coltel di scardova le scaglie
 o d'altro pesce che più larghe l'abbia.
'O tu che con le dita ti dismaglie,'
 cominciò 'l duca mio all'un di loro,
 'e che fai d'esse tal volta tanaglie,
dinne s'alcun latino è tra costoro
 che son quinc'entro, se l'unghia ti basti
 etternalmente a cotesto lavoro.'   90
'Latin siam noi, che tu vedi sì guasti
 qui ambedue,' rispuose l'un piangendo.
 'Ma tu chi se' che di noi dimandasti?'
E 'l duca disse: 'I' son un che discendo
 con questo vivo giù di balzo in balzo,
 e di mostrar lo 'nferno a lui intendo.'
Allor si ruppe lo comun rincalzo,
 e tremando ciascuno a me si volse
 con altri che l'udiron di rimbalzo.
Lo buon maestro a me tutto s'accolse,   100
 dicendo: 'Di' a lor ciò che tu vuoli.'
 E io incominciai, poscia ch'ei volse:
'Se la vostra memoria non s'imboli
 nel primo mondo dall'umane menti,
 ma s'ella viva sotto molti soli,
ditemi chi voi siete e di che genti:
 la vostra sconcia e fastidiosa pena
 di palesarvi a me non vi spaventi.'

Two propped against each other where they sat,
    Like pans propped against pans to be warmed up,
    And both covered with scabs from head to foot;
And I have never ever seen a curry-
    Comb being plied for an impatient master,
    Or plied by one up late and in a hurry,
As I saw both of them go scratch, scratch, scratch,
    Their own nails scratching them in all the fury   80
    Of endless itching to relieve the itch;
And so they scraped their scabs off with their nails,
    Just as a knife does when it strips a carp
    Or any other fish with largish scales.
'O you who scale yourself with your own fingers,'
    My leader chose to speak to one of them,
    'And sometimes have to turn them into pincers,
Tell us if any Latin[8] is within
    That group of yours, so may your scaling nails
    Last out to do that work that's never done.'[9]   90
'The two of us are Latins you see here
    So dreadfully disfigured,' was the answer
    That came with tears; 'but tell us who you are.'
My leader answered: 'I am going down
    From terrace to terrace, for I must reveal
    The whole Inferno to this living man.'
Those sinners broke apart as he replied;
    Then, as they turned to look at me, they trembled,
    With others who by chance had overheard.
My master came up close to me, and told   100
    Me then: 'Say what it is you want of them';
    And I began, since that was what he willed:
'So that you may not fade from minds of men
    In the first world above, but your names live
    Through many revolutions of the sun,
Disclose your stock and your identity;
    And do not let your loathsome punishment
    Deter you from revealing this to me.'

8. Italian.
9. Frequently, to persuade the shades to answer questions, Virgil or Dante expresses a wish to please them. Here the wish is a backhanded one.

'Io fui d'Arezzo, e Albero da Siena,'
    rispuose l'un, 'mi fe' mettere al foco –   110
    ma quel per ch'io mori' qui non mi mena.
Vero è ch'i' dissi lui, parlando a gioco:
    "I' mi saprei levar per l'aere a volo" –
    e quei, ch'avea vaghezza e senno poco,
volle ch'i' li mostrassi l'arte, e solo
    perch'io nol feci Dedalo, mi fece
    ardere a tal che l'avea per figliuolo.
Ma nell'ultima bolgia delle diece
    me per l'alchìmia che nel mondo usai
    dannò Minòs, a cui fallar non lece.'   120
E io dissi al poeta: 'Or fu già mai
    gente sì vana come la sanese?
    Certo non la francesca sì d'assai!'
Onde l'altro lebbroso, che m'intese,
    rispuose al detto mio: 'Tra'mene Stricca,
    che seppe far le temperate spese,
e Niccolò, che la costuma ricca
    del garofano prima discoperse
    nell'orto dove tal seme s'appicca –
e tra'ne la brigata in che disperse   130
    Caccia d'Ascian la vigna e la gran fonda,
    e l'Abbagliato suo senno proferse.
Ma perché sappi chi sì ti seconda
    contra i Sanesi, aguzza ver me l'occhio,
    sì che la faccia mia ben ti risponda:
sì vedrai ch'io son l'ombra di Capocchio,
    che falsai li metalli con l'alchìmia:
    e te dee ricordar, se ben t'adocchio,
com'io fui di natura buona scimia.'

'I was an Aretine,' the first[10] replied.
    'Alberto da Siena[11] had me burnt.   110
    I was not brought here for the way I died;[12]
The truth is, when I told him, jokingly,
    "I could rise up and fly into the air",
    He, with less sense than curiosity,
Desired to see this feat; for this alone –
    Failing to make him Daedalus[13] – he had
    Me burnt by one who held him as a son.[14]
But never-erring Minos had me hurled
    Into the final ditch of all the ten
    For the alchemy I practised in the world.'   120
I asked the poet: 'Were there ever folk
    As hoity-toity as the Sienese?
    Certainly not the French, by a long chalk!'
To which the other leper, who'd heard me,
    Replied: 'Exceptions to all this are Stricca[15],
    Who knew the art of living frugally,
And Niccolò[16], who first revealed to men
    Habitual usage of the costly clove
    In the city where such fashions soon catch on;[17]
And also Caccia d'Asciano's[18] company,   130
    With whom he wasted vineyards and whole woods,
    While Muddlehead[19] showed his sagacity.
But, if you wish to know who's backing you
    Against the Sienese, look hard at me,
    And once you have my visage in full view,
You'll know the shade of old Capocchio[20], who
    Falsified metals with his alchemy;
    And you'll recall, if I remember you,
How I aped nature most successfully.'

10. Griffolino d'Arezzo, an alchemist, who died before 1272.
11. Alive in the second half of the thirteenth century. A favourite of a bishop of Siena.
12. He was burnt alive for annoying Alberto da Siena, but damned for his alchemy.
13. Famous in myth as the first man to fly successfully.
14. The bishop who favoured Alberto da Siena.
15. A notorious spendthrift of Siena in the second half of the 13th century. The word 'exceptions' is ironical.
16. Niccolò dei Salimbeni, still alive in 1311.
17. The city is Siena. Cloves were imported from the Far East and were therefore expensive.
18. Caccia was contemporary with Stricca and Niccolò, and like them devoted to extravagant spending.
19. A nickname, and another member of the band of spendthrifts.
20. A Florentine and an acquaintance of Dante, burnt alive for alchemy in Siena in 1293.

CANTO XXX

This canto begins with two accounts of madness, drawn from myth and Trojan history, which lead into a description of two shades running about wildly and savagely attacking the other shades – Gianni Schicchi, who impersonated someone in order to draw up a false will in his own favour, and Myrrha, who impersonated another woman in order to commit incest with her own father.

Then Dante notices a sinner lying there who is so deformed that he has, if one ignores his legs, the appearance of a lute – his face is shrunken like the neck of the lute and his body bloated like its body. This is Master Adam, damned for coining. He says how he had all he wanted while he was alive, but now is desperately craving a drop of water. He gives a lyrical description of the little streams which run down from the Casentino to join the Arno: this image is always in his mind and forms a great part of his punishment. With a dramatic reversal of tone, any sympathy we might have for Adam is destroyed however when he says that, if he could only see in the Inferno the shades of the three brothers who persuaded him to sin, he would prefer that sight to all the water in Fonte Branda. Adam believes that one of the brothers is already dead and damned, but he cannot move to look for him because of the weight of his dropsical body.

Adam identifies for Dante two sinners huddled together, so hot with fever that steam is rising from their bodies as from 'warm wet hands in winter'. They are Sinon, who lied to persuade the Trojans to take the wooden horse into Troy, and Potiphar's wife, who falsely accused Joseph of attempted rape.

A quarrel breaks out between Sinon and Master Adam, one which is both disgusting and amusing. When Virgil reproves him for his baseness in listening to such bickering, Dante's shame is such that he is quickly forgiven.

Nel tempo che Iunone era crucciata   1
   per Semelè contra 'l sangue tebano,
   come mostrò una e altra fiata,
Atamante divenne tanto insano,
   che veggendo la moglie con due figli
   andar carcata da ciascuna mano,
gridò: 'Tendiam le reti, sì ch'io pigli
   la leonessa e' leoncini al varco,'
   e poi distese i dispietati artigli,
prendendo l'un ch'avea nome Learco,   10
   e rotòllo e percosselo ad un sasso –
   e quella s'annegò con l'altro carco.
E quando la fortuna volse in basso
   l'altezza de' Troian che tutto ardiva,
   sì che 'nsieme col regno il re fu casso,
Ecuba trista, misera e cattiva,
   poscia che vide Polissena morta,
   e del suo Polidoro in su la riva
del mar si fu la dolorosa accorta,
   forsennata latrò sì come cane,   20
   tanto il dolor le fe' la mente torta.
Ma né di Tebe furie né troiane
   si vider mai in alcun tanto crude,
   non punger bestie, non che membra umane,
quant'io vidi in due ombre smorte e nude,
   che mordendo correvan di quel modo
   che 'l porco quando del porcil si schiude.
L'una giunse a Capocchio, ed in sul nodo
   del collo l'assannò, sì che, tirando,
   grattar li fece il ventre al fondo sodo.   30
E l'Aretin che rimase, tremando,
   mi disse: 'Quel folletto è Gianni Schicchi,
   e va rabbioso altrui così conciando.'
'Oh,' diss'io lui, 'se l'altro non ti ficchi
   li denti a dosso, non ti sia fatica
   a dir chi è, pria che di qui si spicchi.'

Of old when Juno was infuriated,   1
    Through Semele, against the Theban blood,
    As time and time again she demonstrated,[1]
Then Athamas was driven so insane
    That, when he saw his wife go passing by,
    Bearing upon each arm a little son,
He cried: 'Let's spread the nets and let me catch
    The lioness and both her cubs at once';
    And then he stretched his talons out to snatch
The child known as Learchus, whirled him round,   10
    And dashed him on a rock – at which his wife
    Leapt in the sea with the other, and they drowned.
And when on Fortune's wheel the Trojan pride,
    That had been full of daring, was brought low,
    So that both King and kingdom were destroyed,
Hecuba, now a wretched prisoner,
    When she had seen Polyxena lie dead,
    And she, in all her mourning, was aware
That it was Polydorus by the sea,
    Then she went howling madly like a dog,   20
    So far had grief driven her wits astray.[2]
But never was Theban fury ever seen,
    Or Trojan either, running so amok,
    Ripping up beasts, and even limbs of men,
As two pale naked shades I saw come by,
    Running, and biting everybody like
    A hog that's just been let loose from the sty.
The one got to Capocchio, and in the nape
    Of the neck he stuck his tusks and, dragging him
    On the hard ground, he made his belly scrape.   30
The one shade left, the trembling Aretine[3],
    Told me: 'That imp of hell is Gianni Schicchi[4]:
    He rages and does this to everyone.'
I answered him: 'Oh! That the other may
    Not sink its teeth in you, be not displeased
    To say its name before it gets away.'

1. Juno, to avenge herself on her husband Jupiter when he was unfaithful to her with Semele, contrived Semele's death. She also took a wider revenge by driving Semele's brother-in-law Athamas mad.
2. After the sack of Troy, the ex-queen Hecuba, by now herself a slave, witnessed the sacrifice of her daughter Polyxena. She also saw the body of her son Polydorus when it was washed up by the sea.
3. Griffolino. See the previous canto.
4. A Florentine (died c.1280) who impersonated Buoso Donati in order to dictate a false will by which he was to inherit a valuable mare.

Ed elli a me: 'Quell'è l'anima antica
    di Mirra scellerata, che divenne
    al padre fuor del dritto amore amica.
Questa a peccar con esso così venne,   40
    falsificando sé in altrui forma,
    come l'altro che là sen va sostenne,
per guadagnar la donna della torma,
    falsificare in sé Buoso Donati,
    testando e dando al testamento norma.'
E poi che i due rabbiosi fuor passati
    sovra cu' io avea l'occhio tenuto,
    rivolsilo a guardar li altri mal nati.
Io vidi un, fatto a guisa di leuto,
    pur ch'elli avesse avuta l'anguinaia   50
    tronca dall'altro che l'uomo ha forcuto.
La grave idropesì – che sì dispaia
    le membra con l'omor che mal converte
    che 'l viso non risponde alla ventraia –
faceva lui tener le labbra aperte
    come l'etico fa, che per la sete
    l'un verso il mento e l'altro in su rinverte.
'O voi che sanz'alcuna pena sete,
    e non so io perché, nel mondo gramo,'
    diss'elli a noi, 'guardate e attendete   60
alla miseria del maestro Adamo:
    io ebbi vivo assai di quel ch'i' volli,
    e ora – lasso! – un gocciol d'acqua bramo.
Li ruscelletti che de' verdi colli
    del Casentin discendon giuso in Arno,
    faccendo i lor canali freddi e molli,
sempre mi stanno innanzi, e non indarno,
    ché l'imagine lor vie più m'asciuga
    che 'l male ond'io nel volto mi discarno.
La rigida giustizia che mi fruga   70
    tragge cagion del loco ov'io peccai
    a metter più li miei sospiri in fuga.

And he replied: 'That is the ancient soul
    Of Myrrha the accursed, who loved her father,
    But in a way that's not permissible.[5]
And this is how that sinner came to sin: 40
    She took upon herself another's figure.
    The other[6], who goes there, took it on him –
He so desired the queen of all the herd –
    To make believe he was Buoso Donati,
    And made a will in due form, word for word.'
And when the two, still raging, had passed on,
    Whom I'd been looking at so fixedly,
    I turned to other shades of the ill-born.
I saw one who'd be fashioned like a lute
    If only at the groin, where human beings   50
    Divide up into two, he'd been cut short.
Ponderous dropsy, working to confound
    The limbs with liquid that will not digest,
    Till face and belly fail to correspond,[7]
Forced him to hold his lips asunder, like
    Consumptives who, dried up and thirsting, turn
    One to the chin, and one lip up and back.
'O you who seem to pay no penalty,
    I don't know why, in this bleak world of ours,'
    He said to us, 'now look this way and see   60
The heartache Master Adam[8] has to suffer:
    Alive, I'd everything I ever wanted,
    And now, alas, I crave a drop of water.
The little streams of the green hills which fall
    From Casentino[9] down into the Arno,
    In channels that are always moist and cool,
Are never out of mind, and not in vain,
    Because their image parches me much more
    Than this illness which makes my face so lean.
The rigid justice that is racking me   70
    Uses the very region where I sinned
    To make my sighs come faster as they flee.

5. The mythical Myrrha disguised herself as another woman in order to commit incest with her father.
6. Gianni Schicchi. See line 32 and note.
7. Dropsy has the effect of swelling the belly while shrinking the flesh of the head.
8. Burnt alive in 1281 for coining.
9. A district in Tuscany which includes the upper Arno valley.

Ivi è Romena, là dov'io falsai
    la lega suggellata del Batista,
    per ch'io il corpo su arso lasciai.
Ma s'io vedessi qui l'anima trista
    di Guido o d'Alessandro o di lor frate,
    per Fonte Branda non darei la vista.
Dentro c'è l'una già, se l'arrabbiate
    ombre che vanno intorno dicon vero –   80
    ma che mi val, c'ho le membra legate?
S'io fossi pur di tanto ancor leggero
    ch'i' potessi in cent'anni andare un'oncia,
    io sarei messo già per lo sentero,
cercando lui tra questa gente sconcia,
    con tutto ch'ella volge undici miglia,
    e men d'un mezzo di traverso non ci ha.
Io son per lor tra sì fatta famiglia:
    e' m'indussero a batter li fiorini
    ch'avean tre carati di mondiglia.'   90
E io a lui: 'Chi son li due tapini
    che fumman come man bagnate 'l verno,
    giacendo stretti a' tuoi destri confini?'
'Qui li trovai, e poi volta non dierno,'
    rispuose, 'quando piovvi in questo greppo,
    e non credo che dieno in sempiterno.
L'una è la falsa ch'accusò Giuseppo,
    l'altr'è il falso Sinón greco di Troia:
    per febbre aguta gittan tanto leppo.'
E l'un di lor, che si recò a noia   100
    forse d'esser nomato sì oscuro,
    col pugno li percosse l'epa croia[a].
Quella sonò come fosse un tamburo –
    e mastro Adamo li percosse il volto
    col braccio suo, che non parve men duro,
dicendo a lui: 'Ancor che mi sia tolto
    lo muover per le membra che son gravi,
    ho io il braccio a tal mestiere sciolto.'

a. A word of doubtful origin and even of meaning, a hapax legomenon in Dante. In combination with 'epa' it suggests common speech, and it fits with the tone of the following line.

There is Romena[10], there is where I coined
    Metal that bore the image of the Baptist[11] –
    And there it was I left my body, burnt.
But, could I see the soul of Alexander
    Being punished here, or Guido's, or their brother's,
    I would not swap that sight for Fonte Branda.[12]
One's here already,[13] if shades running round,
    In such a fury, are to be believed.   80
    But what good's that to me, whose limbs are bound?[14]
If I were still endowed with such great speed
    That I could inch one inch each hundred years,
    I would already be upon the road,
To find him in this crooked crowd, for all
    The ditch's circuit is eleven miles,
    And side to side is more than half a mile.
It is their fault I'm here with folk like this:
    They were the ones persuading me to strike
    Florins containing such a deal of dross.'   90
I asked: 'Who are those two in such a plight
    They send up steam like warm wet hands in winter,
    Lying there close to you upon your right?'
'I found them when I came,' he said, 'and they
    Have not stirred ever since and, I believe,
    They will not stir to all eternity.
One is Sinon of Troy, the lying Greek[15] –
    The other's she who cited Joseph falsely[16] –
    It is their raging fever makes them reek.'
And one of them, who seemed perhaps to blench   100
    At being named and spoken of so badly,
    Landed a punch on Adam's tightened paunch.
The paunch resounded like a beaten drum,
    And Master Adam struck him on the face
    With something that was just as hard – his arm –
And said to him: 'Although my body loses
    The ability to move, with its great weight,
    I have my arm free when the need arises.'

10. A castle in Casentino.
11. Florentine gold florins bore the image of the city's patron, John the Baptist.
12. Guido da Romena and his brothers, Alessandro and Aghinolfo, persuaded Master Adam to counterfeit
    the Florentine florin. There is a famous fountain, Fonte Branda, in Siena; but it seems more likely from
    the context that Adam is referring to Fonte Branda near Romena. Either way the significance is obvious.
13. Guido da Romena had died in 1292.
14. Bound figuratively by the weight of his swollen body.
15. Sinon pretended he had changed sides and persuaded the Trojans to take the wooden horse (secretly
    filled with armed Greeks) into their city.
16. Potiphar's wife falsely accused Joseph of trying to rape her (Genesis 39: 7–20).

Ond'ei rispuose: 'Quando tu andavi
    al fuoco, non l'avei tu così presto: 110
    ma sì e più l'avei quando coniavi.'
E l'idropico: 'Tu di' ver di questo:
    ma tu non fosti sì ver testimonio
    là 've del ver fosti a Troia richesto.'
'S'io dissi falso, e tu falsasti il conio,'
    disse Sinone, 'e son qui per un fallo –
    e tu per più ch'alcun altro demonio!'
'Ricorditi, spergiuro, del cavallo,'
    rispuose quel ch'avea infiata l'epa,
    'e sieti reo che tutto il mondo sallo!'   120
'E te sia rea la sete onde ti crepa,'
    disse 'l greco, 'la lingua, e l'acqua marcia
    che 'l ventre innanzi li occhi sì t'assiepa!'
Allora il monetier: 'Così si squarcia
    la bocca tua per tuo mal come sòle –
    ché s'i' ho sete ed umor mi rinfarcia,
tu hai l'arsura e 'l capo che ti dole –
    e per leccar lo specchio di Narcisso
    non vorresti a 'nvitar molte parole.'
Ad ascoltarli er'io del tutto fisso,   130
    quando 'l maestro mi disse: 'Or pur mira,
    che per poco che teco non mi risso!'
Quand'io 'l senti' a me parlar con ira,
    volsimi verso lui con tal vergogna
    ch'ancor per la memoria mi si gira.
Qual è colui che suo dannaggio sogna,
    che sognando desidera sognare,
    sì quel ch'è, come non fosse, agogna,
tal mi fec'io, non possendo parlare,
    che disiava scusarmi, e scusava   140
    me tuttavia, e nol mi credea fare.
'Maggior difetto men vergogna lava,'
    disse 'l maestro, 'che 'l tuo non è stato,
    però d'ogne trestizia ti disgrava:

To which he answered: 'When you went to burn,
    Your arms were not unbound; and yet they were   110
    Quite free and easy when you went to coin.'
The one with dropsy then: 'What you now say
    Is true: but you were not a truthful witness
    When you were asked to tell the truth at Troy.'
'If I spoke lies, you faked your coins as well,'
    Said Sinon. 'I am here for one fault only,
    And you for more than any devil in hell!'
'Perjurer, bear in mind the horse,' was how
    The one with bloated belly answered him,
    'And be dismayed the whole world knows it now!'[17]   120
'And may your thirst,' the Greek said, 'dismay you,
    Cracking your tongue, while all the filthy water
    Distends your belly, blocking out your view!'[18]
At this the coiner: 'Your mouth has to burst
    Apart with fever as it always does!
    For if I'm bloated and I have a thirst,
You have your fever and your aching head –
    To get you to lap up Narcissus' mirror[19]
    There'd be no need to press you very hard.'
I was wholly intent upon these two,   130
    When my guide said to me: 'Just go on looking,
    And soon there'll be a clash between us too!'
When I heard him address me angrily,
    I turned towards him and I felt such shame
    That even now it haunts my memory.
Like someone who is having a bad dream
    And, dreaming, wishes he were dreaming, therefore
    Wishing what is were happening to him –
Just so was I: I could not say a word –
    I longed to excuse myself, and did excuse   140
    Myself in fact, and did not think I did.
'Less shame would wash away a greater fault,'
    My master said to me, 'than yours has been:
    So do away with any sense of guilt.

17. The incident of the wooden horse is dealt with in detail by Virgil in his *Aeneid*.
18. Adam is supine.
19. Water. The mythical Narcissus fell in love with his own reflection in a pool.

e fa' ragion ch'io ti sia sempre a lato,
    se più avvien che fortuna t'accoglia
    dove sien genti in simigliante piato –
ché voler ciò udire è bassa voglia.'

Always suppose that I am still about,
    If chance again should bring you to a place
    Where there is such another falling-out;
The wish to listen to such things is base.'

CANTO XXXI

When the canto opens Dante is still thinking of his shame at
Virgil's rebuke for his vulgar curiosity. Then the two companions
start to make their way through half-light across the parapet
which bounds the final circle of the Inferno. Suddenly they hear
a horn, so loud that it outdoes even the sound of Roland's at
Roncesvalles. Dante looks round him and sees what appear to
be many towers. To forearm Dante, Virgil explains that they are
really giants, those giants who tried to seize power from the
Olympian gods. They are ranged all round the central lake or
well of this final circle. Again and again their overwhelming size,
much greater than that of any unmythical giant, is emphasised.

The first whom Dante sees clearly is the biblical Nimrod,
'the mighty hunter before the Lord'. It was he who blew
the horn. He speaks briefly in a strange babble which reminds us
of his responsibility for the Tower of Babel, whose construction
led to the multiplication and confusion of human tongues. The
few words which Virgil addresses to him are reproving and
scornful: this sets the tone for Dante's similar attitude towards
the people he will meet in the following canto.

As the pilgrims go on their way, they see Ephialtes, bound
five times round with chains. When they come to Antaeus,
who did not take part in the revolt against the Olympian
gods, Virgil speaks to him fairly and asks him to lift them
down onto the frozen lake of Cocytus. Virgil grasps Dante to
him, and this double burden is lifted by Antaeus and put
down in the first zone of this circle, Caïna (named after
Cain), where those who betrayed relatives are punished.

Una medesma lingua pria mi morse,   I
    sì che mi tinse l'una e l'altra guancia,
    e poi la medicina mi riporse:
così od'io che soleva la lancia
    d'Achille e del suo padre esser cagione
    prima di trista e poi di buona mancia.
Noi demmo il dosso al misero vallone
    su per la ripa che 'l cinge dintorno,
    attraversando sanza alcun sermone.
Quiv'era men che notte e men che giorno,   10
    sì che 'l viso m'andava innanzi poco –
    ma io senti' sonare un alto corno,
tanto ch'avrebbe ogne tuon fatto fioco,
    che, contra sé la sua via seguitando,
    dirizzò li occhi miei tutti ad un loco.
Dopo la dolorosa rotta, quando
    Carlo Magno perdé la santa gesta,
    non sonò sì terribilmente Orlando.
Poco portai in là volta la testa,
    che me parve veder molte alte torri –   20
    ond'io: 'Maestro, di', che terra è questa?'
Ed elli a me: 'Però che tu trascorri
    per le tenebre troppo dalla lungi,
    avvien che poi nel maginare abborri.
Tu vedrai ben, se tu là ti congiungi,
    quanto 'l senso s'inganna di lontano,
    però alquanto più te stesso pungi.'
Poi caramente mi prese per mano,
    e disse: 'Pria che noi siamo più avanti,
    acciò che 'l fatto men ti paia strano,   30
sappi che non son torri, ma giganti,
    e son nel pozzo intorno dalla ripa
    dall'umbilico in giuso tutti quanti.'
Come quando la nebbia si dissipa,
    lo sguardo a poco a poco raffigura
    ciò che cela il vapor che l'aere stipa,

It was the same tongue giving me the wound,   1
    Tinging with red first one cheek then the other,
    Which then made sure that I was medicined:[1]
Just as, so I have heard, Achilles' lance,
    Which was his father's lance before, delivered
    Agony first and afterwards redress.[2]
Turning our backs upon that wretched ditch[3],
    We went up on the bank surrounding it,
    And made our way across without more speech.
It was not night, but certainly not dawn: 10
    I could but see a little way ahead –
    And then I heard a loud blast on a horn,
That would have made a thunderclap seem light,
    And as I traced that sound back to its source,
    I fixed my eyes upon one single spot.
After the dire defeat when Charlemagne
    Lost all his holy band of paladins,
    Not such a shock arrived from Roland's horn.[4]
Not long I tried to pierce the gloom before
    I saw, or so it seemed, many high towers;   20
    'Master,' I asked, 'what city is this here?'
And he replied: 'You'll find, now that you fix
    Your eyes on something far off in the shadows,
    That your imagination's playing tricks.
Once you get there, then you will clearly see
    How much the distance has deceived your sight:
    So let that knowledge urge you on your way.'
Then tenderly he took me by the hand,
    And said: 'Before we go on any further,
    And so that you may not get too alarmed,   30
Know now you are not seeing towers at all,
    But giants[5] round this rampart, who are buried
    Up to their navels in the central well.'
As when a mist begins to dissipate,
    And bit by bit we start to make some sense
    Of what the foggy air hid from our sight,

---

1. See the previous canto, ll. 130–48.
2. Rust from Achilles' spear could heal the wounds the spear had inflicted.
3. The tenth and last ditch of Eviltiers.
4. When Charlemagne's army, in the year 778, was withdrawing from Spain, his rearguard of select warriors under the command of Roland was wiped out at Roncesvalles. Charlemagne learnt of this when he heard Roland blow his horn from eight miles away to summon help.
5. Dante conflates the giants mentioned in Genesis 6: 4–5 with the giants of Greek mythology who tried to storm Mount Olympus but were foiled by the Olympian gods and particularly by Jove's thunderbolts.

così, forando l'aura grossa e scura,
    più e più appressando ver la sponda,
    fuggìemi errore e crescìemi paura,
però che come sulla cerchia tonda   40
    Montereggion di torri si corona,
    così la proda che 'l pozzo circonda
torreggiavan di mezza la persona
    li orribili giganti[a], cui minaccia
    Giove del cielo ancora quando tona.
E io scorgeva già d'alcun la faccia,
    le spalle e 'l petto e del ventre gran parte,
    e per le coste giù ambo le braccia.
Natura certo, quando lasciò l'arte
    di sì fatti animali, assai fe' bene,   50
    per tòrre tali essecutori a Marte.
E s'ella d'elefanti e di balene
    non si pente, chi guarda sottilmente,
    più giusta e più discreta la ne tene,
ché dove l'argomento della mente
    s'aggiugne al mal volere ed alla possa,
    nessun riparo vi può far la gente.
La faccia sua mi parea lunga e grossa
    come la pina di San Pietro a Roma,
    e a sua proporzione eran l'altre ossa,   60
sì che la ripa, ch'era perizoma
    dal mezzo in giù, ne mostrava ben tanto
    di sopra, che di giungere alla chioma
tre Frison s'averìen dato mal vanto,
    però ch'i' ne vedea trenta gran palmi
    dal luogo in giù dov'uomo affibbia 'l manto.
'Raphèl maì amècche zabì almi,'
    cominciò a gridar la fiera bocca,
    cui non si convenìa più dolci salmi.
E 'l duca mio ver lui: 'Anima sciocca,   70
    tienti col corno, e con quel ti disfoga
    quand'ira o altra passion ti tocca!

a. 'La proda' is the object and 'li orribili giganti' the subject, with 'torreggiavano' used transitively – a bold use but not untypical of Dante.

So, as I pierced the murky atmosphere,
    And kept on coming closer to the brink,[6]
    My error vanished, giving way to fear;
For just as round the circle of its wall   40
    Montereggioni crowns itself with towers,[7]
    Just so, above the bank around the well,
The giants tower, half shown, half hidden under,
    So tall, so terrible, but such as still
    Jove threatens out of heaven with his thunder.
Already I could see the face of one,
    His shoulders, breast, a great part of his belly,
    And his high sides by which his arms hung down.
Nature did well to leave off making these
    Creatures and other creatures like them, taking   50
    Such monstrous ministers away from Mars[8].
And, though she still continues with the whale
    And elephant, if one considers subtly,
    That turns out to be well advised as well:
It's where the reasoning of a man of sense
    Combines with evil will and such great power
    That mankind has no adequate defence.
His face seemed every bit as long and round
    As the huge pine cone standing in St Peter's,[9]
    And all his body equally big-boned;   60
Indeed the bank, which served him as a screen
    Down from his waist, revealed so much above
    That three Frieslanders[10] would have hoped in vain
That they might boast of reaching to his hair,
    For downward from the spot where cloaks are buckled[11]
    I could see thirty spans at least laid bare.
'*Raphèl maì amècche zabì almi*,'[12]
    Such were the words which came from that brute mouth
    (Sweeter psalms would have come less suitably).
My leader said to him: 'You babbling fool,   70
    Stick to your horn, and with that vent your feelings
    When ire or other passion stirs your soul!

6. The parapet round the lowest circle of the Inferno.
7. There were originally fourteen high towers round the walls of this fortress near Siena.
8. The Roman god of war.
9. This is the old basilica of St Peter in Rome: the present building was made long after Dante's day.
   However, the giant bronze pine cone is still to be seen in the Vatican Museum.
10. Noted for their stature.
11. The throat.
12. As Dante makes clear in ll. 79–81, this is meaningless babble.

Cercati al collo, e troverai la soga
    che 'l tien legato, o anima confusa,
    e vedi lui che 'l gran petto ti doga.'
Poi disse a me: 'Elli stesso s'accusa –
    questi è Nembròt per lo cui mal coto
    pur un linguaggio nel mondo non s'usa.
Lasciànlo stare e non parliamo a vòto,
    ché così è a lui ciascun linguaggio   80
    come 'l suo ad altrui, ch'a nullo è noto.'
Facemmo adunque più lungo viaggio
    vòlti a sinistra, ed al trar d'un balestro
    trovammo l'altro assai più fero e maggio.
A cinger lui qual che fosse 'l maestro
    non so io dir, ma el tenea soccinto
    dinanzi l'altro e dietro il braccio destro
d'una catena che 'l tenea avvinto
    dal collo in giù, sì che 'n su lo scoperto
    si ravvolgea infino al giro quinto.   90
'Questo superbo volle essere sperto
    di sua potenza contra al sommo Giove,'
    disse 'l mio duca, 'ond'elli ha cotal merto.
Fialte ha nome, e fece le gran prove
    quando i giganti fer paura a' dei:
    le braccia ch'el menò già mai non move.'
E io a lui: 'S'esser puote, io vorrei
    che dello smisurato Briareo
    esperienza avesser li occhi miei.'
Ond'ei rispuose: 'Tu vedrai Anteo   100
    presso di qui che parla ed è disciolto,
    che ne porrà nel fondo d'ogni reo.
Quel che tu vuo' veder, più là è molto,
    ed è legato e fatto come questo,
    salvo che più feroce par nel volto.'
Non fu tremoto già tanto rubesto
    che scotesse una torre così forte,
    come Fialte a scuotersi fu presto.

Feel round your neck, and you will find the strap
    That holds it fast, you poor bewildered creature:
    It lies across your great chest like a stripe.'
Virgil went on: 'By himself he stands revealed –
    For this is Nimrod, through whose evil notion
    One single tongue no longer serves the world.[13]
Let's leave him, let's not talk with him in vain,
    For every other language is to him   80
    As his to others – understood by none.'
So, turning to the left, we went on further,
    Until we found, a crossbow shot away,
    Another giant, more fierce and even larger.
And whosoever was the master-hand
    That tied him I can't tell you, but he had
    His left arm in the front, his right behind,
Both pinioned by a chain that held him bound
    From the neck down, and what was visible
    Was circumvented fully five times round.   90
'This was a giant who wanted, in his pride,
    To pitch his strength against almighty Jove,'
    My guide went on, 'and this is his reward.
He's Ephialtes, strong in that endeavour
    When gods were terror-stricken by the giants:
    The arms he moved then have been stilled for ever.'
To this I answered: 'I am curious,
    If possible, to see with my own eyes
    One above all – the huge Briareus.'
And he replied: 'Antaeus is the one   100
    We'll find nearby, who speaks and is unfettered:[14]
    He'll place us at the centre of all sin.
He whom you want to see's much further on,
    And he is bound and built like Ephialtes,
    Except his face looks even more malign.'
No earthquake ever gave so great a shock,
    So sudden, to a tower to make it tremble,
    As Ephialtes, when he heard this, shook.

13. 'And Cush begat Nimrod: he began to be a mighty one in the earth. He was a mighty hunter before the Lord... And the beginning of his kingdom was Babel...' (Genesis 10: 8–10). It is appropriate for Nimrod, as a hunter, to have a horn. There is also a tradition that he was chiefly responsible for the building of the Tower of Babel, which led to the confusion of tongues (Genesis 11: 1–9).

14. Antaeus is unfettered because he did not take part in the rebellion of the giants against the gods.

Allor temett'io più che mai la morte,
 e non v'era mestier più che la dotta,   110
 s'io non avessi viste le ritorte.
Noi procedemmo più avante allotta,
 e venimmo ad Anteo, che ben cinque alle,
 sanza la testa, uscìa fuor della grotta.
'O tu che nella fortunata valle
 che fece Scipion di gloria reda –
 quand'Annibàl co' suoi diede le spalle –
recasti già mille leon per preda,
 e che se fossi stato all'alta guerra
 de' tuoi fratelli, ancor par che si creda   120
ch'avrebber vinto i figli della terra –
 mettine giù, e non ten vegna schifo,
 dove Cocito la freddura serra.
Non ci fare ire a Tizio né a Tifo:
 questi può dar di quel che qui si brama,
 però ti china, e non torcer lo grifo.
Ancor ti può nel mondo render fama,
 ch'el vive, e lunga vita ancor aspetta
 se innanzi tempo Grazia a sé nol chiama.'
Così disse 'l maestro, e quelli in fretta   130
 le man distese, e prese il duca mio,
 ond'Ercule sentì già grande stretta.
Virgilio, quando prender si sentìo,
 disse a me: 'Fatti qua, sì ch'io ti prenda;'
 poi fece sì ch'un fascio era elli e io.
Qual pare a riguardar la Garisenda
 sotto 'l chinato – quando un nuvol vada
 sovr'essa sì che ella incontro penda –
tal parve Anteo a me che stava a bada
 di vederlo chinare, e fu tal ora   140
 ch'i' avrei voluto ir per altra strada.
Ma lievemente al fondo che divora
 Lucifero con Giuda, ci sposò –
 né, sì chinato, lì fece dimora,
e come albero in nave si levò.

Oh, then I feared to die, so great my fright:
  The fear itself seemed great enough to kill me,   110
  Had I not seen the chains that held him tight.
And so we carried on and went ahead,
  And reached Antaeus, rising up five ells
  Above the rock, not reckoning his head.
'O you who once, within the fateful vale
  Where Scipio inherited such glory
  When Hannibal and all his troops turned tail,[15]
Seized on a thousand lions for your prey,[16]
  And who, if you'd accompanied your brothers
  In their great war, some reckon to this day   120
The sons of earth might well have gained the field,
  Do not disdain to set us down below you,
  Where the Cocytus[17] is locked in with cold.
Must we ask Tityus, Typhon, and so on?
  This man can give you what you all crave here;
  So do not curl your lip, but just bend down.
He can reward you with fresh worldly fame,
  For he's alive, and he expects long life,
  Unless grace summons him before his time.'
So said my master; the other, like a shot,   130
  Reached down and took my leader in that grasp
  Which had onetime held Hercules so tight.[18]
And Virgil, when he felt those fingers, said:
  'Come over here, let me hold onto you.'
  And so the two of us became one load.
The way the Garisenda[19] looks, below
  The side it leans on, when a cloud goes over
  So that it seems to topple – that is how
Antaeus, as he leant down, looked to me
  Who stood in apprehension: at that instant   140
  I would have much preferred some other way.
But down he set us gently in the abyss
  Where Lucifer and Judas are held fast;[20]
  Nor did he lean down long: straight after this
He straightened up again, like a ship's mast.

15. In North Africa at the Battle of Zama in 202 BC the Roman general Scipio (who became known as 'Africanus' in honour of this victory) decisively defeated Hannibal.
16. The number is hyperbolic, but lions were his usual diet.
17. One of the rivers of the underworld which has here spread to a lake and frozen over.
18.When he wrestled with Antaeus, Hercules found that every time he threw him he rose up stronger than ever. This was because Antaeus was born from the earth and drew his strength from it. When Hercules realised this, he held Antaeus above his head and won.
19. A leaning tower in Bologna.
20. The lowest part of the Inferno where the sinners are locked in ice.

CANTO XXXII

Dante stresses the difficulty of describing the ninth and lowest circle of the Inferno – the frozen lake of Cocytus, divided, as it slopes towards the centre, into four concentric zones: Caïna, for betrayers of their relatives; Antenora, for betrayers of their country; Ptolomea, for betrayers of guests; and finally Judecca, for betrayers of benefactors.

This is the cruellest canto so far: in the sinners' punishments, in their attitude to each other, in Dante's own actions, and in the harsh, at times blackly humorous, tone of the canto as a whole. Two brothers who committed mutual fratricide are locked together; they weep, but their tears congeal as they issue: they butt each other like goats. Their names are revealed by another shade, who insists that his own sins pale into insignificance in comparison with those of a cousin whom he is expecting to join him. The shades here are not so quick to name themselves as others are in the Inferno, but they are very quick to name each other: the habit of betrayal sticks. As Dante moves down from Caïna into Antenora he 'happens' to kick a sinner's head. Dante is anxious to know who this shade is; the shade is anxious he should not know. Dante seizes him by the scruff of his neck and threatens to tear all his hair out if he does not reveal his name; the sinner remains adamant, but of course another shade gives the game away: this is Bocca degli Abati, who betrayed the Guelphs at Montaperti. Dante adds to this sinner's suffering by promising to report the truth about him to the world above. Other sinners, who with nice understatement are said to be 'laid out to cool', are dealt with more summarily.

Finally, Dante and Virgil reach two shades engaged in eating and being eaten, and Dante promises the eater that, if he tells his story, it shall be related in the world above.

S'io avessi le rime aspre e chiocce,   I
   come si converrebbe al tristo buco
   sovra 'l qual pontan tutte l'altre rocce,
io premerei di mio concetto il suco
   più pienamente, ma perch'io non l'abbo,
   non sanza tema a dicer mi conduco –
ché non è impresa da pigliare a gabbo
   discriver fondo a tutto l'universo,
   né da lingua che chiami mamma o babbo:
ma quelle donne aiutino il mio verso   10
   ch'aiutaro Anfione a chiuder Tebe,
   sì che dal fatto il dir non sia diverso.
Oh sovra tutte mal creata plebe
   che stai nel luogo onde parlare è duro,
   mei foste state qui pecore o zebe!
Come noi fummo giù nel pozzo scuro
   sotto i piè del gigante assai più bassi,
   e io mirava ancora all'alto muro,
dicere udi'mi: 'Guarda come passi –
   va sì che tu non calchi con le piante   20
   le teste de' fratei miseri lassi.'
Per ch'io mi volsi, e vidimi davante
   e sotto i piedi un lago che per gelo
   avea di vetro e non d'acqua sembiante.
Non fece al corso suo sì grosso velo
   di verno la Danoia in Osterlicchi,
   né Tanaì là sotto 'l freddo cielo,
com'era quivi – ché se Tambernicchi
   vi fosse su caduto, o Pietrapana,
   non avrìa pur dall'orlo fatto cricchi.   30
E come a gracidar si sta la rana
   col muso fuor dell'acqua – quando sogna
   di spigolar sovente la villana –
livide, insin là dove appar vergogna,
   eran l'ombre dolenti nella ghiaccia,
   mettendo i denti in nota di cicogna.

If I could conjure up such raucous, rasping   1
    Rhymes as would suit the melancholy hole
    Where all the other rocks converge, then, grasping
My theme more firmly, I would press the juice
    More fully from it: since I have none such,
    I am, here at the outset, timorous;
This is no May-game for just anybody –
    To sound the depth of all the universe –
    Nor for a tongue that still says *mummy, daddy*:
But may those learned ladies[1] now help me,   10
    Who once helped Amphion throw a wall round Thebes,[2]
    That style and substance may not disagree.
Oh, misbegotten brood, down in this deep
    So hard to talk about, it had been better
    By far had you been born as goats or sheep![3]
As we were standing, down in that dark well,
    Under the giant's feet and much much lower,
    With me still gazing up at the high wall,[4]
I heard this said to me: 'Look how you go!
    And take good care you do not trample over   20
    The heads of the sad brotherhood of woe!'
At this I turned and saw in front there was –
    And underfoot – a lake so frozen over
    It did not look like water, but like glass.
The Austrian Danube's never ever veiled
    Itself to such a depth in winter, nor
    The River Don, for all the northern cold.
This sheet of ice would not – if Tambernic
    Were to crash down on it, or Pietrapana[5] –
    Not even at the edge, so much as creak.   30
Like frogs that keep their muzzles out of water
    To croak, that season[6] when the peasant girl
    So often dreams of what she'll glean and gather,
So, livid, sunken up to where the face
    Can show its shame, and where the teeth can chatter
    In time with storks,[7] shades suffer in the ice.

1. The Muses.
2. The myth has it that Amphion, with the music of his lyre, attracted stones down from the mountains to build the walls of Thebes.
3. They would not then be responsible for, and punished for, their actions.
4. The parapet around this lowest part of the Inferno.
5. Tambernic and Pietrapana are mountains in the Apuan Alps, in the north-west of Tuscany.
6. Early summer.
7. When they rattle their bills.

Ognuna in giù tenea volta la faccia:
 da bocca il freddo, e dalli occhi il cor tristo
 tra lor testimonianza si procaccia.
Quand'io m'ebbi dintorno alquanto visto,   40
 volsimi a' piedi, e vidi due sì stretti
 che 'l pel del capo avìeno insieme misto.
'Ditemi, voi che sì strignete i petti,'
 diss'io, 'chi siete?' E quei piegaro i colli –
 e poi ch'ebber li visi a me eretti,
li occhi lor, ch'eran pria pur dentro molli,
 gocciar su per le labbra, e 'l gelo strinse
 le lacrime tra essi e riserrolli.
Con legno legno spranga mai non cinse
 forte così, ond'ei come due becchi   50
 cozzaro insieme, tanta ira li vinse.
E un ch'avea perduti ambo li orecchi
 per la freddura, pur col viso in giùe,
 disse: 'Perché cotanto in noi ti specchi?
Se vuoi saper chi son cotesti due,
 la valle onde Bisenzo si dichina
 del padre loro Alberto e di lor fue.
D'un corpo usciro, e tutta la Caina
 potrai cercare, e non troverai ombra
 degna più d'esser fitta in gelatina –   60
non quelli a cui fu rotto il petto e l'ombra
 con esso un colpo per la man d'Artù –
 non Focaccia – non questi che m'ingombra
col capo sì ch'i' non veggio oltre più,
 e fu nomato Sassol Mascheroni –
 se tosco se', ben sai omai chi fu.
E perché non mi metti in più sermoni,
 sappi ch'io fu' il Camicion de' Pazzi,
 e aspetto Carlin che mi scagioni.'
Poscia vid'io mille visi cagnazzi   70
 fatti per freddo – onde mi vien riprezzo,
 e verrà sempre, de' gelati guazzi.

They were all looking down – their eyes revealed
    Their inner sadness as they wept – their teeth
    Bore chattering witness to the outer cold.
And, after a short time of looking round,   40
    I, glancing down, saw two so close together
    The hairs upon their heads were intertwined.
'You who are locked in such a strong embrace,'
    I said, 'who are you?' They bent back their necks,
    And as they both looked up and in my face,
Their eyes, which had been only moist within,
    Gushed over at the lids, until the cold
    Congealed those tears, and locked the lids again.
No clamp has ever clamped two beams of wood
    So tight as they were held – whereat they butted   50
    Each other like two billy goats gone mad.
Another who, in this perpetual winter,
    Had lost both ears, kept looking down, and said:
    'Why do you stare at us, as in a mirror?[8]
You want to know who these two are together?
    The Vale of the Bisenzio was theirs,
    After Alberto, and he was their father.[9]
They issued from one body – and when you've seen
    All of Caïna you'll have found no shade
    More suitable to set in gelatine;   60
Not even him whose breast and shadow were
    Pierced by a single blow from Arthur's hand,[10]
    Not Focaccia[11], and not this fellow here
Whose head's so in the way I can't see through;
    Sassolo Mascheroni[12] was his name –
    If you're a Tuscan he'll be known to you.
So that I need not say another word,
    I'll say my name: Camicione de' Pazzi[13];
    And when Carlino[14] comes I'll not seem bad.'
And then I saw a thousand faces, pale   70
    And blue in all that cold – which makes me shudder
    Now to see ice on pools, and always will.

8. The image conveys primarily the intensity of Dante's gaze. Also, the ice acts as a mirror.
9. Napoleone and Alessandro, the sons of Alberto degli Alberti, quarrelled over their inheritance and for political reasons, and in 1286 killed each other.
10. When Mordred, who had rebelled against his uncle King Arthur, was killed, the lance made such a great hole in his body that even his shadow had a hole in it.
11. A citizen of Pistoia, he treacherously killed a cousin, which led to such disturbances that the Florentines were called in to help. This created a feud between the Black and White Guelphs in Florence.
12. A Florentine who murdered a relative for his inheritance.
13. A Tuscan who killed a relative.
14. Carlino de' Pazzi, a relative of Camicione, took a bribe to deliver a castle which he was holding for the White Guelphs into the hands of the Black Guelphs. He was alive at the time of Dante's vision (1300).

E mentre ch'andavamo inver lo mezzo
    al quale ogni gravezza[a] si rauna –
    e io tremava nell'etterno rezzo –
se voler fu o destino o fortuna
    non so, ma, passeggiando tra le teste,
    forte percossi il piè nel viso ad una.
Piangendo mi sgridò: 'Perché mi peste?
    se tu non vieni a crescer la vendetta   80
    di Montaperti, perché mi moleste?'
E io: 'Maestro mio, or qui m'aspetta,
    sì ch'io esca d'un dubbio per costui –
    poi mi farai, quantunque vorrai, fretta.'
Lo duca stette, e io dissi a colui
    che bestemmiava duramente ancora:
    'Qual se' tu che così rampogni altrui?'
'Or tu chi se' che vai per l'Antenora,
    percotendo,' rispuose, 'altrui le gote,
    sì che, se fossi vivo, troppo fora?'   90
'Vivo son io, e caro esser ti pote,'
    fu mia risposta, 'se dimandi fama,
    ch'io metta il nome tuo tra l'altre note.'
Ed elli a me: 'Del contrario ho io brama –
    lèvati quinci e non mi dar più lagna,
    ché mal sai lusingar per questa lama!'
Allor lo presi per la cuticagna,
    e dissi: 'El converrà che tu ti nomi,
    o che capel qui su non ti rimagna.'
Ond'elli a me: 'Perché tu mi dischiomi,   100
    né ti dirò ch'io sia, né mosterròlti,
    se mille fiate in sul capo mi tomi.'
Io avea già i capelli in mano avvolti,
    e tratti li n'avea più d'una ciocca,
    latrando lui con li occhi in giù raccolti,
quando un altro gridò: 'Che hai tu, Bocca?
    Non ti basta sonar con le mascelle,
    se tu non latri? Qual diavol ti tocca?'

a. Weight drawn to the centre of the earth by the force of gravity. There is also the very apposite sense of 'trouble' or 'affliction'.

As we continued downwards and towards
    The centre where all weight and woe converges,
    And shivered in the eternal too-cool shade,
Whether by my intention, or by fate,
    Or chance, I do not know, with all those heads,
    I knocked against a face there with my foot.
He wept, and shouted out complainingly:
    'Unless you're here to add to all the vengeance   80
    For Montaperti[15], why d'you tread on me?'
Then I said: 'Let me linger here, my master,
    Until I have resolved a doubt about him,
    And then I'll hurry up – I'll go much faster.'
My leader did stop, and I asked the one
    I'd kicked, who kept on cursing all the while:
    'Now who are you, to grunt like this and groan?'
'Now who are you, to walk through Antenora[16],
    Kicking us in the cheek?' he asked in turn.
    'That's something which, alive, I would not suffer!'[17]   90
'Now I, I am alive. If you want fame,'
    I said, 'I know the way to make you grateful,
    Setting down, with the other names, your name.'
Then he to me: 'I want the opposite;
    Get on your way – stop causing all this trouble –
    Your flattery is pointless in this pit!'
I grabbed him by his scruffy scruff and said:
    'It is essential that you give your name,
    If you want any hairs left on your head!'
He only answered: 'Though you make me bald,   100
    I'll never say my name, or let it slip,
    However much I'm hauled about and mauled.'
I had by now his hair wrapped round my hand,
    And had already torn some clumps away,
    And he, head down, was howling like a hound,
When someone else cried out: 'What is it, Bocca[18]?
    Can't you be satisfied with rattling jaws,
    But you must bark? Now what the devil's the matter?'

15. A battle in 1260 at which the Tuscan Ghibellines defeated the Florentine Guelphs.
16. Dante and Virgil have now moved down into the second zone of this ninth circle, reserved for betrayers of their country, and named after the Trojan Antenor who was said to have betrayed Troy to the Greeks.
17. He means he would take vengeance.
18. Bocca degli Abati, whose treachery was largely responsible for the Guelph defeat at Montaperti.

'Omai,' diss'io, 'non vo' che più favelle,
    malvagio traditor – ch'alla tua onta   110
    io porterò di te vere novelle.'
'Va' via,' rispuose, 'e ciò che tu vuoi conta –
    ma non tacer, se tu di qua entro eschi,
    di quel ch'ebbe or così la lingua pronta.
El piange qui l'argento de' Franceschi:
    "Io vidi," potrai dir, "quel da Duera
    là dove i peccatori stanno freschi."
Se fossi domandato: "Altri chi v'era?"
    tu hai da lato quel di Beccheria,
    di cui segò Fiorenza la gorgiera.   120
Gianni de' Soldanier credo che sia
    più là con Ganellone e Tebaldello,
    ch'aprì Faenza quando si dormìa.'
Noi eravam partiti già da ello,
    ch'io vidi due ghiacciati in una buca,
    sì che l'un capo all'altro era cappello;
e come 'l pan per fame si manduca,
    così 'l sovran li denti all'altro pose
    là 've 'l cervel s'aggiugne con la nuca:
non altrimenti Tideo si rose   130
    le tempie a Menalippo per disdegno,
    che quei faceva il teschio e l'altre cose.
'O tu che mostri per sì bestial segno
    odio sovra colui che tu ti mangi,
    dimmi 'l perché,' diss'io, 'per tal convegno:
che se tu a ragion di lui ti piangi,
    sappiendo chi voi siete e la sua pecca,
    nel mondo suso ancora io te ne cangi,
se quella con ch'io parlo non si secca.'

'Well now,' I said, 'you need not speak again,[19]
    You wicked traitor – now I'll tell the truth   110
    In spite of you and to your grief and shame.'
'Then go,' he said, 'and say whatever you like –
    But don't be silent, if you do get out,
    About that fellow there, so quick to speak.
He's here atoning for French silver: you'll
    Find time to say, "I saw him of Duera,[20]
    There where the sinners are laid out to cool."
And if you're asked about the other dead,
    You have just there beside you Beccaria[21],
    Legate to Florence, where he lost his head.   120
Gianni de' Soldanieri[22], if I'm right,
    Is there with Ganelon[23] and Tebaldello,
    Who unlocked Faenza in the dead of night.'[24]
We had already gone beyond this shade,
    When I saw two, frozen within one hole,
    Where one head wore the other like a hood;
Like someone who is famished, he on top
    Was digging with his teeth into the other,
    Just where the brain's connected to the nape:
As ancient Tydeus, in a fit of spite,   130
    Gnawed Melanippus' temples,[25] so this shade
    Chewed skin and bone and brain up, every bit.
'O you who show by such a bestial act
    How much you hate him whom you're eating up,'
    I said, 'say why, and we will make a pact:
If you can show good cause for this bad blood,
    I will, when I'm above, return the favour,
    Once I know who you are and what he did,
So long as what I speak with does not wither.'[26]

19. From the mention of Montaperti, Dante had probably already guessed his name.
20. Buoso da Duera, bribed by the French to allow free passage to the troops of Charles of Anjou when they invaded Lombardy in 1265.
21. Tesauro dei Beccaria was charged of conspiring with the Ghibellines, who were banished from Florence.
22. A Florentine Ghibelline who, in 1266, betrayed his own party by allying himself with the Guelphs.
23. After Judas, probably the most famous traitor of all.
24. Tebaldello de' Zambrasi, a citizen of Faenza who, to avenge a private grudge, in 1280 opened the gates of the city to the Bolognese.
25. Tydeus, one of the Seven against Thebes, was mortally wounded by Melanippus as he was killing him. He had the head of Melanippus brought to him and ate it.
26. Dante is referring to his tongue. He is using an accepted formula to emphasise the firmness of his promise.

CANTO XXXIII

The shade mentioned at the end of the previous canto lifts his face from the skull he is gnawing, wipes his mouth on his victim's hair, and tells his own story. He is Ugolino della Gherardesca of Pisa who, damned for treachery, was himself betrayed on the orders of Archbishop Ruggieri, and imprisoned with his sons in a tower, where they were all starved to death. At the end of his account he goes back to gnawing the head of his betrayer.

This account is famous for its pathos, yet it is framed by a bestial action: the horror of Ugolino's earthly punishment is not allowed to obscure his guilt. Dante shows his anger at the cruelty of the Pisans, and pity for the unmerited suffering of Ugolino's sons, but no sympathy for Ugolino. Our sympathy is aroused by Ugolino's account, but so too is our disgust at his revenge upon Ruggieri. The result is to stress the strictness of divine judgement, which is concerned solely with human merit or demerit, and which is not deflected by other considerations.

Dante and Virgil then move down to the next zone of Cocytus, Ptolomea, where those who betrayed their guests lie supine in the ice, with their eyes frozen over so that they cannot vent their grief in tears. Dante makes what seems to be a solemn promise to clear the ice from the face of one of them, Friar Alberigo, in return for his name, but he does not carry out his promise: to do so would be an attempt to interfere with the operation of divine justice.

Alberigo has given much more than his name: he has explained that, for sins as serious as his, it often happens that a soul descends into Antenora while the body is still alive in the world above: he himself is one example of this, and Branca Doria is another.

The canto concludes with an invective against Genoa, the city of which Branca Doria was, in fact still is bodily, a citizen.

La bocca sollevò dal fiero pasto   1
 quel peccator, forbendola a' capelli
 del capo ch'elli avea di retro guasto.
Poi cominciò: 'Tu vuo' ch'io rinovelli
 disperato dolor che 'l cor mi preme
 già pur pensando, pria ch'io ne favelli.
Ma se le mie parole esser dien seme
 che frutti infamia al traditor ch'i' rodo,
 parlare e lacrimar vedrai inseme.
Io non so chi tu se', né per che modo   10
 venuto se' qua giù – ma fiorentino
 mi sembri veramente quand'io t'odo.
Tu dei saper ch'i' fui conte Ugolino,
 e questi è l'arcivescovo Ruggieri:
 or ti dirò perché i son tal vicino.
Che per l'effetto de' suo' mai pensieri,
 fidandomi di lui, io fossi preso
 e poscia morto, dir non è mestieri;
però quel che non puoi avere inteso –
 ciò è come la morte mia fu cruda –   20
 udirai, e saprai s'e' m'ha offeso.
Breve pertugio dentro dalla muda,
 la qual per me ha il titol della fame –
 e 'n che conviene ancor ch'altrui si chiuda –
m'avea mostrato per lo suo forame
 più lune già, quand'io feci 'l mal sonno
 che del futuro mi squarciò 'l velame.
Questi pareva a me maestro e donno,
 cacciando il lupo e' lupicini al monte
 per che i Pisan veder Lucca non ponno.   30
Con cagne magre, studiose e conte,
 Gualandi con Sismondi e con Lanfranchi
 s'avea messi dinanzi dalla fronte.
In picciol corso mi parìeno stanchi
 lo padre e' figli, e con l'agute scane
 mi parea lor veder fender li fianchi.

He raised his mouth from his barbaric feed,   1
    That sinner,[1] and he wiped it on what hair
    There still remained on the half-eaten head.
And then began: 'You ask me to revive
    Death and despair, a weight upon my heart
    Even to think of, never mind describe.
But since my words may bear this bitter fruit –
    Infamy for the traitor I am chewing –
    Then, though I weep, yet will I speak of it.
I don't know you, nor by what ways and means   10
    You've come down here – but certainly I think
    Your way of speaking is a Florentine's.
You must know Ugolino is my name,
    And this man is Ruggieri[2], the archbishop:
    I'll tell you why I am so close to him.
That he had all my trust, and that I fell
    Into the snare he laid, and was imprisoned
    Until I died, there is no need to tell;
But what you can't have heard of, you'll now hear –
    That is, the agonising death I died –   20
    And know the rightness of the grudge I bear.
A tiny aperture inside the Mew[3],
    Called now, on my account, the Tower of Hunger,
    Where others after me will be locked too,
Had let me have a glimpse already through
    Its slit of several moons[4], before my dream
    In which the future's veil was torn in two.
This man appeared,[5] the master of the hunt
    Of wolf and wolf-cubs on that Mount which means
    That Pisans looking to see Lucca can't.[6]   30
With lean and hungry hounds this man had sent
    Gualandi and Sismondi and Lanfranchi[7]
    Up there before him and way out in front.
And then it seemed to me that all too soon
    Father and sons started to tire; sharp fangs
    Invaded them – I saw their bodies torn.

1. See ll. 124–39 of the previous canto. This is Ugolino della Gherardesca, born in Pisa *c.*1230. Although a member of a Guelph family, he conspired to bring the Ghibellines to power in Pisa. This may be the betrayal for which he is damned in Antenora. He was later himself betrayed by the Ghibellines, and imprisoned with two sons and two grandsons in a tower, where all were starved to death in 1289.
2. Archbishop of Pisa 1278–95.
3. Tower belonging to the Gualandi family, which stood in what is now the Piazza dei Cavalieri in Pisa.
4. Months.
5. Ruggieri, in Ugolino's dream.
6. This is Monte di San Giuliano. The periphrastic mention of it here suggests subtly an unfulfilled longing for Lucca, a Guelph stronghold.
7. All members of powerful Ghibellines families in Pisa.

Quando fui desto innanzi la dimane,
    pianger senti' fra 'l sonno i miei figliuoli
    ch'eran con meco, e domandar del pane.
Ben se' crudel, se tu già non ti duoli   40
    pensando ciò che 'l mio cor s'annunziava –
    e se non piangi, di che pianger suoli?
Già eran desti, e l'ora s'appressava
    che 'l cibo ne solea essere addotto,
    e per suo sogno ciascun dubitava;
e io senti' chiavar l'uscio di sotto
    all'orribile torre – ond'io guardai
    nel viso a' mie' figliuoi sanza far motto.
Io non piangea, sì dentro impetrai:
    piangevan elli – e Anselmuccio mio   50
    disse: "Tu guardi sì, padre! Che hai?"
Perciò non lacrimai né rispuos'io
    tutto quel giorno, né la notte appresso,
    infin che l'altro sol nel mondo uscìo.
Come un poco di raggio si fu messo
    nel doloroso carcere, e io scorsi
    per quattro visi il mio aspetto stesso,
ambo le man per lo dolor mi morsi –
    ed ei, pensando ch'i' 'l fessi per voglia
    di manicar, di subito levorsi   60
e disser: "Padre, assai ci fia men doglia
    se tu mangi di noi: tu ne vestisti
    queste misere carni, e tu le spoglia."
Queta'mi allor per non farli più tristi –
    lo dì e l'altro stemmo tutti muti –
    ahi dura terra, perché non t'apristi?
Poscia che fummo al quarto dì venuti,
    Gaddo mi si gettò disteso a' piedi,
    dicendo: "Padre mio, ché non m'aiuti?"
Quivi morì, e come tu mi vedi,   70
    vid'io cascar li tre ad uno ad uno
    tra 'l quinto dì e 'l sesto – ond'io mi diedi,

When I awoke, before the dawn, I heard
   My sons[8], who were imprisoned with me, weeping
   While still asleep, and crying out for bread.
You must be hard of heart, if you can keep   40
   Your tears back, as you guess what I foresaw.
   Oh, if you don't weep now, when would you weep?
They were awake; and it was near the time
   When it was customary to bring us food,
   Who'd all been frightened by the selfsame dream,
When down below I heard the key being turned
   To lock that tower – and it was then I looked
   My children in the face, without a word.
I could not weep, being turned to stone inside:
   They wept; and my poor little Anselm asked: 50
   "Father, why look like that? Are you afraid?"
I did not weep and I did not reply
   All of that day and all the following night,
   Until another sun rose in the sky.
The moment that some light managed to make
   Its way into our jail, and I could see
   Four faces looking as my own must look,
I chewed my two hands in my agony;
   And they, thinking I did this out of hunger,
   Struggled onto their feet immediately,   60
And said: "Father, we'd be in much less pain
   If you were eating us: you clothed us with
   This wretched flesh, so strip it off again."
I calmed myself, not to make them feel worse;
   That day, the next day, no one spoke. Why did
   You, earth, not open up and swallow us?
When our starvation came to its fourth day,
   Gaddo threw himself at my feet, and cried:
   "Father, why can't you do something for me?"
With that he died – and clear as you see me,   70
   I saw the other three fall one by one
   Between the fifth day and the sixth day; I

8. Ugolino refers to all those with him, sons and grandsons, simply as his sons or children.

già cieco, a brancolar sovra ciascuno,
    e due dì li chiamai, poi che fur morti:
    poscia, più che 'l dolor, poté 'l digiuno[a].'
Quand'ebbe detto ciò, con li occhi torti
    riprese 'l teschio misero co' denti,
    che furo all'osso, come d'un can, forti.
Ahi Pisa, vituperio delle genti
    del bel paese là dove 'l sì sona,   80
    poi che i vicini a te punir son lenti,
muovasi la Capraia e la Gorgona,
    e faccian siepe ad Arno in su la foce,
    sì ch'elli annieghi in te ogni persona!
Ché se 'l conte Ugolino aveva voce
    d'aver tradita te delle castella,
    non dovei tu i figliuoi porre a tal croce.
Innocenti facea l'età novella –
    novella Tebe! – Uguiccione e 'l Brigata
    e li altri due che 'l canto suso appella.   90
Noi passammo oltre, là 've la gelata
    ruvidamente un'altra gente fascia,
    non volta in giù, ma tutta riversata.
Lo pianto stesso lì pianger non lascia,
    e 'l duol, che truova in su li occhi rintoppo,
    si volge in entro a far crescer l'ambascia –
ché le lagrime prime fanno groppo,
    e sì come visiere di cristallo
    riempion sotto 'l ciglio tutto il coppo.
E avvegna che, sì come d'un callo,   100
    per la freddura ciascun sentimento
    cessato avesse del mio viso stallo,
già mi parea sentir alquanto vento:
    per ch'io: 'Maestro mio, questo chi move?
    Non è qua giù ogne vapore spento?'
Ed elli a me: 'Avaccio sarai dove
    di ciò ti farà l'occhio la risposta,
    veggendo la cagion che 'l fiato piove.'

a. The suggestion, which has been made, that this means that Ugolino began to eat his children's flesh seems unwarranted. The significance is that, however great Ugolino's grief, it did not kill him, but starvation did. The realism here can be compared with that in l. 73 above where Ugolino is blind, not hyperbolically with tears, but literally, as a result of starvation.

Was blind[9] by now, and called and fumbled over
    Their bodies two days after they were dead –
    Then what grief could not do, was done by hunger.'[10]
He said this, rolled his eyes, and once again
    He got the wretched skull[11] between his teeth,
    As savage as a dog is with a bone.
Pisa! Dishonoured city, dreadful blot
    On that dear country where the word is *si*[12],   80
    Whom your neighbours seem slow to castigate,
Could but Capraia move – Gorgona too[13] –
    And make a dam across the Arno's mouth,
    Until it drowned all living souls in you!
Even with Ugolino said to be
    Betrayer of your castles, was it right
    To put his children to such agony?
New Thebes![14] They were too young to share his blame,
    Brigata and Uguccione, and those others,
    The two[15] already mentioned in my rhyme.   90
We went on further,[16] where the frozen zone
    Has other people wrapped up cruelly,
    Not looking down now: all of them supine.
Their very weeping will not let them weep:
    Their pain, finding obstruction in their eyes,
    Turns back inside them to augment their grief;
Their first tears form a cluster as they freeze,
    Which like a sort of visor made of crystal,
    Fills up the cavities below their brows.
And even though, being in a land of ice   100
    Where everything is harder than a callus,
    I had no feeling in my frozen face,
I felt that I could feel some wind blow there,
    And asked my master: 'What's the cause of this?
    Isn't it true there are no vapours here?'[17]
And he replied: 'You'll find yourself quite soon
    Where your own eyes will come up with the answer,
    And see the reason why this wind blows down.'

9. Through starvation.
10. He did not die from grief, but hunger.
11. Of Archbishop Ruggieri.
12. Italy is distinguished from some other countries with Romance languages by its use of *si* for yes.
13. Two islands just off the mouth of the river, the Arno, which runs through Pisa.
14. Ancient Thebes had a reputation for cruelty.
15. Anselmo (line 50) and Gaddo (line 68).
16. Into Ptolomea, the third zone of Cocytus, reserved for those who betrayed guests or other associates. The name is derived either from Ptolemy, King of Egypt (51–47 BC), or from Ptolemy, governor of Jericho (1 Macc. 16: 11–17): they both murdered guests.
17. The belief was that winds were caused by vapours drawn out of the earth by the sun.

E un de' tristi della fredda crosta
   gridò a noi: 'O anime crudeli,   110
   tanto che data v'è l'ultima posta,
levatemi dal viso i duri veli,
   sì ch'io sfoghi 'l duol che 'l cor m'impregna
   un poco, pria che 'l pianto si raggeli.'
Per ch'io a lui: 'Se vuo' ch'i' ti sovvegna,
   dimmi chi se', e s'io non ti disbrigo,
   al fondo della ghiaccia ir mi convegna.'
Rispuose adunque: 'Io son frate Alberigo –
   io son quel dalle frutta del mal orto,
   che qui riprendo dattero per figo.'   120
'Oh,' diss'io lui, 'or se' tu ancor morto?'
   Ed elli a me: 'Come 'l mio corpo stea
   nel mondo su, nulla scienza porto.
Cotal vantaggio ha questa Tolomea:
   che spesse volte l'anima ci cade
   innanzi ch'Atropòs mossa le dea.
E perché tu più volentier mi rade
   le 'nvetriate lacrime dal volto,
   sappie che tosto che l'anima trade
come fec'io, il corpo suo l'è tolto   130
   da un demonio, che poscia il governa
   mentre che 'l tempo suo tutto sia vòlto.
Ella ruina in sì fatta cisterna –
   e forse pare ancor lo corpo suso
   dell'ombra che di qua dietro mi verna.
Tu 'l dei saper, se tu vien pur mo giuso:
   elli è ser Branca d'Oria, e son più anni
   poscia passati ch'el fu sì racchiuso.'
'Io credo,' diss'io lui, 'che tu m'inganni,
   ché Branca d'Oria non morì unquanche,   140
   e mangia e bee e dorme e veste panni.'
'Nel fosso su,' diss'el, 'de' Malebranche,
   là dove bolle la tenace pece,
   non era ancora giunto Michel Zanche

One of the sinners of the frozen crust[19]
    Cried out to us: 'O souls who are so cruel   110
    The zone that you're assigned to is the last,[20]
Remove these heavy veils from off my face,
    That I may briefly vent heart-swelling grief,
    Before my tears, as always, turn to ice.'
'Tell me your name,' I said: 'that is my price;
    And if I do not liberate you after,
    May I go to the bottom of the ice.'
'Friar Alberigo,' he said straight away,
    'The man whose fruits grew in an evil orchard.[21]
    Here dates for figs are given back to me.'[22]   120
'Oh then!' I burst out. 'You're already dead?'[23]
    'What's happened to my body in the world
    Is something I've no news of,' he replied.
'We have one privilege in Ptolomea:
    Many a soul falls down into this place
    Well before Atropos has sent it here.[24]
And so that you may scrape with better will
    This glazing tears have made from off my face,
    I shall explain: as soon as any soul
Betrays as foully as I did, a fiend   130
    Captures the body and controls its actions
    Until its time on earth comes to an end,
While into this cold well the soul drops down.
    Perhaps the world above still sees the body
    Of the shade that winters here behind my own?
You must know him, if you have only just
    Come here: he's Branca Doria[25], and some years
    Have now gone by since he was so embraced.'[26]
'I think,' I said, 'you're trying to abuse
    My trust, for Branca Doria has not died: 140
    He eats and drinks and sleeps and puts on clothes.'
'Before Michele Zanche reached the hole
    Above, where Clawboys play their games,' he said,
    'Where sticky pitch is always on the boil,[27]

19. Those whose eyes are blocked with ice.
20. Judecca, the fourth and last zone of Cocytus.
21. Friar Alberigo in 1285 invited his brother and a nephew to a banquet. When Alberigo called for the fruit course, hidden assassins killed the guests.
22. Figs were more expensive than dates, and the expression means to pay dearly for a misdeed.
23. Alberigo was still alive at the time of Dante's vision (1300).
24. Before death. The mythical Atropos was one of the three Fates: she cut the thread of life which had been spun and measured out by her sisters.
25. A Genoese who murdered his father-in-law, Michele Zanche, at a banquet to which he had invited him.
26. So closed in ice.
27. In the fifth ditch of the eighth circle, that of the barrators.

che questi lasciò il diavolo in sua vece
    nel corpo suo, ed un suo prossimano
    che 'l tradimento insieme con lui fece.
Ma distendi oggimai in qua la mano –
    aprimi li occhi.' E io non lil'apersi:
    e cortesia fu lui esser villano.   150
Ahi Genovesi, uomini diversi
    d'ogne costume e pien d'ogni magagna,
    perché non siete voi del mondo spersi?
Ché col peggiore spirto di Romagna
    trovai di voi un tal, che per sua opra
    in anima in Cocito già si bagna,
ed in corpo par vivo ancor di sopra.

This soul here left a demon in his stead
    Inside the body – as a relative,
    Who helped in the betrayal, also did.
But now stretch out your hand – this is the time
    To clear my eyes.' But that I did not do:
    Courtesy here meant being rough with him.[28]   150
You, Genoese, so utterly devoid
    Of all good customs, full of every vice,
    Why have you not been driven from the world?
For, with Romagna's foulest shade of all,[29]
    I found a Genoese[30] with sins so grave
    That he bathes in Cocytus in his soul,
And seems in body still alive above.

28. It would have been discourteous (to God) to try to interfere with His justice.
29. Friar Alberigo.
30. Branca Doria.

CANTO XXXIV

Virgil and Dante are now in Judecca. This is the lowest zone of Cocytus, the lowest part of the Inferno: the sinners here (who betrayed their benefactors) are, with a few notable exceptions, covered entirely by the ice.

An atmosphere of mystery and menace pervades this canto. Where does the wind come from? What is the strange building or contrivance, rather like a windmill with turning sails, which Dante glimpses in the distance?

Both of those questions are answered when Dante at last sees Lucifer or Dis or Beelzebub, the source of all the evil in the world. He is a shaggy giant set, up to mid-chest, in the ice. He has three heads, and three mouths, and each mouth is furiously chewing a sinner. These sinners are Judas Iscariot (who gives his name to this region), and Brutus and Cassius, who betrayed Julius Caesar.

Virgil and Dante make their way down the body of Lucifer. There is another mystery (startling at first to Dante and his reader, but soon explained) when Virgil suddenly turns upside down and begins to climb up Lucifer's body, so that, when the pilgrims detach themselves from the body to rest in a cleft in the surrounding rock, Dante finds that Lucifer's legs are upside down.

The atmosphere changes when we learn of a little stream which flows into this cleft from the world outside. Dante and Virgil follow the course of this stream, and eventually they emerge from a hole in the rock and see the stars once more. They are now in the southern hemisphere, and Dante has been told that he will there see some rising land which, although he does not yet know it, is Mount Purgatory and will be explored in the second part of *The Divine Comedy*.

For all the physical horror, perhaps the most striking feature of this canto is that none of the sinners communicates with Dante or Virgil in any way. All human feelings are frozen, and all sense of community is lost.

'*Vexilla regis prodeunt inferni*   1
    verso di noi – però dinanzi mira,'
    disse 'l maestro mio, 'se tu 'l discerni.'
Come quando una grossa nebbia spira,
    o quando l'emisperio nostro annotta,
    par di lungi un molin che 'l vento gira,
veder mi parve un tal dificio allotta –
    poi per lo vento mi ristrinsi retro
    al duca mio, ché non li era altra grotta.
Già era, e con paura il metto in metro,   10
    là dove l'ombre tutte eran coperte,
    e trasparien come festuca in vetro.
Altre sono a giacere, altre stanno erte,
    quella col capo e quella con le piante –
    altra, com'arco, il volto a' piè rinverte.
Quando noi fummo fatti tanto avante
    ch'al mio maestro piacque di mostrarmi
    la creatura ch'ebbe il bel sembiante,
d'innanzi mi si tolse e fe' restarmi,
    'Ecco Dite,' dicendo, 'ed ecco il loco   20
    ove convien che di fortezza t'armi.'
Com'io divenni allor gelato e fioco,
    nol dimandar, lettor, ch'i' non lo scrivo,
    però ch'ogni parlar sarebbe poco.
Io non mori' e non rimasi vivo:
    pensa oggimai per te, s'hai fior d'ingegno,
    qual io divenni, d'uno e d'altro privo.
Lo 'mperador del doloroso regno
    da mezzo il petto uscìa fuor della ghiaccia,
    e più con un gigante io mi convegno,   30
che i giganti non fan con le sue braccia –
    vedi oggimai quant'esser dee quel tutto
    ch'a così fatta parte si confaccia!
S'el fu sì bel com'elli è ora brutto,
    e contra 'l suo fattore alzò le ciglia,
    ben dee da lui procedere ogni lutto.

'*Vexilla regis prodeunt inferni*[1]   1
    Towards us. And so, looking straight ahead,'
    My master told me, 'see if you discern him.'
It looked most like – as when mist gathers round,
    Or night begins to cloak our hemisphere –
    A distant mill, sails whirling in the wind –
At least I thought I saw something like that.
    I shrank out of the wind, behind my guide,
    There being no other rock, or safe retreat.
I fear to set it down: I found I was   10
    Somewhere where all the sinners were iced over,
    Yet seen distinctly, like straws under glass.[2]
Some of them lie there; others are upright,
    Standing apparently, or on their heads;
    Some bowed like bows, face bent towards the feet.
We carried on until, after a while,
    My guide considered it was time to show me
    That creature who had been so beautiful:[3]
He stepped aside, and stopped me, and he said:
    'Look upon Dis! And look upon the region   20
    Where you'll have need of all your fortitude.'
Then how I shuddered, how my blood ran cold!
    Don't ask me, Reader, how: I cannot write it:
    There is no tongue in which it could be told.
I did not suffer death, or live on either:
    Try to imagine, if you have the wit,
    My state, bereft of one and of the other.
The emperor of the empire of despair
    Rose from mid-chest above the ice all round;
    I bear comparison to giants more   30
Readily than giants do to this one's arms:
    So now consider what the whole is like,
    Imagined in proportion to those limbs!
If he was once so beautiful as he
    Is ugly now, yet flouted his Creator,
    No wonder he's the fount of misery.

1. 'The banners of the King of hell advance.' This, with the parodic addition of *inferni* (of hell), is the first line of a sixth-century hymn by Venantius Fortunatus in honour of the Cross.

2. Virgil and Dante are now in Judecca (named after Judas Iscariot) where they see the shades of those who betrayed their benefactors.

3. Satan (aka Dis, Lucifer, Beelzebub) was reputedly the most beautiful of the angels before his fall.

Oh quanto parve a me gran maraviglia
   quand'io vidi tre facce alla sua testa!
  L'una dinanzi – e quella era vermiglia –
l'altr'eran due, che s'aggiugnìeno a questa   40
   sovresso 'l mezzo di ciascuna spalla,
   e sé giugnìeno al luogo della cresta:
e la destra parea tra bianca e gialla –
   la sinistra a vedere era tal, quali
   vegnon di là onde 'l Nilo s'avvalla.
Sotto ciascuna uscivan due grand'ali,
   quanto si convenìa a tanto uccello:
   vele di mar non vid'io mai cotali.
Non avean penne, ma di vispistrello
   era lor modo – e quelle svolazzava,   50
   sì che tre venti si movean da ello:
quindi Cocito tutto s'aggelava.
   Con sei occhi piangea, e per tre menti
   gocciava 'l pianto e sanguinosa bava.
Da ogni bocca dirompea co' denti
   un peccatore, a guisa di maciulla,
   sì che tre ne facea così dolenti.
A quel dinanzi il mordere era nulla
   verso 'l graffiar, ché tal volta la schiena
   rimanea della pelle tutta brulla.   60
'Quell'anima là su c'ha maggior pena,'
   disse 'l maestro, 'è Giuda Scariotto,
   che 'l capo ha dentro e fuor le gambe mena.
Delli altri due c'hanno il capo di sotto,
   quel che pende dal nero ceffo è Bruto –
   vedi come si storce, e non fa motto –
e l'altro è Cassio che par sì membruto.
   Ma la notte risurge, e oramai
   è da partir, ché tutto avem veduto.'
Com'a lui piacque, il collo li avvinghiai,   70
   ed el prese di tempo e luogo poste;
   e quando l'ali fuoro aperte assai,

I found he had three faces on his head,
    Which was not something I had seen before!
    One was in front, and that one was bright red;
The other two were joined onto the first   40
    At just about the mid-point of each shoulder;
    And all were joined together at the crest:
That on the right was white to yellow, while
    The one upon the left had the complexion
    Of those who live along the Upper Nile.[4]
Under each face two monstrous wings were spread,
    Proportionate to such a monstrous bird:
    I never saw sails on the sea so broad.
They were not feathered, but of such a kind
    As bats have – and the fiend was beating them   50
    So that he blew at once three blasts of wind:
And hence Cocytus is all frozen over.
    With six eyes he was weeping; down three chins
    The tears were dripping, mixed with bloody slaver.
In every mouth, as with a rake or comb,
    The teeth were scraping, grinding up a sinner:
    There were three simultaneously in pain.
And yet to him in front being so gnawn
    Seemed nothing to the clawing: very often
    This sinner's back was bare down to the bone.   60
'That soul up there that is worst scarified,'
    My master said, 'is Judas Iscariot[5],
    His head within, his wriggling legs outside.
Of the other two, dangling with swinging head,
    The one who's hanging from the black snout's Brutus[6]:
    Look how he writhes, and does not say a word;
That other's Cassius[7], who looks strong and tall.
    But night is coming on – now is the time
    To go from here, since now we've seen it all.'
Just as he told me to, I held him tight   70
    Around the neck; he looked for time and place,
    And when the wings were wide enough apart,

4. The three faces are a parody of the three persons of the Holy Trinity. The symbolism is complex and disputed: the different colours seem to cover the whole human race – the red indicating Europeans, the yellowish the Asiatic races, and the black the Africans; also different colours suggest qualities in opposition to those God personifies – red indicating hatred (as against love), yellow impotence (as against power), and black ignorance (as against omniscience).
5. Who betrayed Christ.
6. The leader of the conspirators who murdered Julius Caesar.
7. Another of the murderers of Caesar.

appigliò sé alle vellute coste:
    di vello in vello giù discese poscia
    tra 'l folto pelo e le gelate croste.
Quando noi fummo là dove la coscia
    si volge, a punto in sul grosso dell'anche,
    lo duca, con fatica e con angoscia,
volse la testa ov'elli avea le zanche,
    e aggrappossi al pel com'uom che sale,   80
    sì che 'n inferno i' credea tornar anche.
'Attienti ben, ché per cotali scale,'
    disse 'l maestro, ansando com'uom lasso,
    'conviensi dipartir da tanto male.'
Poi uscì fuor per lo foro d'un sasso,
    e puose me in su l'orlo a sedere –
    appresso porse a me l'accorto passo.
Io levai li occhi, e credetti vedere
    Lucifero com'io l'avea lasciato,
    e vidili le gambe in su tenere;   90
e s'io divenni allora travagliato,
    la gente grossa il pensi, che non vede
    qual è quel punto ch'io avea passato.
'Lèvati su,' disse 'l maestro, 'in piede:
    la via è lunga e 'l cammino è malvagio,
    e già il sole a mezza terza riede.'
Non era camminata di palagio
    là 'v'eravam, ma natural burella
    ch'avea mal suolo e di lume disagio[a].
'Prima ch'io dell'abisso mi divella,   100
    maestro mio,' diss'io quando fui dritto,
    'a trarmi d'erro un poco mi favella.
Ov'è la ghiaccia? E questi com'è fitto
    sì sottosopra? E come, in sì poc'ora,
    da sera a mane ha fatto il sol tragitto?'
Ed elli a me: 'Tu imagini ancora
    d'esser di là dal centro, ov'io mi presi
    al pel del vermo reo che 'l mondo fora.

a. 'Lack'.

He grabbed tight hold upon the shaggy sides,
    And made his way down slowly, tuft to tuft,
    Between thick fur and the encrusting ice.[8]
When we had reached the point at which the thigh
    Curves round, just on the swelling of the haunch,[9]
    My leader, struggling, breathing heavily,
Turned his head round to where his legs had been,
    And grasped the fur as though to climb: I thought   80
    That we were going back to Hell again.
'Now hold on tight, for it is by such ladders,'
    My master said, panting in his exhaustion,
    'That we must say goodbye to so much badness.'
At last he issued by a rocky vent,
    And set me on the edge of it to rest;
    Then placed himself there, minding how he went.
I raised my eyes, believing I'd be faced
    With Lucifer once more, as I had left him;
    And saw his legs stick up, feet uppermost!   90
Now how I was bewildered and aghast
    Slow-witted people may imagine, they
    Who do not realise what point I'd passed.[10]
'Get up,' my master said to me, 'stand steady:
    The way is long, the road is difficult;
    The sun has gone halfway through terce[11] already.'
It was no palace chamber where we were,
    But simply a rough tunnel made by nature,
    With little light on the uneven floor.
'Even before I'm out of this abyss,   100
    Master,' I asked, once I was on my feet,
    'Settle the problems that come out of this:
Where has the ice gone? Why's he upside down?
    And how has evening been transformed to morning
    By such a rapid journey of the sun?'
He answered: 'Do you think you're still withheld
    North of the centre, where I grasped the fur
    Of this damned grub that hollows out the world?

8. The ice encasing the hole in which Dis is fixed.

9. The broadest part of the hips, regarded as the centre of the body.

10. Virgil and Dante have passed through the centre of the earth.

11. The first of the four canonical hours (set hours for prayers) of the daytime.

Di là fosti cotanto quant'io scesi –
    quand'io mi volsi, tu passasti 'l punto   110
    al qual si traggon d'ogni parte i pesi.
E se' or sotto l'emisperio giunto
    ch'è contraposto a quel che la gran secca
    coverchia, e sotto 'l cui colmo consunto
fu l'uom che nacque e visse sanza pecca:
    tu hai i piedi in su picciola spera
    che l'altra faccia fa della Giudecca.
Qui è da man, quando di là è sera:
    e questi, che ne fe' scala col pelo,
    fitto è ancora sì come prim'era.   120
Da questa parte cadde giù dal cielo;
    e la terra, che pria di qua si sporse,
    per paura di lui fe' del mar velo,
e venne all'emisperio nostro – e forse
    per fuggir lui lasciò qui luogo vòto
    quella ch'appar di qua, e su ricorse.'
Luogo è là giù da Belzebù remoto
    tanto quanto la tomba si distende,
    che non per vista, ma per suono è noto
d'un ruscelletto che quivi discende   130
    per la buca d'un sasso ch'elli ha roso
    col corso ch'elli avvolge, e poco pende.
Lo duca e io per quel cammino ascoso
    intrammo a ritornar nel chiaro mondo,
    e sanza cura aver d'alcun riposo
salimmo su, el primo e io secondo,
    tanto ch'i' vidi delle cose belle
    che porta 'l ciel, per un pertugio tondo –
e quindi uscimmo a riveder le stelle.

You were still there while I was climbing down;
    When I turned over, we went past the point   110
    To which all weights from every part are drawn.[12]
Now you're beneath the hemisphere of sky[13]
    Antipodal to that[14] which arches over
    The great dry land,[15] under whose zenith[16] He[17]
Was killed who lived, as He was born, sinless:
    You're standing on a little circular
    Region[18] which forms Judecca's other face.
Here it is morning, when it's evening there;
    And he whose fur was useful as a ladder
    Is still fixed firmly as he was before.   120
When he fell down from heaven, he fell here;
    And all the land which had before protruded
    Veiled itself under water out of fear,
And fled until it reached our hemisphere;[19]
    And, fleeing him perhaps, this hollow space
    Was left by land which you'll see rising here.'[20]
There is a place down there, far underground,
    Far from Beelzebub as his tomb reaches,[21]
    And not perceived by sight, but by the sound
Of a small stream which makes its trickling way   130
    Through the hollow of a rock it has eroded
    In its winding course which slowly slopes away.
My guide and I followed that hidden route
    To bring us once more to the light of day;
    And, with no rest from the fatigue of it,
We clambered up, he first, till finally
    I saw the glory of the heavenly spheres,
    Through a round hole, the aperture whence we
Emerged to look once more upon the stars.

12. Virgil is referring to the force of gravity.
13. The southern celestial hemisphere.
14. The northern celestial hemisphere.
15. It was a common medieval belief that the northern hemisphere contained all the land in the world.
16. Jerusalem was believed to lie at the mid-point of the habitable world.
17. Christ.
18. One facet of a small sphere at the centre of the earth, an opposite facet of which is Judecca.
19. This is the origin of the land in the northern hemisphere.
20. Mount Purgatory, which Dante will see in the second part of *The Divine Comedy*.
21. Beelzebub's 'tomb' is the 'rough tunnel made by nature' of line 98, and Dante and Virgil are now
    at the far end of it from Beelzebub.

AFTERWORD

The Chief Imagination Of Christendom[1]

After seven hundred years, and after many rereadings by in-
dividuals, Dante's *Inferno* remains a shocking poem. The physical
torments of the damned are so horrific as to make the first-time
reader feel that he has strayed into some super Grand Guignol:
shades are immersed in boiling pitch, or in human excrement,
or running on burning sand under a hail of fire; and these are
only the first few torments that spring to mind. And those
punishments are less horrifying than the ones which reveal an
apparently fiendish ingenuity: the simoniac popes placed upside
down in holes in the rock with only their feet showing, around
which flames flicker in a parody of the haloes of the saints; or
sinners like Bertran de Born, the sowers of discord, who tore
apart the fabric of society, and whose bodies are now torn and
mangled. One of the most ingenious punishments, and perhaps
the most affecting, is that of the sinners frozen in the ice of
Caïna, those who betrayed their kindred, and who are desperate
to weep but cannot:

> Their eyes, which had been only moist within,
>   Gushed over at the lids, until the cold
>   Congealed those tears, and locked the lids again.[2]

It is apparent that the punishments are not designed to display
ingenuity for its own sake. It seems fitting that those who
flattered others for their own ends should wallow in excrement:
after all, that is what they chose to do. Again, Bertran de Born,
who stirred sons up to make war upon their father, thus wrench-
ing apart natural and honourable ties, receives a justice which is
poetic in more ways than one:

> I really saw, and still I seem to see,
>   A trunk without a head, moving along
>   With all the others in that company;
> It held its severed head up by the hair,
>   Swinging it in one hand just like a lantern;
>   The head saw us and moaned in its despair...
> And thus fit retribution is delivered.[3]

1. W.B. Yeats, 'Ego Dominus Tuus'.
2. XXXII: 46–8.
3. XXVIII: 118–23, 142.

We are bound to recognise what may be, to many modern readers, the most shocking feature of all. That is, that Dante's universe is strictly moral; it is one where no one asks whether it is nature or nurture which leads us to do what we do, one where no excuses can avail; it is one where human beings do what they do of their own choice, and live, even when dead, with the consequences of their choices, live with what they have themselves chosen: they have what they wanted all along.

To convey this sense of a just and moral order behind the spectacle of human existence Dante uses allegory. Many may find that word more off-putting than the idea of eternal damnation, but we need not make heavy weather of it: Dante himself does not. It can be analysed and categorised in a hundred and one ways, but it is in its essence very simple – a manner of expression, and a way of understanding, which comes naturally to human beings. Boccaccio puts it succinctly:

'What other thing is it than poetic fiction in Scripture when Christ says that He is now a lion, and now a lamb, and now a serpent, and then a dragon, and then a rock?... What else do the words of the Saviour in the gospels contain if not a meaning different from the plain sense, a way of speaking which we call by the common term allegory?'[4]

Ordinary conversation never proceeds far without words being used in such ways. And, as with all expression, there are occasional difficulties. This is particularly so when emblems – devices whose meaning exists *only* figuratively, and often needs interpretation – are used. I mean such devices as a red cross on a field ambulance (the same emblem, but with a very different meaning, as on a crusader's chest), or a red crescent, or any number of political and commercial logos which we can think of, and – last but not least – the leopard, the lion, and the she-wolf in the first canto of the *Inferno*. These creatures are hardly realistic: they appear out of the blue for no apparent purpose other than to convey something of the state of Dante's mind at that stage; above all, they need interpretation, interpretation which is often uncertain and disputed.

Most of the allegory, however, is not like that. Objects in the poem are there in their own right, as things in themselves, while they also have deeper symbolic meanings which coexist with the

4. *Life of Dante*, translated by J.G. Nichols, Hesperus Press, 2002, p. 52.

literal ones. This is the kind of allegory in which Dante excels. Consider the dark wood which Dante, and we, come across in the second line of the poem, or the hill which Dante then attempts to climb, or the huge hole in the ground in the shape of an inverted cone down which Dante and Virgil climb as they sink into the very depths. The single most important feature of the *Inferno*, and of *The Divine Comedy* as a whole, is that it is presented to us as fact, physical fact which bristles with spiritual, psychological, and eschatological meaning.

The *Inferno* contrasts sharply with another justly famous Christian allegory. *The Pilgrim's Progress* (1678) begins:

'As I walked through the wilderness of this world, I lighted on a certain place, where was a den; and I laid me down in that place to sleep: and as I slept I dreamed a dream.'

Dante's journey is not a dream: it is given as history. We do not therefore have to be always interpreting: as we follow the story, the deeper significance of it enters into our minds without further effort. (This is not to suggest that, if we make the effort, even more interest will not be revealed.) Dante's 'dark wood' is not labelled with an abstract word: this is something which is more likely to happen in works that are more obtrusively allegorical, or emblematic: it happens in *The Faerie Queene* (1590) in a similar situation:

'This is the wandring wood, this *Errours den*.'[5]

Bunyan is always careful to explain his allegory as he goes along: when Pilgrim climbs a hill we are told that it is 'Hill Difficulty'. His characters have names which reveal their significance, their significance being the only reason for their appearance in the narrative. In Dante there is no one, as there is in Bunyan, called 'Mr Facing-bothways'. There is, however, Guido da Montefeltro, a complex historical character who does indeed face both ways and comes to grief accordingly. There is in Dante a slough of despond, where the souls of those who willed to live in sadness wallow in the mud; but Dante does not call it such. Bunyan tells us clearly that 'the name of the Slough was Despond': Dante leaves us to realise that for ourselves, and his characters and their circumstances are much more than simple allegorical abstractions:

5. I.i: 13.

363

'Beneath the surface many people sigh,
   With lots of little bubbles rising up,
   As you can see, wherever you cast your eye.
They say, stuck in the mud: "Our minds stayed dark
   In the sweet air enlightened by the sun.
   Inside us was a sort of sluggish smoke.
Now we are sullen in the gloomy mud." '[6]

It is here that the English reader is irresistibly reminded of Shakespeare, whose characters too are seen not only in a moral light but in all their human complexity. So, for instance, we have in the *Inferno* no one known as Pliable or Obstinate, but we do have Farinata, who is as proud in the Inferno as he was on earth, and who has other human qualities, like his snobbery and his concern with the politics of his city. And it is not just little intriguing foibles, little humanising details, which Dante reveals along with the reasons for damnation. Farinata is allowed to manifest even in the Inferno his good qualities – the strength and determination which saved the city of Florence from destruction:

'Yet there at Empoli I was the one –
   When all agreed on Florence's destruction –
   Who set his face against it, I alone.'[7]

Despite this, Farinata, who is an enemy of Dante's party, might seem to provide some justification for the assumption, frequently made by those who have not read the poem, that Dante placed his enemies in Hell and his friends in Heaven. The lie is given to this assumption most obviously when Dante, on the burning sand of the seventh circle, comes across 'the dear, the kindly, the paternal image' of his old friend and mentor Brunetto Latini. Our judgements are not as God's, and so Brunetto, damned for sodomy, reveals in his damnation the qualities for which he was loved: not just his beguiling pride in his writings, but also his intellectual achievement which is not nullified either by death or by damnation:

'I recommend to you my *Treasury*,
   In which I'm still alive: that's all I'll say.'
Then he turned round, and looked like one of those
   Who race, to win the green cloth at Verona,

6. VII: 118–24.
7. X: 91–3.

Across the fields; and looked, among all these,
Most like the winning, not the losing, runner.[8]

It is well known how the eponymous hero of *Piers Plowman* (from the second half of the fourteenth century) sees at the beginning of that poem 'a fair field full of folk'. One could hardly describe the Inferno as a 'fair field', but it is certainly full of folk in all their various human complexity. One must also bear in mind that Dante's 'fair field' will come later, glimpsed at times in his *Purgatory*, and in full bloom in his *Paradise*. The greatest mistake we could make as readers of the *Inferno* would be to stop short once we had read it and go no further. Dante's vision in the *Inferno* is overwhelming, but still only partial. The best, morally and poetically, is yet to come.

– J. G. Nichols, 2005

Acknowledgements
This translation is based on the edition of *Inferno* by Natalino Sapegno, La Nuova Italia, 1985, reprinted 1991, with frequent reference to the edition by Umberto Bosco and Giovanni Reggio, Le Monnier, 1979, reprinted 1982. I have also benefited from reading the translations by Allen Mandelbaum, Everyman's Library, 1995, and John E. Sinclair, second edition, Oxford University Press, 1948. For biblical quotations, in the notes only, I have used the Authorised Version of the Bible, as the one most familiar and congenial to English readers.

I am very grateful to Alessandro Gallenzi, who has checked this translation throughout, and provided many valuable criticisms and suggestions. The publisher wishes to acknowledge the helpful suggestions made by Mike Stocks, and the patience and dedication of William Chamberlain in checking the text and the translation. Our thanks also go to Fraser Muggeridge for his typesetting work and to Stephen Parkin for his help with the illustration of the Inferno.

8. XV: 119–24.

INDEX

Abati, see Bocca degli Abati.
Abel (son of Adam), IV: 56.
Abraham (patriarch), IV: 58.
Absalom (son of King David), XXVIII: 138.
Accorso, see Francesco d'Accorso.
Acheron (river of Inferno), III: 78; XIV: 116.
Achilles (Greek hero), V: 65; XII: 71; XXVI: 62; XXXI: 4.
Achitophel (advisor to David), XXVIII: 137.
Acquacheta (river of the Appennines), XVI: 97.
Acre (Syrian city), XXVII: 89.
Adam – see Master Adam.
Adam (first man), III: 115; IV: 55 (see note).
Adige (river), XII: 5.
Aegina (island), XXIX: 59.
Aeneas (son of Anchises), I: 74 (see note); II: 13
  (see note), 32; IV: 122; XXVI: 93.
Aeneid, I: 73 (see note); XX: 112 (see note); XXVI: 82
  (see note).
Aesop (Greek writer), XXIII: 4.
Agnolo (Florentine), XXV: 68.
Alardo (advisor to Charles of Anjou), XXVIII: 18.
Alberigo (Frisky Friar), XXXIII: 118.
Alberto da Siena, XXIX: 110.
Alberto degli Alberti (count), XXXII: 57 (see note).
Alchemy, XXIX: 120 ff.
Alecto (one of the Furies), IX: 47.
Alessandro degli Alberti (count), XXXII: 55 (see
  note).
Alessio Interminelli (from Lucca), XVIII: 122.
Alexander (count of Romena), XXX: 76 (see note).
Alexander the Great, XII: 107 (see note); XIV: 31
  (see note).
Ali (son-in-law of Mahomet), XXVIII: 32 (see note).
Alpe (Alps), XVI: 101.
Amphiaraus (Greek king and soothsayer), XX: 34
  (see note).
Amphion (mythical musician), XXXII: 11 (see note).
Amphisboenae (snakes), XXIV: 86 (see note).
Anastasius II (pope), XI: 8 (see note).
Anaxagoras (Greek philosopher), IV: 138 (see note).
Anchises (father of Aeneas), I: 74.
Andrea de' Mozzi (bishop of Florence), XV: 112
  (see note).
Angiolello (from Fano), XXVIII: 77.
Anselm (nephew of Ugolino), XXXIII: 50, 90
  (see note).
Antaeus (giant), XXXI: 100 (see note), 113–45;
  XXXII: 17.
Antenora (second zone of Cocytus), XXXII: 88
  (see note).
Antiochus (king of Syria), XIX: 86 (see note).
Appennines, XVI: 95; XX: 65; XXVII: 30.
Apulia (region of Italy), XXVIII: 9 (see note).
Aquarius (constellation), XXIV: 2.
Arachne (mythical weaver transformed into a
  spider), XVII: 18 (see note).
Arbia (Tuscan river), X: 86.
Arethusa (nymph transformed into a spring),
  XXV: 98 (see note).
Aretines (citizens of Arezzo), XXII: 5.
Argonauts, XVIII: 86 (see note).
Ariadne (daughter of Minos), XII: 20 (see note).

Aristotle (Greek philosopher), IV: 131 (see note).
Arles (city in Provence), IX: 112.
Arno (river in Florence), XIII: 146; XV: 113; XXIII 95;
  XXX: 65; XXXIII: 83.
Arrigo (possibly one of the Fifanti family), VI: 80.
Aruns (Etruscan soothsayer), XX: 46 (see note).
Asdente (cobbler from Parma), XX: 118 (see note).
Athamas (mythical king of Boeotia), XXX: 3 ff
  (see note).
Athens (city of Greece), XII: 17.
Atropos (one of the Fates), XXXIII: 126 (see note).
Attila the Hun (king of Huns), XII: 134 (see note);
  XIII: 149 (see note).
Augustus (imperial title), XIII: 68 (see note).
Augustus Octavius (emperor), I: 71 (see note).
Aulis (Greek port), XX: 111.
Averroës (Arabic philosopher), IV: 144.
Avicenna (Arabic philosopher), IV: 143.

Bacchiglione (river in the Veneto region), XV: 113
  (see note).
Bacchus (god), XX: 59.
Baptistery (baptistery of San Giovanni in Florence),
  XIX: 18 (see note).
Barrators, XXI, XXII.
Beatrice, II: 53 ff; X: 131 (see note); XII: 88 (see
  note); XV: 90 (see note).
Beccaria – see Tesauro dei Beccaria.
Beelzebub (Lucifer), XXXIV: 128 (see note).
Benaco (Lake Garda), XX: 61 ff (see note).
Bergamese (citizens of Bergamo), XX: 71.
Bertran de Born (troubadour), XXVIII: 118 ff
  (see note).
Betrayers, XXXII–XXXIV.
Bisenzio (tributary of the Arno river), XXXII: 56.
Blacks (Black Guelphs), XXIV: 143 (see note).
Bocca degli Abati (Florentine), XXXII: 106 (see note).
Bologna (city), XXIII: 142; XXIII: 103 (see note).
Bolognese (citizens of Bologna), XVIII: 58 ff
  (see notes).
Boniface VIII (pope), VI: 69 (see note); XIX: 53
  (see note); XXVII: 70 ff (see note).
Bonturo Dati (barrator from Lucca), XXI: 41
  (see note).
Branca Doria (Genoese), XXXIII: 137 ff (see note).
Brenta (river in the Veneto region), XV: 7.
Brescia (city), XX: 68.
Brescians (citizens of Brescia), XX: 71.
Briareus (giant), XXXI: 99.
Brigata (nephew of Ugolino), XXXIII: 89.
Brunetto Latini (writer and mentor to Dante), XV:
  22 ff (see notes).
Brutus (assassin of Julius Caesar), XXXIV: 65
  (see note).
Brutus (leader of a rebellion against Tarquin),
  IV: 127 (see note).
Bulicame (lake near Viterbo), XIV: 79 (see note).
Buoso (possibly one of the Abati family), XXV: 140.
Buoso da Duera (from Cremona), XXXII: 106, 114,
  116 (see note).
Buoso Donati (Florentine), XXX: 44.

Epicurus (Greek philosopher), X: 14 (see note).
Erichtho (witch), IX: 23 (see note).
Erinyes (the Furies), IX: 45 (see note).
Eteocles (son of Oedipus), XXVI: 54 (see note).
Ethiopia, XXIV: 88.
Etna (volcanic mountain), XIV: 56 (see note).
Euclid (Greek mathematician), IV: 142 (see note).
Euryalus (Trojan hero), I: 108 (see note).
Eurypylus (Greek writer), XX: 112 (see note).
Ezzelino III da Romano (tyrant), XII: 110 (see note).

Faenza (city), XXXII: 123 (see note).
Falsifiers, (of metal – alchemists) XXIX: 40–139;
    (of money, people) XXX: 25 ff.
Fano (city), XXVIII: 76.
Farinata degli Uberti (Florentine), VI: 79; X: 22–121
    (see note).
Fiesole (city), XV: 62, 73.
Filippo Argenti (Florentine), VIII: 31 ff (see note).
Flatterers, XI: 58; XVIII: 104 ff (see note).
Flemings, XV: 4.
Flibbertigibbet (devil), XXI: 118; XXII: 133.
Florence, VI: 50 (see note), 61; X: 26, 92; XIII: 143;
    XV: 78; XVI: 9 (see note), 74; XXIII: 95 (see note);
    XXIV: 144; XXVI: 1.
Florentines, XV: 61 (see note); XVI: 73; XVII: 70.
Florins (gold currency), XXX: 90.
Focaccia (from Pistoia), XXXII: 63 (see note).
Focara (mountain in the Marche region), XXVIII: 90.
Fonte Branda (spring near Siena), XXX: 78
    (see note).
Forlì (city), XVI: 99; XXVII: 43 (see note).
Fortune, VII: 62 ff; XV: 70, 93, 95 (see note).
France, XIX: 87.
Francesca da Rimini, V: 74 ff (see notes).
Francesco d'Accorso (jurist), XV: 110 (see note).
Francesco dei Cavalcanti (Florentine), XXV: 151
    (see note).
Franciscan friars, XXIII: 3 (see note); XXVII: 92 ff
    (see note).
Fraud, XI: 52 ff (see note).
Fraudulent, XI: 26, 58 ff (see note); XVIII: 25; XXVI:
    31 ff; XXXIV: 69.
Frederick II (Emperor), X: 119 (see note); XIII: 59
    (see note), 68 (see note); XXIII: 66 (see note).
French, XXVII: 44 (see note); XXXII: 115 (see note).
Friar Gomita (from Sardinia), XXII: 81 ff (see note).
Friars Minor, XXIII: 3 (see note).
Frieslanders, XXXI: 63 (see note).
Frisky Friars, XXIII: 103 (see note).
Fucci, Vanni – see Vanni Fucci.
Furies, IX: 38 ff.

Gaddo (son of Ugolino), XXXIII: 68, 90 (see note).
Gaeta (city), XXVI: 92 (see note).
Galen (Greek physician), IV: 143 (see note).
Gallura (Sardinian district), XXII: 82 (see note).
Ganelon (traitor), XXXII: 122 (see note).
Garda (lake), XX: 65.
Gardingo (area of the city of Florence), XXIII: 108
    (see note).

Garisenda (tower in Bologna), XXXI: 136 (see note).
Gaville (town), XXV: 151 (see note).
Genesis (book of the Bible), XI: 107 (see note).
Genoese, XXXIII: 151 ff.
Geri del Bello (relative of Dante), XXIX: 27 (see note).
Geryon (winged monster), XVII: 97, 113 ff; XVIII: 20.
Ghisolabella (sister of Venedico Caccianemico),
    XVIII: 56 (see note).
Gianfigliazzi (Florentine family), XVII: 60 (see note).
Gianni Buiamonte dei Becchi (Florentine usurer),
    XVII: 73 (see note).
Gianni de' Soldanieri (Florentine), XXXII: 121
    (see note).
Gianni Schicchi (Florentine), XXX: 32 (see note),
    42 ff (see note).
Giants, XXXI: 43 ff.
Gluttony, VI: 7–99.
God, I: 40, 124 (see note), 126, 131; II: 16, 91, 103;
    III: 4, 39, 63, 103, 108, 122; IV: 38; V: 91; VII: 19,
    73; VIII: 60; XI: 22, 26, 31, 51, 74, 81, 84, 105; XII:
    119; XIV: 16, 69; XIX: 2, 10; XX: 19; XXIV: 119;
    XXV: 3; XXXIV: 35.
Gorgona (island in the Tyrrhenian Sea), XXXIII: 82
    (see note).
Governolo (town), XX: 78.
Greece, XX: 108 (see note).
Greeks, XXVI: 74 (see note); XXX: 97 (see note), 121.
Griffolino d'Arezzo (alchemist), XXIX: 109 (see
    note); XXX: 31 (see note), 37.
Gualandi (Pisan family), XXXIII: 32 (see note).
Gualdrada (daughter of Bellincion Berti), XVI: 37
    (see note).
Guglielmo Borsiere (Florentine), XVI: 70 (see note).
Guido (count from Romena), XXXIII: 77.
Guido Bonatti (astrologer from Forlì), XX: 118
    (see note).
Guido Cavalcanti (poet and friend of Dante), X: 60
    (see note), 63, 111 (see note).
Guido da Montefeltro (Ghibelline captain), XXVII:
    4 ff (see note).
Guido Guerra (leader of the Florentine Guelphs),
    XVI: 38 (see note).
Guinevere (wife of king Arthur), V: 128 ff (see
    note).
Guy de Montfort (deputy of Charles of Anjou),
    XII: 118 (see note).

Hacksore (devil), XXI: 123; XXIII: 40.
Hannibal (Carthaginian leader), XXXI: 117
    (see note).
Harpies (winged monsters), XIII: 10 (see note), 101.
Hautefort (fortress in France), XXIX: 29.
Hector (Trojan hero), IV: 122 (see note).
Hecuba (wife of Priam), XXX: 16 (see note).
Helen of Troy (wife of Menelaus), V: 64 (see note).
Hellhound (devil), XXI: 119; XXII 106, 120 (see
    note).
Henry II (king), XXVIII: 136 (see note).
Heraclitus (Greek philosopher), IV: 138 (see note).
Hercules (Greek hero), XXV: 32 (see note); XXVI: 107
    (see note); XXXI: 132 (see note).

Heresiarchs, IX: 112 ff; X: 7.
Hippocrates (Greek physician), IV: 143 (see note).
Hogwash (devil), XXI: 122; XXII: 55.
Holy Face, XXI: 47 (see note).
Holy Mother Church, XIX: 57 (see note).
Homer (Greek poet), IV: 88 (see note).
Homicide, XI: 37; XII: 48 ff.
Horace (Roman poet), IV: 89 (see note).
Hound, I: 101 ff (see note).
Hypocrites, XXIII: 58 ff.
Hypsipyle (queen of Lemnos), XVIII: 92 (see note).

Icarus (son of Dedalus), XVII: 109 (see note).
Ida (mountain in the island of Crete), XIV: 98
    (see note).
Imola (city), XXVII: 50 (see note).
Incontinent, XI: 70–90.
India, XIV: 31.
Isaac (patriarch), IV: 59.
Israel (Jacob) (patriarch), IV: 59 (see note).
Italy, I: 107; IX: 114; XX: 61; XXVII: 26 (see note);
    XXVIII: 72; XXXIII: 80 (see note).

Jacopo da Santo Andrea (Paduan), XIII: 133 (see
    note).
Jacopo Rusticucci (Florentine), VI: 80 (see note);
    XVI: 44.
Jaculi (snakes), XXIV: 86 (see note).
Jason (leader of the Argonauts), XIX: 85–6 (see note).
Jehoshaphat (the place of Judgement Day), X: 11
    (see note).
Jerusalem (city), XXXIV: 114 (see note).
Jesus, IV: 53 (see note); XII: 38 (see note); XIX: 90;
    XXXIV: 114–5.
Jews, XXIII: 123 (see note); XXVII: 87.
John the Baptist, XIII: 143; XXX: 74 (see note).
Joseph (patriarch), XXX: 98 (see note).
Jove (god), XIV: 52; XXXI: 45, 92.
Jubilee (of the year 1300), XVIII: 28 (see note).
Judas Iscariot, IX: 27 (see note); XIX: 96 (see note);
    XXXI: 143; XXXIV: 62 (see note).
Judecca (lowest zone of Cocytus), IX: 27 (see note);
    XXXIV: 117 (see note).
Julia (daughter of Julius Caesar), IV: 128 (see note).
Julius Caesar, I: 70 (see note); IV: 123 (see note);
    XXVIII: 98 (see note).
Juno (goddess), XXX: 1 (see note).
Justice, III: 4, 50, 125 (see note); XXIX: 56.

King Arthur, XXXII: 62 (see note).
King Latinus (king of Latium), IV: 125 (see note).
King Thibaut, XXII: 52 (see note).

Laertes (father of Ulysses), XXVI: 95 (see note).
Lake Garda – see Benaco.
Lamone (river in the Romagna region), XXVII: 50
    (see note).
Lancelot (knight of the Round Table), V: 128
    (see note), 134 (see note).

Lanfranchi (Pisan family), XXXIII: 32 (see note).
Lano (squanderer), XIII: 120 (see note).
Lateran (palace in Rome), XXVII: 86 (see note).
Latin land (Italy), XXVII: 26 (see note); XXVIII: 72.
Latinus – see King Latinus.
Lavinia (daughter of king Latinus), IV: 126 (see
    note).
Learchus (son of Athamas), XXX: 10.
Lemnos (island), XVIII: 88 (see note).
Leopard, I: 32 (see note); XVI: 108.
Lethe (river in the Earthly Paradise), XIV: 131, 136
    (see note).
Libya, XXIV: 85.
Limbo (the first circle of the Inferno), IV: 31 ff.
Linus (mythical Greek poet), IV: 140 (see note).
Lion, I: 44 (see note).
Livy (Roman historian), XXVIII: 12 (see note).
Loderingo (Frisky Friar), XXIII: 104 (see note).
Logudoro (Sardinian region), XXII: 88.
Lombards (citizens of Lombardy), XXII: 99.
Lombardy, I: 68; XXVII: 20 (see note).
Looters and pillagers, XI: 38.
Lucan (Roman poet), IV: 90 (see note); XXV: 94
    (see note).
Lucca (city), XXI: 38 (see note); XXXIII: 30
    (see note).
Lucchese (citizens of Lucca), XVIII: 122.
Lucifer, XXXI: 143; XXXIV: 89.
Lucrece, IV: 128 (see note).
Luni (Etruscan city), XX: 47.
Lustful, V: 32 ff.

Maccabees (book of the Bible), XIX: 86 (see note).
Maghinardo Pagani da Susinana (lord of Faenza),
    XXVII: 49 (see note).
Mahomet, XXVIII: 31 ff (see note).
Majorca (island), XXVIII: 83.
Malatesta da Verrucchio (lord of Rimini), XXVII: 46
    (see note).
Malatestino da Verrucchio (son of Malatesta da
    Verrucchio), XXVII: 46 (see note); XXVIII: 81
    (see note), 85 (see note).
Malice, XI: 82.
Manto (soothsayer), XX: 55 ff (see note).
Mantua (city), XX: 92.
Mantuans (citizens of Mantua), I: 69; II: 58.
Marcabò (fortress in the Ravenna area), XXVIII: 75.
Marcia (wife of Cato of Utica), IV: 128 (see note).
Maremma (Tuscan region), XXV: 19 (see note);
    XXIX: 48 (see note).
Marquis – see Obizzo da Esti.
Mars (god), XIII; 144 (see note); XXIV: 146; XXXI: 51
    (see note).
Mary – see Virgin Mary.
Master Adam, XXX: 49 ff (see notes).
Medea (witch), XVIII: 96 (see note).
Medicina (description), XXVIII: 73.
Mediterranean Sea (description), XIV: 94; XXVI: 100,
    105 (see note); XXVIII: 79.
Medusa (mythical monster), IX: 52 (see note), 56.
Megaera (one of the Furies), IX: 46.

BIOGRAPHICAL NOTE

Dante Alighieri was born in Florence in 1265, into a noble but impoverished Guelph family; his father was the notary Alighiero di Bellincione Alighieri. Dante was educated in rhetoric, grammar, philosophy, literature and theology and was a pupil of the great orator and politician Brunetto Latini (c.1210–94), who later became the subject of an encounter in *Inferno*. As a poet, however, Dante was virtually self-taught, and formed strong friendships with other poets, such as Guido Cavalcanti and Cino da Pistoia, with whom he originated the '*stil novo*', a 'new style' of poetry, influenced by the medieval troubadours and adapted for the poets' innovative philosophical and courtly love poetry. When he was still very young, he met for the first time Beatrice (thought by some to be Bice Portinari), who was to be his spiritual muse and the inspiration for his *Vita nova* [*New Life*], a series of love poems with prose links in his own *stil novo*, completed four years after her death in 1290.

In around 1285 Dante married Gemma Donati, a distant relative, by whom he had two sons and two daughters. In order to assume a role in public life, Dante enrolled in the guild of physicians and apothecaries; he proved a success in politics, rising to become one of the municipal priors of Florence by 1300. A Guelph more by birth than spirit, Dante was a member of the moderate faction – the Whites – at the end of the thirteenth century, and when the Blacks seized power in 1301 he was dismissed from office and, along with the rest of his party, was permanently banished from the republic.

After a few initial attempts to make common cause with other exiles against Florence, Dante eventually abandoned politics and devoted himself to writing. In the early years of the fourteenth century Dante travelled widely in central and northern Italy, and was welcomed at many courts. His exile acted as a new artistic stimulus and he wrote a series of odes (*canzoni*), one of which depicted Justice and her children as outcasts, and glorified his own banishment. At about this time he also composed his treatise on vernacular poetry *De Vulgari Eloquentia* [*On Vernacular Language*], a piece of enormous importance in the literary theory of the late middle ages; though it spoke of an ideal form of Italian as necessary for the composition of high literature, Dante himself produced his most beautiful works in his own native Florentine dialect.

In 1309, Dante turned once more to politics, filled with optimism at the appointment of a new emperor, Henry VII, whom he hoped would be able to resolve the situation in Florence. He wrote his political essay *De Monarchia* [*On Monarchy*], which held that both temporal and spiritual government was necessary. Dante's hopes came to nothing, and in 1317 he finally settled in Ravenna. Here he was to complete his greatest work, *La Divina Commedia* [*The Divine Comedy*], an epic poem in three parts – '*Inferno*', '*Purgatorio*', and '*Paradiso*' – which laid out, in the form of an allegory, Dante's entire philosophy of life. *La Divina Commedia* has come to be hailed as one of the greatest works of literature of all time, and has earned Dante his reputation as the master of pre-Renaissance literature and the founder of Italian poetry. Dante died and was buried in Ravenna in 1321.

J.G. Nichols is a poet and translator. His published translations include the poems of Guido Gozzano (for which he won the John Florio Prize), Giacomo Leopardi, and Petrarch (for which he won the Monselice Prize). He has also translated prose works by Ugo Foscolo, Giovanni Boccaccio, Giacomo Leopardi, Leonardo da Vinci, Luigi Pirandello, Petrarch, Giacomo Casanova, Giovanni Verga, Dante Alighieri, Gabriele D'Annunzio and Italo Svevo, all published by Hesperus Press.